ROUTLEDGE LIBRARY EDITIONS: ALCOHOL AND ALCOHOLISM

I0127754

Volume 12

ALCOHOL: THE PREVENTION DEBATE

ALCOHOL:
THE PREVENTION
DEBATE

MARCUS GRANT
AND
BRUCE RITSON

Routledge
Taylor & Francis Group

LONDON AND NEW YORK

First published in 1983 by Croom Helm

This edition first published in 2024
by Routledge
4 Park Square, Milton Park, Abingdon, Oxon OX14 4RN

and by Routledge
605 Third Avenue, New York, NY 10158

Routledge is an imprint of the Taylor & Francis Group, an informa business

© 1983 Marcus Grant and Bruce Ritson

All rights reserved. No part of this book may be reprinted or reproduced or utilised in any form or by any electronic, mechanical, or other means, now known or hereafter invented, including photocopying and recording, or in any information storage or retrieval system, without permission in writing from the publishers.

Trademark notice: Product or corporate names may be trademarks or registered trademarks, and are used only for identification and explanation without intent to infringe.

British Library Cataloguing in Publication Data
A catalogue record for this book is available from the British Library

ISBN: 978-1-032-59082-0 (Set)
ISBN: 978-1-032-63986-4 (Volume 12) (hbk)
ISBN: 978-1-032-63992-5 (Volume 12) (pbk)
ISBN: 978-1-032-63990-1 (Volume 12) (ebk)

DOI: 10.4324/9781032639901

Publisher's Note
The publisher has gone to great lengths to ensure the quality of this reprint but points out that some imperfections in the original copies may be apparent.

Disclaimer
This book is a re-issue originally published in 1983. The language used and views portrayed are a reflection of its era and no offence is meant by the Publishers to any reader by this re-publication.

Alcohol
the Prevention Debate

Marcus Grant and Bruce Ritson

CROOM HELM
London & Canberra

© 1983 Marcus Grant and Bruce Ritson
Croom Helm Ltd; Provident House, Burrell Row
Beckenham, Kent BR3 1AT

British Library Cataloguing in Publication Data

Alcohol.
  1. Alcoholism
  I. Grant, Marcus   II. Ritson, Bruce
  362.2'92   HV5035

  ISBN 0-7099-1133-5

Printed and bound in Great Britain
by Billing & Sons Limited, Worcester.

CONTENTS

This book is dedicated to the memory of Dr. David L. Davies, whose vision inspired it in the first place and whose death now leaves an irrevocable gap amongst the ranks of those concerned with the prevention of alcohol problems.

CONTRIBUTORS

Mr. **Tim Ambler**, International Distillers and Vintners Ltd., London

Dr. **Dan E. Beauchamp**, Department of Health Policy and Administration, School of Public Health, University of North Carolina at Chapel Hill, USA

Dr. **Sally Casswell**, Alcohol Research Unit, University of Auckland, New Zealand

Mr. **John Cavanagh**, Institute for Policy Studies, Washington, D.C., USA (Formerly World Health Organisation, Geneva, Switzerland)

Mr. **Sam Docherty**, Scottish Health Education Group, Edinburgh

Mr. **Martin Evans**, Teachers' Advisory Council on Alcohol and Drug Education, Manchester

Dr. **Michael Goodstadt**, Education Research Section, Addiction Research Foundation, Toronto, Canada

Mr. **Marcus Grant**, Alcohol Education Centre, London

Ms. **Peggy Gray**, Centre for Mass Communication Research, University of Leicester

Mr. **Richard Grindal**, Scotch Whisky Association, London

Ms. **Denise Herd**, Alcohol Research Group, Institute of Epidemiology and Behavioral Research, Medical Research Institute of San Francisco at Pacific Medical Center, Berkeley, California, USA

Ms. **Joy Moser**, Formerly World Health Organisation, Geneva, Switzerland

Dr. **Robin Murray**, Institute of Psychiatry, University of London

Dr. **Martin Plant**, Alcohol Research Group, University of Edinburgh

Dr. **David Player**, Health Education Council, London

Dr. **Bruce Ritson**, University Department of Psychiatry, Royal Edinburgh Hospital, Edinburgh

Dr. **David Robinson**, Institute for Health Studies, University of Hull

Dr. **Robin Room**, Alcohol Research Group, Institute of Epidemiology and Behavioural Research, Medical Research Institute of San Francisco at Pacific Medical Center, Berkeley, California, USA

Mr. **Philip Tether**, Institute for Health Studies, University of Hull

Dr. **I.E. Thompson**, Scottish Health Education Group, Edinburgh

Contributors

Dr. Lawrence Wallack, Alcohol Research Group, Institute of Epidemiology and Behavioural Research, Medical Research Institute of San Francisco at Pacific Medical Center, Berkeley, California, USA

Professor Brendan Walsh, Department of Political Economy, University College Dublin, Eire

Mr. M.J. Waterson, The Advertising Association, London

Ms. Margaret Whitehead, Scottish Health Education Group, Edinburgh

Dr. Friedner Wittman, Alcohol Research Group, Institute of Epidemiology and Behavioural Research, Medical Research Institute of San Francisco at Pacific Medical Center, Berkeley, California, USA

ACKNOWLEDGEMENTS

Thanks are due to the contributors to this book, all of whom have shown considerable patience, tolerance, tact and good humour in the face of interminable delays, impossible deadlines and a variety of *ad hominen* attacks, now couched in more scholarly terms. We were sorry to lose some other contributors along the way and would like to apologise in particular to David Pittman, Mike Daube and the Brewers' Society, who obviously found the delays too irksome, the deadlines too demanding or the scholarly attacks too heady.

Very special thanks are due to Beryl Skinner, whose attentions have extended far beyond typing the final version of this book. Some chapters she has nursed like sickly children through draft after draft. No manuscript proved too scrappy for her, no reference too elusive. Without her long-suffering commitment, this book would never have seen the light of day.

Thanks, too, to Annie Grant, who put up with countless editorial conferences over the years, both in London and in Berkeley, which must surely have tested the boundaries of friendship, hospitality, scholarship and marriage.

And thanks, finally, to Tim Hardwick, our editor at Croom Helm, who never betrayed the sense of futility he must have felt when we told him yet again that we would not be able to deliver the typescript on time.

INTRODUCTION

This is not the first book to be written on the prevention of alcohol problems. Its justification is more, however, than that it simply provides an update on previous attempts to deal with this topic from a theoretical or empirical point of view. The last decade has seen an unprecedented rise in interest in the potential of preventive strategies as a means of countering a worldwide increase in alcohol problems. This upsurge in interest reached a watershed in the Technical Discussions at the 35th World Health Assembly in Geneva in 1982. Reviewing local, regional and global patterns of alcohol consumption and relating these to the wide range of alcohol problems manifest in different parts of the world, a strong recommendation emerged (WHO, 1982) that countries should develop explicit national alcohol policies. Inevitably, such policies must rely upon some concept of how alcohol problems are to be prevented as well as how they are to be treated.

Debates about the merits of particular preventive strategies have been growing increasingly vigorous, so that issues previously seen as having relatively marginal importance to alcoholism (issues such as the portrayal of drinking on television or the market domination of transnational corporations) have now become much more central to the prevention debate. What this book does, therefore, is to try to set out the new terms for debate, in the light of the call for national alcohol policies. We make no attempt to judge who has won or even who is winning the various debates. In truth, it would be premature to make such judgements. Instead, what interests us is who it is that is debating, where the debates are taking place and what it is exactly that is being debated.

Much of this book, therefore, consists of exchanges of short contributions from a variety of individuals in different parts of the world who are all, in their various ways, championing particular points of view. In order to set the scene for these exchanges, the first eight chapters try to provide general answers to some very basic questions. Then, following the debates themselves (Chapters 9-16) relying also upon some other contextual material, we attempt to draw out in the final chapter the salient strands which run through the whole of the prevention debates.

1 WHY IS ALCOHOL A PROBLEM?

In most parts of the world, alcohol consumption is increasing rapidly. A major cause of this global trend must be that alcoholic beverages are being produced in continuously increasing quantities and are becoming more widely and readily available. This book examines the effects of unrestrained productivity and raises the question of whether normal market forces should determine levels of production and consumption or whether there should be national or international endeavours to influence consumption trends in order to minimise social and personal harm. The question has not yet been adequately answered. What happens as the market is flooded with alcohol? Do good sense and moderation prevail? Or is satiety reached only at the expense of unacceptable social and physical harm?

The evidence of world-wide increased beverage alcohol productivity can be deduced only from those countries which keep reasonably accurate records. These data indicate that between 1960 and 1972, production increased by 19 per cent for wine, 61 per cent for spirits and 68 per cent for beer (Bruun, et al 1975). Between 1960 and 1980 the global increases in production reached 40 per cent for wine and 124 per cent for beer. The increase in the latter was particularly rapid in developing countries. For example, the registered output of commercially produced beer grew by over 50 per cent in 46 countries (of which 43 were in the developing world) and by over 100 per cent in 17 (of which 16 were developing countries). Beer production increased by nearly 200 per cent in Latin America, more than 400 per cent in Africa and 500 per cent in Asia in the period 1960-80.

Beer, wine and spirits are all relatively easy to produce, with the result that the constraints on the limits of production lie principally in terms of what the market will consume. If some countries like France appear to be saturated, there is room for expansion into new markets, for instance the developing countries, where commercially produced alcoholic beverages are a relatively recent arrival. Women, traditionally modest drinkers or abstainers, can form a source of new recruits to the drinking classes in many countries. The balance between supply and demand and the endeavour to tilt it in a way which enhances profitability will be a recurrent theme in later chapters.

Improved production methods and the increased centralisation of

1

brewing and, to a certain extent, distilling, may also contribute to greater availability and a pressure to expand the market if the enhanced production skills are to pay off. This commonly leads to greater investment in advertising and marketing in an attempt to recruit new drinkers and to the development of overseas markets. These issues are debated in greater detail in Chapter 13.

Trends in alcohol use may be assayed in two principal ways: the first by monitoring reported sales of alcohol and the other by sampling segments of the population and asking them directly about their drinking habits. Both methods present problems and require a degree of investment in research and data collection that is outside the means of many developing countries. Where studies have been possible, the upward trend has been clear and consistent. The only exception to this continuous growth in alcohol consumption is France, where there was a 12 per cent reduction in alcohol consumption between 1960 and 1976 which contrasts with a 22-25 per cent increase in countries such as the USA, UK and Poland, and a doubling of consumption in the Netherlands during a similar period. It is worth noting that, despite the reduction reported, France still has the highest reported *per capita* consumption of alcohol in the world.

There are doubtless many reasons for these striking increases. Increased availability is widely acknowledged to be a very important factor, since liberalising trends in recent years have promoted an increased number of sales outlets which are a necessary corollary to the growth in production. A walk around a typical British town will quickly remind the reader that many of the coffee bars of the 1950s have become licensed premises and that increasing proportions of grocers and more significantly supermarkets have moved into the drink trade.

The growth in licensed clubs in recent years has been even more marked. The Clayson Committee in Scotland (Clayson 1973) noted that the number of licensed clubs in that country had risen substantially in the last 20 years. It is increasingly rare to find sporting or social facilities which are without a bar. Few countries have been able to observe the effect of increasing numbers of outlets on availability. In Finland, however, when this did prove possible, it seemed that increased ease of access was linked to increased consumption (Bruun *et al* 1975).

There is evidence that most of us are willing to acquire new drinking habits without relinquishing those developed previously. For instance, it has been suggested that experience of wine drinking encountered by many British tourists in Spain has been brought back so that a bottle of wine is now added to Saturday night in addition to regular beer drinking.

Some support for this hypothesis may be deduced from the remarkable growth in wine sales in this country during the past decade. Similarly, expense account lunches with free alcohol will be taken without any commensurate reduction in evening drinking with friends. Ten years ago, most heavy drinking in England was confined to weekends and 'special' occasions. Evidence suggests (Edwards, Chandler and Hensman 1972) that weekend habits are extending to week-days. As we shall see, the hazardous effects of alcohol on health are cumulative. Perhaps, therefore, we should be more concerned, both personally and socially, by this steady recruitment of new drinking habits and occasions.

While availability is very important, we also need to be able to afford to drink. Despite appearances to the contrary, alcohol in Britain is relatively cheaper in terms of available disposable income, than it has been at any time during this century. In 1950 a labourer needed to work for 6½ hours for a bottle of whisky; he now need only work for 2 hours, a 68 per cent reduction (Kendell 1979). In Britain consumption levelled off in the early 1980s. This coincided with an economic recession and a 20 per cent rise in the cost of alcoholic beverages. We do not, however, know in sufficient detail which segment of the drinking population is most affected by price rises − is it the majority of moderate drinkers who forgo their extra pint, leaving the heavier drinker undeterred and willing to make economies elsewhere in the family budget?

In situations where a country or district is enjoying new found wealth, one of the easiest consumer goods to acquire is alcohol. It also has the added advantage of being quickly used up so that the newly rich may spend again. This contrasts with durable goods such as deep freezers, cars and televison sets, which even the most acquisitive would feel could not be replaced at such frequent intervals. These and similar issues concerning availability and consumption of alcohol are considered in Chapters 7, 14 and 15.

In most countries, women have traditionally either abstained or drunk very little. This situation is changing rapidly and is reflected in the growing prevalence of alcohol-related harm being reported amongst females, particularly in Europe and North America (Kricka and Clark 1979). In these areas, most young women drink, whereas amongst older women there is a considerable proportion who have never drunk or drink only very occasionally. It has been estimated that between 1.5

and 2.5 million females in the USA have some form of alcohol related disabilities. We may anticipate a growing concern with alcohol use amongst women as their social lives and aspirations become more like those of males. The issue may be all the more urgent because of evidence that women are physically more vulnerable to certain forms of alcoholic liver disease (Saunders, Davis and Williams 1981) so that safe levels of drinking for men are relatively higher than for women. As little as two pints of beer or four measures of spirits daily may be the upper level of harmfree drinking for the latter.

A feminist analysis of this trend may suggest that such reports are typical male scaremongering in an attempt to reinforce traditional male preserves. While more women are drinking, and are drinking more, so is everybody else — the increase amongst women is not so much disproportionate as novel. Women should, of course, feel as free as men to choose to harm themselves, but they have a right to be given an accurate picture of the hazards involved. The question of individual freedom in relation to this and many other issues will be a recurring theme in this book and will receive closer examination in Chapter 16.

Lamentations about the behaviour of young people are littered throughout history and have often been attributed either to 'sour grapes' or short memories. In most European and North American countries, people drink more in their youth than they do when older. It does, however, appear that the consumption of alcohol amongst young people, and even children, has increased rapidly in the last decade. Studies in Britain and the USA show that in the past 20 years teenagers are now getting drunk and getting into difficulties as a result of their drinking more frequently. Increased freedom, ease of access, greater affluence, peer pressure, parental values and many other factors seem to influence this trend.

As a group, adolescents are both physically and psychologically vulnerable to the effects of alcohol. From society's point of view, they are our investment in the future and it is particularly tragic to see their lives being impaired by drinking. Although risk taking is almost a required part of adolescent life, the presence of alcohol will often turn the challenge of a calculated risk into a foolhardy act, when inexperience and alcohol-impaired judgement can lead to disastrous, perhaps fatal consequences. The special problems of young people and how they form their attitudes and behaviour patterns in relation to drinking will be debated in Chapters 5 and 9.

These two examples — women and young people — of special areas of concern have in common the factor of relative novelty. What is the responsibility of the manufacturer, or of the educator, or indeed of society as a whole, in helping novitiates acquire moderate and enjoyable drinking habits? Lest the reader accuse us of paternalistic moralising, we should recall that young people are a part of this society that is designing a more appropriate response to alcohol use. The design of participative prevention strategies at community level may be an important trend and is debated further in Chapter 14.

In some situations, whole societies are in the process of acquiring new drinking customs. Developing countries face a particular problem in their approach to alcohol. Some national leaders such as Dr. Kaunda of Zambia and Mr. Desai of India, have spoken out very strongly against the dangers of alcohol. Many Islamic countries have recently awoken to the damaging effects which the introduction of alcohol may have on their established way of life and have tried to reinforce restrictions and penalties for drinking. Whilst we should never attempt any simplistic translation of control strategies between very different cultures, it does seem evident that when alcohol is introduced into a society which does not possess established norms of usage, there is a particular risk of damage through excessive drinking.

Most developing countries have long established home produced sources of alcohol; the traditional beverages have usually been relatively weak in strength and prepared only in sufficient quantity for immediate village and family use. In some areas stronger or imported drink was prohibited by colonial powers. It can be argued, of course, that such prohibition was a repressive artefact of imperialism, particularly since these same authorities often drank extremely heavily themselves and possibly created a role model of drinking as a hallmark of privilege and high life. Whatever the reasons, the advent of commercially produced alcohol in countries which have been denied access in the past has certainly had disastrous consequences. Imported whisky and champagne quickly become status symbols of the new rich.

The central question to be examined is, of course, whether the rapid and ubiquitous growth in alcohol consumption should be regarded simply as the acquisition of civilised pleasures, the natural expansion of trade in a desirable and harmless commodity, an understandable expression of an improved standard of living or whether it should be a cause for concern. If we are to conclude that it is the latter because of the association between increased consumption in a society and increased harm, we need to look more closely at the evidence for this association.

The clearest link lies between consumption and the incidence of cirrhosis of the liver. This association is demonstrated in Figures 1.1 and 1.2 which compare consumption data with liver cirrhosis deaths, over time in one country (Figure 1.1) and between different countries (Figure 1.2). In most countries there is a close parallel between the

Figure 1.1: Per Capita Alcohol Consumption Arrests for Drunkenness (Thousands) and Deaths from Liver Cirrhosis, per 100,000 population, Finland, 1950-1975

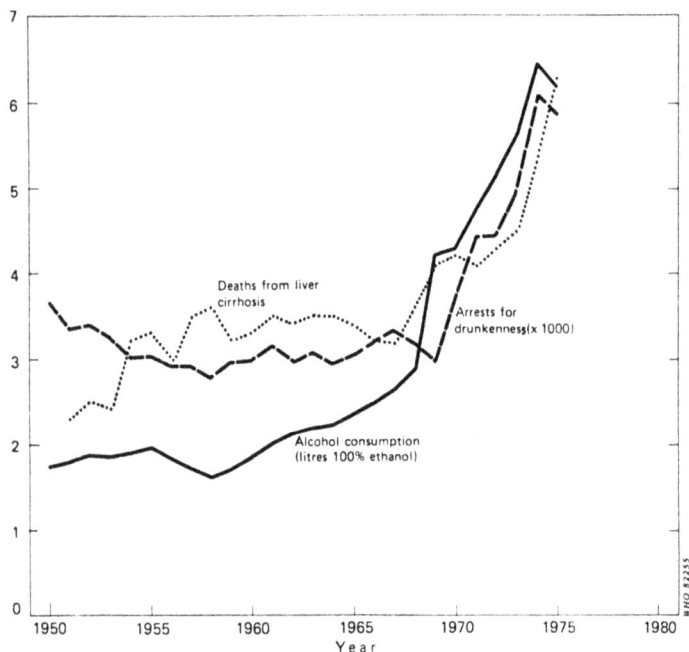

Sources: (With permission) WHO Document A35/Technical Discussions/1 (1982) — derived from data by E. Österberg

number of deaths due to liver disease and the *per capita* alcohol consumption. During times of prohibition, the incidence of cirrhosis drops dramatically as it has done when relative abstinence has been enforced on a population — for instance, during the occupation of Paris during the Second World War (Kendell 1979).

Recent research suggests (Pequignot, Tuyns and Beuta 1978) that we may be able to predict the level of drinking which is likely to cause liver damage. There is considerable individual variation in susceptibility to alcohol induced liver damage, and, as we have seen, women are

Figure 1.2: Liver Cirrhosis Mortality and Alcohol Consumption, Selected Countries mid 1970s

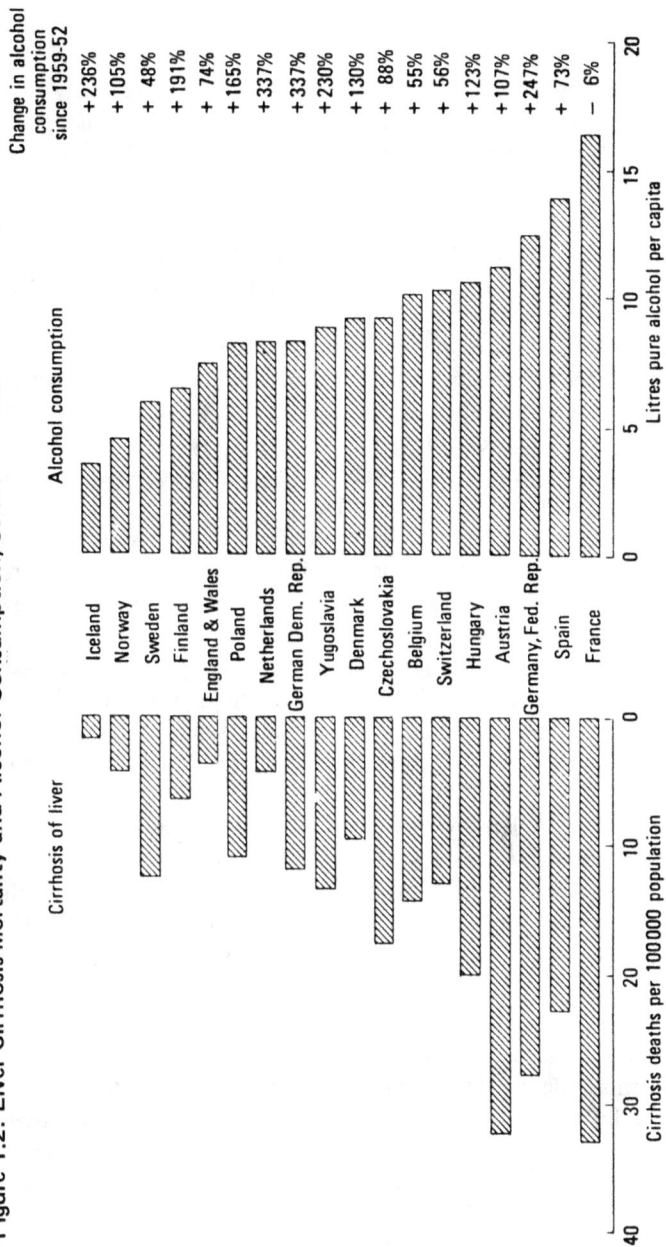

	Change in alcohol consumption since 1959-52
Iceland	+236%
Norway	+105%
Sweden	+ 48%
Finland	+191%
England & Wales	+ 74%
Poland	+165%
Netherlands	+337%
German Dem. Rep.	+337%
Yugoslavia	+230%
Denmark	+130%
Czechoslovakia	+ 88%
Belgium	+ 55%
Switzerland	+ 56%
Hungary	+123%
Austria	+107%
Germany, Fed. Rep.	+247%
Spain	+ 73%
France	– 6%

Cirrhosis of liver

Alcohol consumption

Litres pure alcohol per capita

Cirrhosis deaths per 100000 population

82256

Reproduced from: Office of Health Economics (1981) Alcohol: Reducing the Harm, London, with the kind permission of David Taylor.

markedly more vulnerable than men.

It seems (for males at least) that any individual who regularly drinks more than four pints of beer, or its equivalent, has a five times greater chance of developing liver cirrhosis, and that beyond this level of consumption the risk increases rapidly. The regular tippler seems more likely than the bout drinker to damage his liver in this way. It is now possible to give relatively clear-cut guidelines about safe levels of drinking as far as this common physical consquence is concerned. Liver cirrhosis is ranked sixth most common cause of death in the USA and up to 95 per cent of these deaths are regarded as alcohol related. The prevalence of cirrhosis is particularly high in countries such as France, Italy and Portugal, where regular wine drinking is so much a part of life and regarded by some as a necessary ingredient of diet.

Our concern with prevention cannot simply stop at aiming to reduce the prevalence of alcohol induced liver disease, although that in itself would create a very worthwhile reduction in human suffering, morbidity and reduced life expectancy. While the association between liver cirrhosis and increased *per capita* consumption is the best known evidence of the physical harm induced by excessive drinking, there is a much longer list of disabling or fatal conditions for which excessive drinking is a potent cause. These are discussed in greater detail in the next chapter. As we know, alcohol is a drug, taken for its effect on our minds and behaviour. It is therefore hardly surprising that many of the harmful consequences of drinking are caused by its effect on behaviour and judgement. Relatively low doses of alcohol have been shown to impair eye-hand co-ordination; the eye also proves less able to adapt to rapid changes from light to dark and tunnel vision develops so that objects at the periphery of the field of vision may not be seen. In view of these physiological consequences, it is hardly surprising that alcohol reduces our capacity to carry out skilled tasks. When this biological consequence is linked to the well-known confidence and bravado which come with excessive drinking, then it is hardly surprising that the risk of accidents at home, at work, and most notably on the road are greatly increased by drinking. In countries where effective drinking and driving laws have been introduced, there has usually followed a dramatic decline in the number of road accidents and fatalities.

In 1967, when the British Road Safety Act was introduced, there was a 40 per cent drop in the number of road casualties on Saturday night and Sunday morning. It is interesting to see a single Act have such a preventive influence. It has been estimated that about 5,000 lives have been saved and 200,000 casualties prevented by this measure.

Unfortunately, this drop has often proved short lived when drivers realised that the likelihood of detection was small. The possible impact of legislative measures upon alcohol problems is discussed further in Chapter 15.

Accidents at work, absenteeism and lost productivity all add to the cost of alcohol problems in the community. It has been estimated that alcohol abuse and alcoholism cost the United States nearly $43 billion in 1975, including $19.64 billion in lost production, $5.14 billion in motor vehicle accidents and $2.86 billion in violent crimes. Rather than allow ourselves to be overwhelmed by such figures, we should try to break down the magnitude of the problem into manageable parts. We need to recognise the extent of the harm which drinking causes and then identify parts of the total picture which are recognisable and susceptible to existing preventive strategies.

It is tempting to fix our minds primarily on the socially identifiable consequences of alcohol misuse but it is important not to forget the domestic and personal hidden tragedies which exist within the daily experience of those who have to live with a problem drinker. The incidence of divorce, domestic violence, child abuse and neglect are all higher where a man or woman drinks excessively. For some individuals, alcohol comes to dominate their lives and they become physically and psychologically dependent on this drug so that other concerns, such as family, friends and work, become quite secondary. Thus, when we look at the range of problems which we seek to minimise, they extend from the occasional misuse of alcohol that may result in an accident or some uncharacteristic act of violence or despair, to the problem drinker whose physical and social effectiveness has become chronically impaired. We can no longer regard these casualties as chance occurrences. We know that they are predictable and hopefully preventable, but it may well require a change in our comfortable assumption that we can go on producing and consuming more and more alcohol, secure in a spurious sense of invulnerability.

2 WHAT PROBLEMS ARE PREVENTIBLE?

It is reasonable to think of the 1970s as a decade during which the emphasis of health care planning moved from a predominantly treatment bias, towards an increasing prevention bias. This shift can certainly be recognised in the area of alcohol problems, both at a national and an international level. Nationally, the various circulars, advisory committee reports and white papers of the Department of Health and Social Security, which in the early years of the decade were concerned mainly with the treatment and rehabilitative needs of alcoholics, had, by the early 1980s tended to suggest, implicitly and explicitly, that it was through the development of preventive strategies that the biggest pay-offs were likely to be achieved. Then, at an international level, the reports of the World Health Organisation and of the influential Addiction Research Foundation in Toronto have both paid increasing attention to issues of prevention as well as, and even to an extent in place of, issues of treatment. This trend reached a watershed, as has been noted in the introduction to this book, with the Technical Discussions at the 35th World Health Assembly in 1982.

What emerges from the previous chapter is, however, that there is not a single 'alcohol problem' which has to be prevented and which therefore requires the development of a single 'alcohol prevention strategy'. Much of this book will be devoted to charting just how wide and how diverse the prevention debates currently are. For the time being, however, beginning with the proposition that alcohol *does* cause problems and that these problems are both widespread and serious, it is worth considering whether all these problems are equally preventible and what sort of strategies might be adopted to deal with them.

Some indication has already been given of the size of the shopping list of alcohol-related problems. Physical damage is certainly not restricted to the liver, although cirrhosis and hepatitis are common enough. There is also an association beween heavy drinking and cancers of the upper digestive tract (tongue, mouth, pharynx, larynx and oesophagus). Virtually all forms of circulatory disease seem to be related to excessive drinking and some, such as alcoholic cardiomyopathy, are specifically caused by it. Raised death rates amongst alcoholics occur in relation to ulcers of the stomach, duodenum and oesophagus as well as for diseases of the lower intestine. Acute pancreatitis, which is currently increasing as a cause of death in Britain, is also associated with excessive drinking, as are tuberculosis and respiratory diseases such as bronchitis. Peripheral neuropathy develops in alcohol-dependents and leads in turn to severe disablement. In addition, the role of alcohol in relation to accidents should not be overlooked. Whilst many people acknowledge the importance of this factor in traffic accidents, it has been suggested that it relates also to about a third of all accidents in the home, to a high proportion of drownings and to many more accidents in the workplace than is generally recognised.

In terms of mental illnesses other than alcohol addiction itself, alcohol can cause brain atrophy, dementia and conditions, including Korsakoff's psychosis, which involve memory loss and hallucinations. Psychiatric disorders such as depression, anxiety and morbid jealousy are also liable to be related to alcohol use. Suicide rates amongst alcoholics are strikingly higher than for any other category of the population.

The social costs of alcohol abuse are also considerable, both at an individual and societal level. Family problems, leading often to domestic violence, child abuse and divorce, are associated with excessive drinking. Petty crime of various sorts, as well as alcohol-related offences themselves, have to be taken into account, as do the costs to industry through absenteeism, accidents and inefficiency. This lost productivity, although difficult to quantify, is now attracting increasing attention. In general, it is recognised that the economic costs of alcohol to society are very considerable. Without even claiming anything like comprehensiveness, these examples of alcohol-related harm are summarised in Tables 2.1 and 2.2.

After reading that shopping list of physical, mental and social damage, the first reaction of a rational person must be to question why, if indeed all this is true, anybody ever takes a drink in the first place. The point to be made here, and it is of central importance to the theme of this book, is that most alcohol problems are associated with *excessive* drinking only and not with drinking as such. The task facing those concerned to develop preventive strategies is therefore to try to stop people drinking *so much* (however much that might be) that they do themselves and others harm.

As well as being impressive for its sheer length (and it would, of course, have been possible to go into each item in greater detail) that shopping list of problems is also impressive for its diversity. This too has important implications for prevention. Is it likely, for example, that

Table 2.1: Damage Caused by Excessive Drinking (Alcoholism or Alcohol Dependence)

Medical Problems	Cancers of mouth, throat and gullet Gastritis Stomach ulcer Duodenal ulcer Stomach haemorrhage Pancreatitis Diabetes Vitamin deficiency Feminisation Sexual impotence Testicular atrophy Anemia Chronic myopathy Cardiomyopathy Peripheral neuritis Wernicke's encephalopathy Korsakoff's psychosis	Minor brain damage Dementia Fatty Liver Alcoholic hepatitis Liver cirrhosis Liver cancer Fat metabolism diseases Gout Fetal alcohol syndrome Epilepsy Depression Anxiety Phobic illnesses Hallucinations Paranoid states Delerium tremens Withdrawal epilepsy Alcoholic psychosis
Social problems	Financial debt Homelessness Family problems Marital problems	Sexual problems Absenteeism Employment problems Stigma
Legal problems	Theft Fraud	Deception Vagrancy

the same strategy which is proposed to reduce liver cirrhosis death rates will have much impact upon football hooliganism?

If, therefore, alcohol problems have such a capacity to reach into the widest range of life, it is going to be essential to see if, for the purposes of strategic planning, particular strands of preventive policy have the capacity to bind groups of problems together and make them more manageable. In order to discover whether or not this is possible, it is necessary to take a step back from the heterogeneity of the problems and also from the weight of human misery associated with them. Considering this multitude of problems simply as phenomena and noting its relationship with alcohol simply as a causative association, it gradually becomes clear that we are dealing with two apparently similar but actually quite distinct phenomena. We are dealing with, on the one hand, chronic alcohol problems, called, for the sake of convenience, alcoholism or alcohol dependence, and with, on the other hand, acute alcohol problems, called, also for the sake of convenience, drunken-

Table 2.2: Damage Caused by Intoxication (Drunkenness)

Medical problems	Acute alcohol poisoning or overdose Amnesic episodes Drug overdose Suicidal behaviour Acute gastritis Diabetic symptoms	Pancreatititis Trauma Head injury Accidents Epilepsy Hangover Fetal alcohol syndrome
Social problems	Social isolation Aggressive behaviour Passive behaviour Domestic violence Child abuse Child neglect	Sexual problems Domestic accidents Industrial accidents Absenteeism Poor time-keeping
Legal problems	Driving offences Drunkeness offences Theft Shop-lifting Taking & driving a vehicle	Criminal damage to property Fraud Deception Assault Homicide

Source: Adapted from Thorley, A. (1982) In: Plant, M.A. (ed.) *Drinking and Problem Drinking*, Junction Books, London

ness or intoxication. A careful reading of Tables 2.1 and 2.2 will show the important differences between these two categories of damage.

It is rather like staring out from the shore on a misty day. The sea and the sky are more or less the same colour, but we know that they are actually quite different from each other. The horizon is impossible to distinguish and the two elements seem to blend into each other as if they were interchangeable. But just try to row a boat through the sky or fly a 747 into the sea and the difference will become clear.

And that is the position with regard to the prevention of alcohol problems. Strategies which are likely to have some impact upon acute problems may well be inappropriate for chronic problems, and vice versa. Referring to the tables printed above, it is generally not difficult to see how particular items could be assigned to the acute or to the chronic side. But, of course, alcoholics can be regarded simply as chronic drinkers. That is like the mist which covers the seascape, preventing an accurate assessment of the real condition of the sea and the sky. In order to blow away the mist we need to disaggregate the problems as far as is possible.

It has, nevertheless, been assumed, for different reasons at different times, that it would be possible to prevent all alcohol problems by means of a single solution. A Victorian view, for example, would tend to aggregate alcohol problems under the heading of 'public inebriety' and, as a consequence, see control over the liquor supply coupled with vigorous and sustained policing as a solution likely to prove successful in reducing such problems to tolerable levels. Equally, in the middle years of this century, with the rise of Alcoholics Anonymous and its enormously influential view of alcoholism as a discrete disease entity, it was possible to see how an efficient early detection system together with suitably expanded treatment services would impose a pragmatic cut-off point in the process of the disease.

Neither view is in itself wrong. It is simply that neither view is in itself adequate. Each fails to take account of the presumptions of the other. The Victorians were not concerned with a disease called alcoholism, because they did not have any good reason to suppose that such a disease existed. Alcoholics Anonymous is not much concerned with public drunkenness, because not everybody who gets drunk is an alcoholic. Thus, as the twin potencies of the medical profession and self-help groups rose in parallel during this century, interest moved away from the messy phenomenon of public drunkenness to something which was conceptualised as the underlying *cause* of problems rather than just their manifestations in the health and social functioning of particular individuals. In terms of the extended metaphor developed above, the Victorians were looking into the sea, whilst in this century we have been staring at the sky. The purpose of this book is to sketch the whole landscape and to suggest ways of understanding it.

In moving away from the view of alcohol problems as alcoholism or alcohol problems as drunkenness, the comfort of any possible single solution soon vanishes. This does not relate only to the diversity of the nature of alcohol problems. It relates also to a diversity in their severity. Although there are, of course, definitional problems associated with both unitary concepts (alcoholism and drunkenness) the broader scale of problems now invoked clearly precludes any but the most general description. Something, it could be argued, is an alcohol problem as soon as somebody (anybody) defines it as such. Drinking a single glass of whisky in Saudi Arabia could certainly be viewed as an alcohol problem, for example, just as, at the other end of the scale, losing one's balance whilst fishing from an open boat in Finland is almost invariably associated with heavy alcohol consumption. Both are serious problems, the first carrying severe legal penalties and the second a high chance of freezing to death. Yet in both cases, it is the special local conditions which change a trivial matter into a problem. These local conditions − cultural, environmental, climatic, religious, legal, economic, and so on − all contribute to the process of defining a particular event or sequence as an alcohol problem.

When, later in this book, we examine the issues which inform the various debates about the prevention of alcohol problems, it will frequently become apparent that the strategies which are being examined are determined in large part by the terms of that process of definition. Thus, a country like Saudi Arabia will share with the Victorians a tendency to see solutions in terms of proscription, enforcement and deterrents, whilst Finland, where drink is made available through the State Alcohol Monopoly, is much more concerned with attempting to persuade individuals to moderate the level and context of their drinking so as to reduce the possibility of harmful consequences.

Equally, however, strategies relate to the severity of the alcohol problem along some more general scale which rates various consequences from mild discomfort to loss of life. The same drinking bout which gives one individual a slight hangover might, if that individual happened to be the pilot of a jumbo jet, contribute significantly to the deaths of many others, sober or intoxicated, who happened to be passengers at the moment when his concentration fatally lapsed. Thus, it is not necessarily the drinking itself, but the context of the drinking and the context of the consequences of the drinking which will define the problem and point towards a particular solution which is appropriate.

A question which has to be raised here is how, in view of this diversity of problems and solutions, anything approaching an integrated preventive policy can possibly be envisaged. For a book like this presumes, by its very existence, the possibility of integration. The answer to the question lies in the fabric of the debates themselves, and the common strands (see Chapter 17) which emerge. There is no obvious integrative strategy, since there is not even agreement as to what it is that is being integrated. All we can be sure of is that, as in other areas where pleasure impinges upon health and well-being, society does not put an infinite value upon the life of the individual. We pay a price for having alcohol around in society and will go on doing so, as long as we continue to want the opportunity to drink. There is every indication that the world, as a whole, values alcohol more highly than most, if not all, other mood-altering substances. It certainly seems to believe, if the consumption figures quoted in the previous chapter are anything to go by, that the benefits still outweigh the costs. There will always come a point, for the individual, for the country or the world, when the benefits cease to look so attractive when compared to a mounting column of casualties. If we are not yet at that point with alcohol (though some, a minority, believe we have already passed it) then we still need to recognise that one function of a book like this is to assist in the process of determining, in the light of available resources and knowledge, where it is that the point is to be found. The value of prevention is to ensure that we stay as far on the credit side as we can.

This can, perhaps, be best illustrated by an example. One alcohol problem which causes a great deal of concern in virtually every country (certainly in every developed country and increasingly in developing ones too) is that of road casualties associated with drunk driving. Such casualties are known to peak towards the end of the evening and in the very early hours of the morning (at times, in other words, when those who have been drinking as a leisure activity away from home are driving back). There are, of course, differences between countries regarding the timing of this social phenomenon and its associated mortality and morbidity. Taking such differences into account, it might well seem that an attractive strategy would be for each country to devise appropriate but not necessarily identical curfew speed limits. This step would undoubtedly have a positive impact upon the extent of alcohol-related road casualties. Yet the feasibility of the strategy would depend less upon the perceived costs of such casualties than upon the perceived benefits accruing from unfettered motoring. It would depend upon the state of the roads, the quality of street lighting, the tenacity or corruptibility of the traffic police, the pressure upon the courts and the integrity of the justice system. But it would depend, most of all, on the value people put upon drinking and on driving. Since, frequently, both activities are highly valued, the strategy might be dismissed as unattractive by far more countries than a rational Martian looking down upon this planet could ever believe possible.

3 WHAT CAN BE ACHIEVED THROUGH PROHIBITION?

What has been established so far is that alcohol problems are serious and widespread, affecting all levels of society in most countries in the world. The current upward trend in global consumption has led to the need to pay increasing attention to the prevention of alcohol problems at an individual, community, national and global level. When, however, we come to look more closely at what is meant by 'alcohol problems' we find that the term seems to cover an extraordinary range of different phenomena. Since these problems are so ubiquitous and because they are integrated in such a complex way with personal and social functioning, the possibility of finding a single, final solution to all alcohol problems seems very remote. Indeed, the more disaggregated our concept of alcohol problems, the more heterogeneous the range of preventive strategies becomes.

There is, however, one strategy which appears, at least at first sight, to have all the advantages of the absolute. Since, this strategy states, alcohol consumption is a necessary prerequisite of alcohol problems, these problems could easily be eliminated if alcohol consumption ceased. The single, final solution to alcohol problems consists, therefore, in the total prohibition at a global level of all forms of beverage alcohol.

Two questions have to be raised in connection with this strategy. The first is to ask whether it is practicable and the second whether it is desirable. Whilst it is hardly possible to give an unambiguous response to either of these questions, it is important to delineate the issues which lie behind them, to examine the historical and scientific evidence that should be brought to bear, and to recognise that each question is only really meaningful in the context of the other.

To begin, however, with the question of the practicality of a preventive strategy aimed at the total elimination of alcohol, it is worth remembering that such a strategy is nothing new. It lay behind much though not all of the nineteenth century temperance movement; it lay behind the United States sixteen year experiment with Prohibition; and it lies behind the increasingly influential position adopted by orthodox Islam. Whilst the energising fervour may often have its origin in deeply held religious beliefs, it is important to remember that religious beliefs, like drinking practices themselves, are culturally determined. A simple cause and effect logic lies behind them, a logic persuasive enough to have ensured, for example, that other, less hot-headed countries, such as the United Kingdom and New Zealand, have also from time to time taken very seriously the idea that beverage alcohol should be banished from their shores.

The three examples mentioned above (the temperance movement, Prohibition in the USA, spread of orthodox Islam) are not, of course, identical. The efforts of the temperance movement were directed towards a goal of prohibition but were persuasive in nature as well as interventionist. In a sense, it was a measure of the success of their persuasive and interventionist efforts that Prohibition was attempted in America at all. The question, therefore, of how far total prohibition is seen as a desirable state and how far it is a political end legitimately to be imposed upon unwilling populations remains an important differentiating characteristic. What remains common to these three examples is that none represents an unalloyed success. Even the temperance movement, which might have drawn strength from its temporary success in securing the introduction of Prohibition in America, inevitably suffered a major and possibly irretrievable setback at the time of Repeal.

Whilst relative lack of success of past or present efforts need not lead to the conclusion that no subsequent efforts are likely to be any more effective, it is, certainly, grounds for pausing to discover what lessons might be learned from the failure, in absolute terms, of such initiatives.

Firstly, of course, it can be argued that each of these examples relates to what is essentially an isolated attempt to move against a headlong global trend. Is it likely, such an argument asks, that efforts within a single country or group of countries, even when these efforts spring from a powerful popular sentiment, could ever be sufficient to swim against the global alcohol tide? It may be that, at least temporarily, such efforts can have a significant impact within their country or countries of origin. It may even be that they will have some influence upon geographical or political neighbours. In the long term, however, the overall world trend cannot but prove the more potent force, if only by virtue of providing the line of least resistance. Thus, runs such an argument, for a prohibitionist policy to have even the most remote chance of success, it must have strong and sustained international support. It is all very well for the World Health Organisation to deplore the upward trend in alcohol consumption and to consider banning champagne from its official receptions. Rather more to the point would be a powerful alliance of all members of the United Nations family, rallying behind a common call for a ban on the manufacture, distribution and consumption of beverage alcohol.

In the absence of any such alliance, runs the argument, the very possibility of any success for prohibitionist policies is vitiated. Nor does it seem even remotely likely that such international consensus will emerge in the near future. Even amongst those organisations, such as WHO, which attest to a relationship between *per capita* alcohol consumption and the prevalence of alcohol-related problems, the conclusion which is drawn from the available data relates more to the necessity of establishing optimum drinking levels for individuals and for countries than to the suggestion that alcohol *per se* should be eliminated. At the same time, the vigorous expansion of the beverage alcohol industry at international level, the growth in the extent to which that industry is dominated by trans-national corporations and the internationalisation, through various trade agreements, of the marketing of beverage alcohol, all serve to increase the volume and velocity of the alcohol tide, rather than to stem it. Issues to do with international trade are debated in Chapter 13. Equally, however, factors within countries, such as the popularity of home production of beer and wine, the inertia of consumer habits and, most simple of all, the increased salience of drinking, all contribute to an upward trend in consumption. What signs are there, in such circumstances, of any real, sustained and integrated call for prohibition? Do not those attempts which have been made seem, by contrast with the flow of world events, fragmentary, ineffective, even freakish?

There is, let it be said, at least a partial response to the argument that no call for prohibition can succeed without international consensus. It lies in the increasing attention which is being paid at international level to the public health aspects of alcohol availability. Springing as it does from the distribution of consumption model of alcohol problems (which posits a relationship between consumption trends and rates of problems) and supported by the carefully argued reports of the International Study of Alcohol Control Experiences (ISACE), this approach is gaining weight currently with a wide range of people (including politicians) concerned with social policy development. Dubbed by the beverage industry as neo-prohibitionists, proponents of this view argue that the most effective way of limiting the range and severity of alcohol problems seems, on the basis of the best available evidence, to lie in imposing stricter controls over its manufacture, distribution and price. Thus, whilst not actually advocating the elimination of beverage alcohol, such a view certainly seems to take some steps down the road which leads to curbing the unfettered interplay of market forces. More to the point, in relation to the issues of international consensus as a prerequisite for progress, it does seem to be gaining a degree of international respectability and influence which would have seemed unlikely as little as a decade ago.

Turning, however, to the first of the three examples mentioned above, there are at least two aspects of the temperance movement which require investigation in order to clarify the social factors which operate to challenge the practicability of prohibitionist policies. Even at its height, in the mid-nineteenth century in England and slightly later in America, the temperance movement failed to engage sufficiently broadly based support to carry national consensus on the liquor question. This aspect of the history of the temperance movement may perhaps be interpreted as a reflection of the fundamental ambiguity which lies at the root of man's relationship to alcohol. It is clear, from an anthropological point of view, that alcohol is a special commodity, carrying ritual significance and associated with altered states of consciousness. Equally, it is clear, even from medieval sources, that the association between excessive drinking and social disruption has long been recognised. Thus, both at an individual and community level, there can hardly be such a thing as a holistic response to alcohol. It is a complex substance and its consumption involves complex behaviours. Certainly, different social groups are likely to adopt different sets of values with regard to drinking and are therefore likely to respond differently to any suggestion that it should be proscribed.

It can be argued, therefore, that in its single-minded fervour, the nineteenth century temperance movement simply failed to take account of the complexity of the values associated with alcohol and underestimated the extent to which it was integrated with all levels of personal and social functioning. Whether this integration is viewed in terms of ambiguous symbolic meaning or economic determinism or even the ruthless pursuit of the pleasure principle, is probably less important than recognising the extent to which, in a pluralistic society, it is seldom likely to be possible to achieve consensus on any alcohol policy other than one based upon a compromise between the principles of market justice and the principles of social justice.

The second aspect of the history of the temperance movement which is relevant here concerns the substantial decline in its scope of influence occurring since its heyday in the nineteenth century. There is insufficient space here to do justice to the interplay of social forces involved in the decline of the temperance movement. Rather, it is worth trying to understand how it is that particular social movements with particular goals are clearly energised by, and therefore defined as belonging to, particular sets of historical circumstances. It is difficult, for the temperance movement *not* to seem old fashioned now, simply because its influence was so great in the nineteenth century. Had it been less successful, more marginal then, it would have been easier for it to seem more successful and less marginal now. What is being suggested here is that particular strategies may be viewed as having a greater or lesser potential for effective influence, not so much because of intrinsic qualities susceptible to analytic examination and assessment, but rather because of the accident of having been tarred with a particular historical brush. The very term temperance, which is, after all, an unexceptionable concept, now has the power to conjure up images of the most dull and kill-joy forms of bigotry.

The question of the practicality of a preventive strategy aimed at the elimination of alcohol is brought into sharp focus by the history of the introduction of Prohibition in the USA in 1917 and its subsequent repeal in 1933. The failure of efforts to enforce the regulations, both as a result of the corruptibility of enforcement agencies and the energy and imagination of those seeking to evade the regulations, has been well documented and is indeed part of popular culture through its frequent representation in feature films. What is interesting is the extent to which absolute proscription actually permitted the principles of market justice to operate at their most crudely opportunistic level, unimpeded by a socially sanctioned code of restraining influences. The growth in criminal activity associated with bootlegging and the operation of speakeasies (as distinct from, and in addition to, the illegal act of supplying the liquor) clearly posed individual and social problems that arguably caused far greater damage than the alcohol problems which Prohibition was supposed to alleviate. It has been suggested that the growth of organised crime in the USA and, in particular, the spectacularly rapid rise of the Mafia, was stimulated and encouraged by the special conditions prevailing during the period of Prohibition. An unanticipated effect of Prohibition was to make criminals of large numbers of otherwise law abiding citizens.

Developing social policy always involves establishing priorities. Whether the basis of prioritisation has to do with the strict economic cost to society of particular problems or sets of problems, or whether it is underpinned by some less utilitarian and more arbitrary moral system, there can be little doubt that, despite the fall in the liver cirrhosis death rate, Prohibition failed in the USA. The other costs were simply, whatever the system of arithmetic used, too high. Again, we have an example of an attempt to impose an absolute solution which is evidently out of step with the wishes of a substantial proportion of the population and which is actively opposed by a small but influential group who have a vested interest in promoting its failure. In such circumstances, and particularly at a time of economic uncertainty, as in the USA during the 1920s, the opportunities for exploitation soon came to seem like a way of life. When Repeal was finally introduced, all it did was to regularise drinking practices which, though formally illegal, were already and always had been well integrated into the social fabric.

Finally, then, and most relevantly from a contemporary point of view, in terms of the practicality of imposing a ban on alcohol, there is the case of orthodox Islam, and its increasing influence, expressed both economically and militarily, upon the world. Unlike the example of Prohibition in the USA, here we have a case where the absence of alcohol represents the normative position of a particular society. The elimination of alcohol from non-Islamic countries is, in a sense, part of an evangelical activity, since in the Islamic countries themselves total abstinence is not culturally dissonant. On the other hand, one important point to be made here is that the position of Islamic countries is, in actual practice, much less absolutist than is often supposed. Apart from Iran, where vigorous (some might say savage) enforcement of prohibition has apparently reduced the availability of alcohol to negligible amounts, changing socio-economic conditions in other Middle Eastern countries are eroding the extent to which the Koran, which constitutes a code of civil and criminal law as well as advocating a religious doctrine, is being interpreted literally with respect to its injunctions against alcohol. At present, the production, importation, sale and consumption of beverage alcohol are still completely prohibited in Saudi Arabia, Libya, the Yeman Arab Republic, Kuwait and Qatar. In Bahrain and Pakistan, however, importation and use by foreigners is permitted, although the production and consumption by Moslems is not. Other countries, such as Iraq, Egypt, Lebanon and Sudan do not enforce prohibition.

This rather confused picture has two layers to it since it is necessary to ask first whether laws prohibiting the supply of alcohol exist and secondly, if they do, whether they are enforced. In general, as oil-producing countries establish increased communications with other cultures, stimulating the availability of consumer goods, tourists and foreign workers, so a widening gap appears between traditional orthodox abstinence and the growth in opportunities for smuggling and illegal production of alcohol. Currently, Iran's response has been to harden its attitude to the punishments imposed for infractions of the regulations, whilst some other countries have tended to relax the laws and customs, either through legislative change or through the simpler process of turning a proverbial blind eye.

Obviously, where there is widespread popular adherence to a religious doctrine which is seen as being integrated with civil and criminal law prohibiting the use of alcohol, prohibition is likely to prove an effective control policy. Where, however, that belief system is being challenged, or where enforcement is seen to be ineffective or tokenistic, other, less traditional influences are likely to predominate, particularly when these are perceived, as is the case of Western drinking practices, as being in some important way more 'civilised' than the traditional orthodoxy.

Turning, therefore, from the practicality of prohibition to its desirability, the issue becomes one of testing whether Western drinking practices, moderate or immoderate, can be deemed worthy of the epithet 'civilised'. Is it, the neoprohibitionists may legitimately ask, civilised to die of liver cirrhosis? Is it civilised to drive your motor car whilst drunk, perhaps killing or maiming bystanders? Is it civilised to beat your wife, to run into debt, to lose your job and your self-respect? Such rhetoric, superficially unassailable, requires a rational response. Certainly, it is not sufficient to set against it some vague images of middle class families drinking fine vintages with their steak suppers, or the purportedly therapeutic advantages of the cameraderie of the good olde English pub. The question is a serious one, posing, as it does, a doubt about the quality of particular modes of life and suggesting that some (and not necessarily those which simply have the lowest rates of damage) are, in a fundamentally moral, social and aesthetic sense, qualitatively superior.

To an extent, recalling the compromise between the principles of market and social justice which was mentioned earlier in this chapter, John Stuart Mill's contention that 'each is the proper guardian of his own health, whether bodily, or mental and spiritual' requires to be re-examined in the light of the principles of public health, but not without losing sight of the spirit of vital libertarianism which echoes through the concept of civilised drinking. What is civilised, surely, is the presumption that rational choice remains within the grasp of the individual and that social policy provides an arena within which that rational choice can be legitimately exercised. In such a context, a strategy designed to eliminate beverage alcohol from the world can only be seen as working against the rational process. Whilst it is true that real free-dom exists only in a willing adherence to objectively determined rules, rationality is demonstrated only when a real choice exists. The belief that the only hope for mankind with respect to the reduction of alcohol-related mortality and morbidity is to eliminate alcohol alto-gether is, finally, both pessimistic and inhumane.

All of that is not to say, however, that unfettered market justice is the right way ahead. It is, presumably, the optimisation of drinking practices rather than the maximisation of alcohol consumption that is the objective of an integrated preventive policy. Just as the problems of undertaking cost-benefit analyses with respect to alcohol at a national or international level are bedevilled as much by ethical as methodo-logical considerations, so the process of social policy development is influenced as much by empirical as theoretical considerations. If, in its call for the establishment of explicit national alcohol policies, WHO is once again, as indeed it should, entering a political arena, then it is important to recognise the force of the old adage that politics is the art of the possible. Clearly, especially when viewed from an international perspective, what is possible by way of workable alcohol policies, will be different in different cultures. The purpose of this chapter has been to assess the extent to which policies based upon prohibition of alcohol might have shown themselves capable of fulfilling an attractive or prag-matic promise. The conclusion seems to be that, by and large, they have not.

4 WHAT CAN BE ACHIEVED THROUGH TREATMENT?

The traditional medical response to the prevention of any health hazard involves three phases. The first, *primary prevention*, seeks to prevent harm occurring. For instance the provision of a clean water supply is clearly a more effective means of eradicating water-borne infections than early detection and treatment, however vigorous and well organised. When the cause is less clearly known or understood or the social and economic cost of eradication seems unacceptably high, then *secondary prevention* places greater emphasis on early case detection which minimises harm. Finally, *tertiary prevention* seeks to ensure that, when harm has occurred, the sufferer is effectively rehabilitated with minimal residual damage.

This trinity of preventive strategies has its origins in a medical tradition of the last century when infectious disease was a major cause of morbidity and the dominant model of illness. We may question how well the model serves in the context of alcohol problems. The causal agent is clear enough — alcohol — but the cost of eradication by prohibition, as has been argued in the previous chapter, is unacceptably high in most societies where alcohol has gained an established place. When the USA and some other countries were smarting under the consequences of a prohibitionist era, the pendulum of informed public opinion swung away from a concern with the agent, toward the sufferer — the drinker. Most people drink without coming to any harm, ran the new argument, and therefore there must be something special about the alcoholic. As we noted in relation to Victorian perceptions of alcohol problems, this contrast between the social versus the individual attribution of causation was voiced at a time when moral weakness or vice were the attributes assigned to drunkards. This century, the social climate was inhospitable to such moralistic epithets and, as a consequence, there emerged the concept of the alcoholic as a victim suffering from a medico-social disease. This did nothing to modify the basic tenet that the flaw lies in the individual drinker — the victim continues to bear the blame.

Even within this later context, those with alcohol problems were viewed as specially vulnerable people who for reasons of biological constitution, allergy or psychic tensions were unable to use alcohol like

25

the rest. This was a comfortable enough philosophy for those who could enjoy drinking since it left the detection and treatment of the unfortunate few to the appropriate specialist agencies. This is probably still the most widely held view of alcohol problems today and it has fostered an unprecedented growth in the past thirty years in facilities for the early detection of alcohol problems (secondary prevention) and the treatment and rehabilitation of alcoholics (tertiary prevention). Such facilities have proliferated in the statutory and voluntary sectors, as well as in the special world of private health care provision.

In 1935 the American Medical Association passed a resolution that alcoholics were to be regarded as valid patients. Ten years earlier, Alcoholics Anonymous was founded in Ohio, and has ever since played a major part in continuing to define alcoholism as a disease. During the 1940s, the Yale Centre of Alcohol Studies opened two clinics for alcoholics. Treatment was on an out-patient basis and groups, which were often of a didactic kind, formed a major part of therapy. At about the same time, the National Council on Alcoholism was formed in the USA with one of its principal aims being the dissemination of 'the facts' about alcoholism. In 1952 WHO added its *imprimatur* to the emphasis on treatment in its definition:

Alcoholics are those excessive drinkers whose dependence on alcohol has attained such a degree that it shows a noticeable mental disturbance or interference with their bodily or mental health, their interpersonal relations and their smooth social and economic functioning, or who show the prodomal signs of such developments. They therefore require treatment.   (WHO, 1952)

Ten years later, the Ministry of Health in Britain advised health authorities to establish specialised units for the treatment of alcoholism in their areas. A National Council on Alcoholism was established around the same time and, although at inception its tasks were primarily to inform and advise, its affiliated councils quickly became involved in the provision of direct services to alcoholics and their families. Similar trends were echoed in other developed countries throughout the world so that alcoholism was soon established as a major medical concern. In the USA it came to be regarded as a major health problem and led to the creation of a National Institute on Alcohol Abuse and Alcoholism, which prepares regular major reports to the US Congress.

Meanwhile, in Britain the growth of specialised services continued relatively slowly, so that by 1975 there were 21 special treatment units providing a total of 434 beds — a considerable investment but not nearly adequate to confront a problem which was estimated at that time to affect about 86,000 adults in England and Wales — a number which it was agreed would have to be multiplied by a factor of three if it were to include other alcohol related problems, such as drunk driving offences, industrial accidents and alcohol induced sickness.

The *size* of the problem alone is enough to raise doubts about the likelihood of specialised treatment facilities ever being a sufficient response to alcohol problems. Advocates for continuing expansion of specialist treatment and counselling must also answer the question of effectiveness. There remains an ominous silence over the question of whether there is a well recognised treatment for alcoholism or at least for some recognisable part of the range of alcohol related problems as currently described.

There have always been individual physicians who have recognised that regular excessive drinking caused a state which was recognisably different from simple drunkenness. For instance, Seneca noted that the affects of prolonged drinking were 'quivering of the muscles soaked in wine, and an emaciation due to indigestion and not to hunger. Hence, the uncertain and faltering gait and constant stumbling as if they were actually drunk; hence the swelling of the skin and distension of the belly, which has taken more than it can hold; hence the jaundiced and discoloured complexion and the nerves dulled without feeling.'

Various remedies for chronic drunkenness, some moral or penal, others medical or psychological, have been suggested over ·the centuries. One of the first medical theses on the treatment of chronic inebriety was written by Thomas Trotter in Edinburgh in 1778. His description of the physicians' attitude and therapeutic approach contains much of the essence of contemporary treatment, although it has been elaborated by each passing fashion in medical and psychiatric thought.

On such an occasion it is difficult to lay down rules. The physician must be guided by his own discretion: he must scrutinise the character of his patient, his pursuits, his modes of living, his very passions and private affairs. He must consult his own experience of human nature, and what he has learned in the school of the world. The great point to be obtained is the confidence of the sick man; but this is not to be accomplished at a first visit. It is to be remem-

bered that a bodily infirmity is not the only thing to be corrected.
The habit of drunkenness is a disease of the mind.   (Trotter, 1804)

A recent leader in the Lancet commented that reviewing alcoholism
treatment in this country was like looking at layers of geological
strata:—

> It is possible to discern the deposits, akin to geological layers, of a
> sequence of therapeutic fashions — the residue of almost forgotten
> enthusiasm for in-patient psychotherapy units, for group processes
> and the therapeutic community, for family therapy, and later for
> community psychiatry. To say that treatment for alcoholism is only
> an accretion of fads and fashions would be too harsh, for it is also
> built on much clinical experience; but it must be admitted that we
> have not done enough to assess scientifically the effectiveness of
> treatment methods.   (Lancet, 1977)

We are not concerned here with the way in which these complex treatment philosophies have developed. Almost every psychiatric innovation
of the past fifty years has been applied to the alcoholic at some time or
other. This in itself shows that there is no certainty about the best
approach.

More recently, it has been possible to test some of our assumptions
about treatment by carefully comparing different approaches, when
during the 1960s a small number of studies began to look more closely
at the claims of certain treatment programmes. It is not sufficient
simply to report the success of a new treatment; certain supplementary
questions must be asked: What would have happened if no treatment
had been offered? Were any patients made worse by this treatment? We
also need to know more about the population being treated, since there
is ample evidence that those patients who have the strongest suite of
social attributes — well motivated people of stable personality, secure
job and a supportive family — fare best in treatment, almost irrespective
of the type of intervention, while seriously damaged individuals with
a poor work record and no social stability will have a very unfavourable
outcome. When questions of this kind came to be asked of a plethora of
therapeutic endeavours, considerable doubts arose about the value of
intensive and expensive in-patient programmes and a recent study
(Orford & Edwards 1977) raises some important questions about
elaborate out-patient counselling and other social therapies.

This research was undertaken in London and focused on a group of

100 married male alcoholics. After initial assessment, they were randomly allocated to advice or treatment groups. When advice was given to the couple, it consisted of the simple message that the husband was suffering from alcoholism, the solution to which was abstinence and that it was his responsibility to achieve this. In contrast, those offered treatment were given an individually tailored programme containing many elements of established contemporary therapy.

At the counselling session all husbands in the treatment group were offered an introduction to Alcoholics Anonymous, offered a prescription of citrated calcium carbimide, and prescribed drugs to cover withdrawal if this was indicated. A further appointment was then made for the husband to see the psychiatrist whose personal responsibility it was to evolve a continuing treatment programme with the husband, while the social worker took a similar responsibility for the wife. The husband's care subsequently continued on an out-patient basis with emphasis on strategies for abstinence, reality problems, and interpersonal and particularly marital interactions. Some other psychotherapeutic explorations were made when indicated, but with generally a rather cautious approach in this regard. If the husband failed to respond to out-patient care he was offered admission to a specialized in-patient alcoholism unit for detoxification, and subsequent involvement in in-patient group therapy, occupational therapy, and the ward milieu: the expected stay was about six weeks. The social worker was, if required, available to all husbands in the treatment group for advice on problems such as employment, housing, family finances, and court involvement. She largely, however, worked with the wife, on reality problems and the marital situation. The psychiatrist and social worker regularly discussed their cases together. Information was regularly passed to the GP and care was taken to establish effective liaison with any agencies which might already be involved with the case. The total treatment programme thus allowed wide latitude for varying intensities as determined by the needs and responses of individual couples, rather than the programme being conceived in terms of a stereotyped regime: the general strategy was to give more intensive care at the beginning of the twelve month treatment period and then, as indicated by individual response, to widen if possible the intervals between appointments. When a husband failed an appointment he was offered another, and the social worker might through the wife, or directly on a home visit, encourage the patient to re-attend.

The progress of these two groups of married couples was carefully monitored for one year. No appreciable difference between the groups could be detected at this time and there was still no trend favouring the intensive treatment group after a further year.

This study is clearly of great importance in questioning established treatments, although we must recognise that it was concerned only with married men and that the findings might not apply to other groups, such as female problem drinkers, the homeless, the young or the elderly. There is plenty of scope for continued exploration of specialised techniques and attempts at refining the match between patient needs and treatment offered. Nonetheless, we can say with some confidence that no single, clear, special treatment policy exists which is so certain that it would warrant investing in the training of a cadre of specialists sufficiently numerous to combat alcohol misuse by this means alone.

Treatment services in Britain are at present a patchwork of varied styles and commitments. The alcoholism treatment units still represent the main specialist health service contribution to treatment, research and education. They have recognised that traditional approaches have proved of doubtful merit and now offer a wide range of differing, often experimental, services incorporating traditional individual and group counselling along with newer behavioural approaches and social skills training. The emphasis is now on out-patient and day care with relatively short in-patient stays for detoxification and assessment.

Alcoholics Anonymous continues to grow in the UK at the rate of 15 per cent annually. This growth is paralled in the USA and other English speaking countries. It has had much less impact in France and Southern European countries. It offers a system of recovery which involves adopting a new life style within the fellowship of AA. Whilst it is difficult to evaluate (Robinson 1979) it obviously works for those who stay with it, although an unknown number attend only once or twice and find it uncongenial.

Councils on alcoholism are to be found in many British towns. They offer free counselling and advice and are supported by voluntary subscription. Voluntary counselling of this kind is less well established in many other countries. It is a very low-cost service, considering the numbers involved, but it is still relatively unevaluated and there is no reason to suppose it is more effective than other counselling approaches.

These specialist resources are further supported in some areas by hostels and day centres which cater for the more socially deteriorated alcoholic. This group is particularly difficult to help, because it has few resources on which to draw in staging a re-entry into the mainstream of society. Although it is numerically small, it will probably always require special provision of accommodation and support in the initial stages of recovery. The habitual drunken offender is a further extreme category of problem drinker for whom special provision is required and Britain is slowly joining countries like Poland, Sweden and parts of the USA in diverting drunkenness offenders from the penal system into a medico-social network of support which starts with the need to provide simple detoxification services.

Some countries, notably the USA, have been in the forefront of developing special services within major industries for those with alcohol problems apparent in the context of their employment. At best, these combine preventive and therapeutic approaches. The company will make its employees aware that alcohol is a work hazard and will combine this with advice about safe drinking practices. Unions and management will also work out a joint policy which offers help to employees at all levels, whether senior executives or shop floor workers. When declining work performance is noted and drinking identified as a possible cause, the employee can choose either to receive help for his or her drinking problem or submit to the ordinary disciplinary procedures agreed in the organisation. If treatment is chosen, the worker's job is secured. Reports suggest that this approach, sometimes called constructive coercion, is extremely effective at least in terms of restoring work function. Britain has been slow to introduce these policies but they are becoming increasingly common, particularly in industries like the drink trade, where the level of alcohol related problems is comparatively high.

Research suggests that we are justified in looking for simple modes of intervention which can be employed by non-specialists. If appropriate advice and simple counselling prove sufficient to help many problem drinkers, then we should invest in educating those individuals who are best placed to identify alcohol problems, helping them provide effective intervention at an early stage, before the sufferers have lost their jobs or caused further damage to their families and interpersonal relationships.

The policy of bringing knowledge and skills to a wider range of professions can cause a number of additional problems. If we see therapeutic concern extending to a wide range of alcohol related problems, then it is unlikely that even the wealthier nations would have sufficient resources to create specialised 'alcohologists' to treat or counsel all those with drinking problems. The need to develop low cost solutions is even more evident in developing countries, where alcohol problems are burgeoning.

Quite apart from such numerical arguments, simplicity of access is important for the problem drinker. It has been estimated that only one in ten of problem drinkers is in touch with any appropriate agency. This does not mean that for the rest their drinking causes no problems, since they frequently consult their doctors with stomach upsets and hangover symptoms, and they are involved in accidents, lose time off work, get into debt, and so on. Thus, whilst remaining high users of care-giving services of various kinds, the underlying drinking problem commonly passes unrecognised. If skills in recognition can be improved, then the crises which bring such people to a social work department or into a police court can be used as opportunities for change.

Even when an alcohol problem is recognised, the client may often refuse referral to a specialist facility. As many as half of the alcoholics referred for specialist advice simply do not turn up for their appointments. A prominent reason for this reluctance is an unwillingness to accept the label of alcoholic and the stigma of needing treatment. There are various ways in which this resistance may be overcome but one simple strategy is to avoid the necessity of referral by offering effective counselling at the place of first contact. This also overcomes the feeling of rejection which often accompanies referral between agencies. The alcoholic who has plucked up courage to tell his story once may feel let down by simply receiving a referral note to go and tell his story somewhere else.

The current state of treatment research suggests that heavy demands in the immediate future are likely to be placed on education. The task is to raise the overall level of understanding about alcohol and its effects, to enhance recognition of harmful drinking both in the mind of the sufferers and those whom they encounter and to reduce the stigma and misunderstanding which surround our knowledge of alcoholism. For some, this task involves the acquisition of specialist counselling skills; but in many instances, there will be considerable overlap between general education initiatives concerning alcohol and programmes specifically geared to special categories, such as industry or the helping professions. The planning of appropriate alcohol education policies will be the focus of Chapters 9 and 10. The evident conclusion at this point is that we are wrong to view therapy and education as separate entities, since they are closely interwoven at every level.

5 WHAT CAN BE DONE TO INFLUENCE CHILDREN AND ADOLESCENTS?

We know that problem drinking runs in families. Not only is this part of well established folk lore, but it has been shown in every research investigation aimed at examining this association. While the association is not in doubt, the mode of transmission has been the focus of argument for many years. At one extreme, there are those who see alcoholism as inherited, rather like eye colour is genetically transmitted; while at the other extreme, there are those who see the link being forged in family tradition, parental example, and environmental exposure. Comparatively few researchers or clinicians would now espouse one or other of these extreme views and the majority agree that the misuse of alcohol in general is the outcome of a wide range of influences. A decision that a series of phenomena are determined by many factors should not, however, allow us to retreat into woolly generalisations or to feeling that the task is too formidable to be undertaken. In this chapter, we shall explore what is known about the influences on the child which go to forming subsequent attitudes towards alcohol and its use in adolescence and beyond. It is hoped that the evidence will highlight specific areas which form the focus of closer examination in Chapters 9 and 10.

A few years ago, the nature/nurture argument seemed to have been settled in favour of the latter. Life experiences and opportunities for drinking were what determined drinking habits and the task of treatment and of education was to understand why certain individuals came to drink so much. This is still a central issue but the potent influence of genetic factors, particularly in severe early onset alcoholism, has recently received renewed support. A number of Scandinavian studies have shown that identical twins seem more likely than non-identical twins to show a diagnosis of alcoholism, and that the sons of alcoholics who were adopted early in life still retained an increased risk of alcoholism. While other findings have not always proved so clear cut, the evidence of some form of genetic influence in alcoholism seems strong. It is interesting to note that this trend does not seem to hold true in the same way for women.

The precise nature of this genetic transmission is not known, and it may in fact be a particular kind of emotional predisposition which is being transmitted. Animal studies show that it is quite possible to breed strains which appear particularly excitable and submissive but which have a preference for alcohol and this may be based on inherited bio-chemical differences. The implications of genetics resarch will be examined in more detail in Chapter 17, but it is important to recognise at the outset that we cannot discount the importance of differences in biological make-up nor should their presence make us feel fatalistic about influencing them. If those at risk in this way could be identified by some biological test, then one segment of the at-risk population would be clearly known. This might allow them to receive advice about the levels and styles of drinking which were safe for them and it would certainly be possible to counsel them about avoiding those at-risk occupations and situations.

In addition to his or her genetic make-up, over which the child has no control, there is also the impact of maternal drinking on the babies' development. Most evidence suggests that excessive drinking in pregnancy constitutes a hazard to the unborn child. Some countries, notably the USA, are now investing heavily in advising mothers either not to drink at all or to drink with care, particularly in the early stages of pregnancy. Beyond producing quite severe and characteristic damage to the child in extreme cases, such as in the foetal alcohol syndrome, the physical effects of lesser degrees of drinking during pregnancy are only now coming to be recognised. Thus, even before birth, alcohol may be having a material influence on the child's life.

Let us now consider the family and social influences which go to shape the child's understanding of alcohol. As we do so, we should have an eye for opportunities to strengthen the process which fosters moderate and enjoyable drinking and to counteract influences which seem to promote harmful drinking. There is no reason to suppose that excessive drinking would ever be explained simply by examining the roots from which the individual has sprung. Nonetheless, such a study does provide some clues toward the development of attitudes. In the early years of childhood, the family provides the model for the child's understanding so that the importance of parents as models for behaviour continues throughout childhood and remains a part of that individual for life. It is quite a common experience for us to realise that we are behaving just like our parents, even when this is something we have consciously tried to avoid. The childhood images of the father with his can of beer at his side, watching football on television, or of the parent serving drinks to friends at a party are taken in and often enacted in children's play. It is commonplace that children copy what parents *do* more often that what they *say*. This is entirely satisfactory when the parental model is desirable, but what happens when the parents' drinking is excessive and harmful?

We know that the children of alcoholics are more likely to have behavioural problems in childhood and to become abnormal drinkers in later life. Cork (1969) in a very sensitive study of 115 children of alcoholics revealed many of the pressures to which these children were exposed and felt that at least half had been seriously damaged by the experience. It is interesting that these children were less upset by drinking and even drunkenness *per se* than they were by the constant parental fighting and quarrelling for which they often blamed both parents. They were also aware of the inconsistency of their parents – the father who, when drunk, was a violent overbearing individual who controlled with his remorseless belt, would, when sober, try to buy back the family's affection with ostentatious shows of generosity and concern. This stress or inconsistency is particularly interesting because other observers have noted the prevalence of weak and inconsistent parents in the life history of many problem drinkers. Most of the children whom Cork interviewed said they would not drink through fear of becoming like the alcoholic parent. It seemed likely that this extreme position might change as they got older since one third had already taken alcohol. These children of alcoholics, who were themselves taking an active interest in drinking, caused her particular concern, and she concluded, 'They were amongst the most disturbed members of the group. Unless they get outside help, they would appear to be among those most likely to misuse alcohol or become dependent on it as adults.'

One task of any preventive programme must be to influence such children, whom we know to be at risk. There has been a tendency for alcoholism treatment programmes to focus on the alcoholics and ignore those around them, assuming that if their drinking improves, the other wounds within the family will heal. This view overlooks the psychological damage which already exists. The growing interest in family therapy for alcoholics will hopefully enable those children at risk to be reached and offered help at an early stage. Al-Ateen, which is an organisation for the children of alcoholics, has developed considerable expertise as a self help group for these young people and assists them to live with the drinking parent. It would be interesting to know how far such groups have any long-term preventive function for this acknowledged at-risk population.

Although it might well be undesirable to stigmatise the children of alcoholics by offering them counselling or education, none the less teachers should be aware of the stress engendered in pupils of parents with alcohol problems. They should also recognise that, for some children, education about alcohol will have a very special personal significance, which they may wish to discuss and that for such children special help should be available.

Because of their importance, we have been dwelling on some rather extreme parental models. The majority of parents drink in a responsible way and maintain the tradition of their particular culture's drinking habits. Some cultural traditions seem associated with much lower levels of problems. The low incidence of alcohol problems amongst Orthodox Jews has been attributed, in part, to the way in which drinking small quantities of alcohol is introduced as part of religious ritual within the family. The differences between cultural traditions must have their impact upon chidren. Some nations, for example Italy, commonly drink only with meals, which forms an important centrepiece of family life; while in others, drinking is mostly done away from the home and therefore away from the children. This is certainly the case in Scotland and the North of England, where children are specifically excluded from most drinking places. The child may therefore be particularly aware of the extreme consequences of drinking where these are very evident — father returning drunk from the pub — and have little personal experience of seeing moderate alcohol use. Techniques for changing the drinking habits of a society will be discussed in Chapters 10, 14 and 15 but it should be borne in mind that in most cases the family will be the mediator between general drinking customs and the child's experience.

Sex differences in drinking habits probably have their origins in the family. Most children, from as early as six, have some concept of alcohol and view it as more commonly taken by fathers than mothers. As they grow older, most prove more condemnatory of maternal drinking, a view which persists into the teenagers' view that drunkenness amongst girls is much less tolerable than amongst boys. This is a view held by both sexes. As more women come to drink like men, it will be important to consider how this may influence the young child's perception of maternal drinking. As women come to drink more and more frequently, educational programmes may have to be geared to their special needs and self-perceptions. The foetal alcohol syndrome is one reason for women taking particular care about their drinking, as is the current evidence that women seem to be particularly vulnerable physically to the harmful effects of alcohol. Such concerns will, however, need to be explored within the context of a larger re-assessment of women's position in society if the prospect of further stigmatisation is to be avoided.

Quite young children form concepts of alcohol as a special drink, different from the orange juice and milk which form their daily fare. They are also aware that drinking produces special effects, including drunkenness. An enquiry amongst Scottish school children, aged six, eight and ten showed that as early as six, only one in seven children failed to interpret correctly a film of a drunk man. The same enquiry revealed an increasingly critical view of alcohol consumption by adults. 70 per cent of the youngest children were confident that they would drink when they were older, while less than half of the ten year olds said they would drink (Jahoda & Crammond 1972). This trend towards an increasingly negative attitude contrasts with the observation that most Scots adolescents are drinking regularly by the time they are fourteen.

The negative attitude of ten year olds could not be attributed to alcohol education since they had received almost none. Parents very rarely talked about alcohol; if they did, it was commonly in condemnatory tones, although their own drinking behaviour conveyed a contrary message. Jahoda and Crammond suggested that 'children gradually learned that alcohol is frowned upon by people in such institutions as school and church'. While there may not be much evidence that either school or church are much given to asserting the 'evils of alcohol' at present, it does seem that children pick up an implicit view that alcohol is disreputable, dangerous and unwholesome. This contrasts with the experience of their eyes at home, in the streets and in advertisements. In Scotland, it certainly would appear that children are regularly confronted with society's ambivalence toward alcohol, without any sustained attempt being made to equip them with available facts about alcohol or to attempt to explore their own attitudes toward drinking in the future.

It seems probable that this incorporation of the conventional conscience about drinking quickly becomes one of the encumbrances of adult morality which is shed as children bid for independence in early adolescence. They recall the frequent comments that alcohol is not for children and therefore take alcohol as a symbol of adulthood. This distinction between adult and childhood behaviour is further underlined in many countries by licensing laws which forbid alcohol to those under a certain age.

Jessor and Jessor (1977) showed that young college students in Colorado engaged in a cluster of behaviours such as drinking, drug taking and sexual experiments at a time when they were asserting their independence from traditional values embodied in the school system and parental aspirations. While it is probably true that one attraction of drinking is that it marks a *rite-de-passage* from childhood to the adult state, this is clearly insufficient to account for the complexity of the changes in attitude and behaviour observed between the ages of 10 and 14.

Most parents do not deny alcohol to their children. It is common-place for French and Italian children to be offered diluted wine with meals from an early age. Aitken (1978) explored the habits and attitudes of Scottish school children between the ages of 10 and 14 and found very little support for the adolescent rebellion concept. For instance, most (88 per cent) of the children who drank had been offered a drink at home, usually by their father, and anti-drink views seemed uncommon amongst parents. Far from drinking being a reaction against parental inhibition, it seems that fathers particularly try to introduce their children (especially their sons) to drink. Children at this age remained critical of spirit consumption and of drunkenness, viewing boys or girls who drank a lot as having characteristics disliked by both parents and children themselves. Thus, even in the virtual absence of formal education about alcohol, quite discerning attitudes seem to prevail. How does this good sense equate with the observed increase in alcohol misuse and alcohol related problems amongst young people?

As age increases, progressively more alcohol is consumed outside the home and research shows that young people tend to consume more once they are away from adult influence. Parents in Britain seem to offer alcohol to children on 'special' occasions such as Hogmanay and at weddings. As the children grow older, the occasions become less special and more frequent. No particular excuse is needed for drink. Thus, young people increase both quantity and frequency of drinking as they move away from home influence and become sensitive to peer pressure. The influence of friends' drinking behaviour is particularly marked for boys. Peer group pressure and the need for approval are very important influences at this age. Davies and Stacey (1972) asked a large number of Scottish teenagers how they felt about the drinking behaviour of their peers. The subsequent analysis suggested that tough-ness and sociability were important attributes of the drinker. Although heaviest drinkers were viewed as tough and *un*sociable, this still seemed preferable to the weak and friendless image conjured up by the teetot-aller. They conclude, 'It appears that many young people are motivated to drink both in order to avoid the 'weak/unsociable' stigma associated with no-drinking and to achieve the 'toughness' which they associate with the consumption of alcohol.' The association between toughness, sociability and drinking is well recognised in the adolescent mind, as it is in the advertisements which reinforce the link.

Observations in many countries suggest that those adolescents who drink excessively are most likely to be those males who number other heavy drinkers amongst their friends, where parental controls are less evident (so that a lot of drinking takes place away from the home) and having one or both parents who either drink very heavily or paradoxically, have extreme teetotal views. It is interesting that while children of teetotallers are more likely to remain abstainers than others, those who do drink have a tendency to do so abnormally. It appears that a household in which alcohol is given great symbolic importance, either as something which is so dangerous that it is taboo or so regularly used that it is the focal point of family disputes, may in either case engender deviant drinking behaviour amongst the offspring.

In many cultures, there has been a tendency for women to be abstinent or drink moderately. Remnants of this practice are still evident and the majority of excessive drinkers remain men, although recent surveys show that the situation is changing rapidly so that young adolescent girls in Britain now appear to be drinking as frequently as boys.

Family and peer group influences operate effectively for the 'normal drinkers' who form the majority. Our concern is to enhance the normative influences which promote moderate drinking, while identifying and modifying factors which seem to foster deviant drinking behaviour. In Chapter 9, we explore how education about alcohol may be effectively introduced into the school curriculum in a way which recognises the developmental stages of the child's cognitive skills and capitalises on what is already known about attitude formation. While it is only reasonable to assume that a basic aim of alcohol education in schools should be the provision of accurate information, it is unrealistic to suppose that this is sufficient in itself.

As indicated earlier, attitudes towards drinking are formed by an amalgam of life experiences, such as the drunk in the street, the highly prized television detective who drinks when faced with a difficult case, the bottle of wine with family meals on special occasions, the ritual drunkenness of Saturday night and so on. Much more needs to be known about attitude formation but as research in this area progresses, a further doubt arises: what is the relationship between reported attitudes and behaviour? We are all aware that knowing what is right is often very far from actually doing what is right. It is equally true that reported attitudes toward behaviour may prove very different from what that individual does when confronted with the real situations. A recent Canadian case study of school children showed that knowledge about alcohol was not related to reported drinking habits. They concluded, 'The lack of predictive power of knowledge scores suggests that little influence over drinking might be obtained by cognitively orientated presentation.' (Smart, Gray and Bennal, 1978). Such rather bleak conclusions should not make us despair about educational endeavour but should help us guard against launching simplistic factual programmes which fail to account for the complex influences at work in determining drinking behaviour.

It is easy to see school as the natural focus for influencing the young, since the audience is held captive there, waiting to be educated. Unfortunately, evaluation studies have not been very encouraging about the benefit of alcohol education in schools (Plant & Peck, 1981). We should also recall that peer groups and particularly parents are much more influential than schools, although they are inevitably rather more difficult to reach. Youth clubs and parent-teacher associations, which seem at first sight to be fertile ground for alcohol education, suffer from attracting an audience representing an interested minority. Those who might most usefully receive information about alcohol tend not to come to the meetings. Whilst not wishing to decry the values of such endeavours, it is important to remind ourselves that a fine message which does not reach the relevant audience is of no value. It may be useful therefore to examine the status of the media, particularly radio and television, both as a purveyor of ready-made attitudes and behaviour concerning drinking, and as a means of reaching an otherwise inaccessible audience. The screen images of drinking and advertising may exert a powerful impact on young people where they are particularly susceptible to outside influence. These issues are discussed in greater detail in Chapter 11.

6 WHAT CAN BE DONE TO INFLUENCE ADULTS?

Whilst young people remain the most popular target for alcohol education, increasing attention is now being paid to more broadly based preventive strategies designed to influence the drinking behaviour of adult society. In the next chapter, we will look at the use of sociopolitical and economic measures as controlling factors in the supply of beverage alcohol and at the legal framework which seeks to impose constraints upon availability and upon the behaviour of intoxicated individuals. In this chapter, however, we will examine strategies, usually educational strategies, which are intended to influence the attitudes and behaviour of adults, particularly those deemed to be specially at risk.

The current popularity of such educational approaches could hardly be more widespread. In the UK, for example, 1981 saw the publication of the DHSS's 'Prevention and Health: Drinking Sensibly', (DHSS, 1981) and the Brewers' Society (1981) 'Strategy for the Prevention of Problem Drinking' both of which lay their principal emphasis upon education, and the announcement by the United Kingdom Temperance Alliance of a new national educational campaign. Clearly, the DHSS, the Brewers' Society and the UK Temperance Alliance make unlikely bedfellows: yet here they are united in a common call for more alcohol education. Although a cynic might doubt the sincerity of the Brewers' Society, the political honesty of the DHSS and the compatibility of the UK Temperance Alliance with the real issues of today, it is difficult not to see in their unholy alliance a kind of desperate presumption that these strategies represent a last ditch effort to stave off other, less palatable strategies which might have a more restrictive impact upon individual freedom.

There is little reason to suppose education is likely in itself to have more than a marginal influence over alcohol-related mortality and morbidity. In a review of approximately 150 alcohol education impact studies, one of the authors of this book (Grant, 1982c) has found that virtually all those programmes which tested for increased knowledge found that measurable improvements had indeed occurred. By contrast, those which tested for changes in attitudes, behavioural intentions or current behaviour displayed far more ambiguous results.

The extent of the ambiguity and the marginality of the positive results tended to increase, the closer the evaluation came to examining

41

actual drinking behaviour rather than hypothetical reactions to fictional situations or reported attitudes to purportedly differentiating statements about the place of alcohol in society. There is nothing to be surprised about in that. It confirms the conclusions of researchers who have reviewed drug education on a similar basis. The central question here, as in many areas of health education, is whether attitude changes precede and predict behaviour change. At its simplest, the issue is one of consistency, and its examination as a phenomenon of social functioning begins with the classic 1934 study by La Piere. In this study, La Piere (1934) reports on his cross-country travels in America with a young Chinese couple. He observed that out of 251 separate transactions for accommodation, the travellers were refused service only once. However, six months after each contact La Piere sent a questionnaire to the establishments they had visited asking whether members of the Chinese race were acceptable as guests there. Of those responding (128 of the 151) only one said 'yes', 7 per cent were uncertain and all the rest replied that Chinese guests were unacceptable.

Chastening though this fable is, the temptation must be avoided to reject totally the concept of a causative relationship in this area. The important work of Ajzen and Fishbein (1977) on attitude behaviour variables led them to conclude that 'a person's attitude has a consistently strong relation with his or her behaviour when it is directed at the same target and when it involves the same action'. It is this conclusion which provides the basis for sharpening the focus of alcohol education. Many educators would now suggest that if indeed it is behaviour change which is being sought, then the form, content and explicit aims of the programme, however defined, should directly confront behavioural rather than attitudinal issues.

That is why it is so important to have a clear sense of which problems it is that the education is seeking to prevent. There is sometimes, particularly amongst people who are not themselves directly involved in health education, an unrealistic expectation that massive changes in drinking habits can be brought about as the result of the most meagre of educational interventions. In truth, the process is a much slower and more gradual one. Arguing for a recognition that alcohol education is designed to increase rationality both at an individual and societal level, Juha Partanen has stressed the necessity to leave recipients sufficient leeway in which to consider matters for themselves. 'The success of education,' he suggests, 'depends on how well the campaign really knows the behaviour which is its target and the attitudes which serve to reinforce the particular habits.'

Thus, where a general aim such as reducing harmful drinking or, more positively, 'promoting moderation' is not subsequently broken down into much more exact and particular educational objectives, success rates appear to be comparatively low. In part this may be because the variable which those evaluating the programmes are attempting to measure is therefore so vaguely defined as to elude even the most imaginative, flexible and optimistic methodologies. It is also possible that lack of precision in defining objectives is paralleled in lack of clarity over other aspects of programme design. Where a clear if limited, objective is set, it is likely that greater care will be taken to achieve consistency between that objective and the actual experience of the educational programme. Thus, for example, a thoughtful programme which aims 'to improve assessment skills amongst community workers encountering alcohol problems in West Indian immigrant populations' is not likely to waste much time on liver cirrhosis death rates analysed by occupation for fifteen European countries. Yet many alcohol education programmes today proceed to squander relevance for spurious attempts at comprehensiveness.

Coupled with specificity comes the notion of pragmatism. If an attempt is being made to encourage particular changes in behaviour, then the desired behaviour should not only be clearly specified, the instructions for how to achieve the change should be explicit and accessible to the target audience. Again, it is perhaps worth considering an example. There is evidence that heavy drinking during pregnancy can have an adverse effect upon the health of the unborn child. A precise objective for an educational campaign might, therefore, quite properly be 'to limit or eradicate drinking during pregnancy'. For such an aim to have any chance of success, the educational programme would have to explain how to deal with social pressures, how to develop alternative behaviours and how to adapt to an altered and possibly threatening lifestyle. It would not be sufficient simply to be aware that heavy drinking was hazardous. Knowledge, even relevant knowledge, does not carry with it instructions for its application.

The characteristics of the target group towards which the education is directed have to be consistent with the aims and the instructions. There would be little point, other than to promote liberal education in its vaguest sense, in giving the programme on assessment skills to the pregnant ladies and the programme on drinking in pregnancy to the community workers.

Another issue which these two examples serve to illustrate is the extent to which, in segmenting the target audience, a choice has to be made with regard to priorities. This certainly lies behind the concept that certain groups within the adult population are more likely to be at risk than others. Clearly, different groups are not just more or less at risk; they are also at risk in different ways and from different influences. As soon as the whole range of alcohol problems is considered, it becomes necessary to establish priorities between different kinds of damage (liver cirrhosis, traffic accidents, marital disharmony) as well as between different groups of people (barmen, drunk drivers, pregnant ladies, community workers). Often, judgements about these priorities will have to do with the ease of access to the target populations and their presumed susceptibility to positive educational influences. Equally, however, the aggregate cost to society of particular kinds of damage will have to be taken into account. The issue, therefore, is not simply one of taking careful aim.

Be your aims never so well defined, the next problem is to ensure that the attention of the audience is caught and retained. There are circumstances, such as those which surround alcohol education programmes located within the formal school curricula, where the audience is already captive. Equally, there are training programmes where, since attendance is voluntary, it might be presumed that those self-selected were committed to learning. Even in those two circumstances, however, attendance at an educational event does not presume participation in an educational process.

In any case, gaining the attention of the audience is clearly a prerequisite of encouraging that participative process. Broadly speaking, there are three distinct areas in which the appropriateness of the material to its intended target audience requires careful review during the planning stages. The first of these is the actual content of the material. Appropriateness of content extends beyond the criterion of relevance. This is the most useful baseline to adopt since material perceived as irrelevant is likely to fail to attract attention, but even relevant material can appear less worthy of attention unless care has been taken to ensure that it is expressed in terms which are acceptable to the target audience. An example here may serve to emphasise this point. The relationship between heavy alcohol consumption and various kinds of liver disease is relevant to barmen (who have the highest liver cirrhosis mortality rates of all occupations in the UK) and to medical students (who are being trained to respond to such problems when qualified as well as having, when qualified, rather high mortality rates themselves from this cause) yet the terms which would be selected for communicating this information to these two target groups would be different.

Liver cirrhosis mortality figures are themselves both potentially helpful in enabling education to be targeted towards those with higher rates of damage and also potentially misleading in implying that liver cirrhosis deaths are in some way the most preventable kind of damage, just because they happen to be one of the better documented. Of greater value may be an attempt to describe the common features of occupations featuring high liver cirrhosis death rates and then seeking ways of minimising or counteracting these predisposing characteristics. It has been suggested that the most influential factors here are the availability of free or cheap alcohol, the social pressure to drink, higher than average mobility (removing the stabilising influence of home) and the absence of supervision. Not all of these are likely to be equally susceptible to educational interventions, but all are capable of manipulation and it is possible that coherent initiatives could certainly make some impact, particularly with regard to the availability of alcohol and the explicit or tacit encouragement of regular drinking.

It could be argued that what the liver cirrhosis mortality figures do is point towards those people in the community who are simply the heaviest consumers. Certainly, in terms of targeting, since the more somebody drinks the more likely he is to suffer some kind of alcohol problem, it would seem sensible to select as a priority group for educational or intervention strategies those whose consumption is highest. Survey research in various countries has indicated that a relatively small proportion of the population consumes a disproportionate amount of alcohol. Whether, as in the case of Scotland, it is 3 per cent of the population drinking 30 per cent of the alcohol, or, as in the case of New Zealand, it is 11 per cent of the population drinking 50 per cent of the alcohol, the message is the same. If only that minority could be persuaded to alter its drinking behaviour, the impact upon every index of alcohol-related damage would be gigantic, since it is likely that the majority of those damaging themselves are members of this heavy drinking subgroup.

The difficulty, of course, lies in identifying the heavy drinkers. Sometimes, as through drunken driving convictions, they surface in a particularly visible form. Such opportunities are increasingly being used, both educationally and in terms of more rigorous legal sanctions, to attempt to influence the subsequent behaviour, particularly of those who have re-offended or whose blood alcohol levels are unusually high. Most heavy drinkers, however, keep their heads well down and only become visible when the damage has already occurred and prevention is, by definition, too late. Mass media campaigns, saturating whole countries, are arguably neither well enough targeted nor sensitive enough to individual variations to be likely to produce significant impact. Whilst energies can be devoted to refining and specifying their aims and to improving the methods of delivery, it may well be that the heaviest drinkers are the least likely to be influenced by such approaches, if only because it will appear to them that they have a vested interest in resisting such messages. It must always be remembered that even the most damaged individuals, as long as they continue to drink, are experiencing, in their own terms, benefits from their drinking. A presumption of rationality with respect to alcohol consumption simply does not stand up to empirical examination. It ignores the addictive qualities of the substance and the symbolic values associated with its consumption.

Thus, whilst it is theoretically possible to identify the subgroup in the population most at risk of encountering the most severe and most frequent alcohol problems, it is practically impossible to identify members of that subgroup until it is too late. One solution which has been suggested to this dilemma lies in encouraging the self-monitoring of drinking habits. Self-monitoring can be seen both as a stabilising influence, ensuring that moderate consumers do not drift towards higher consumption and also a potentially reactive influence, pulling heavier consumers back towards more moderate levels. Since, it is argued, so many people take their drinking so much for granted, simply raising the level of awareness to the extent that the process of deciding to have a drink, to continue drinking and to stop at a particular level becomes a conscious process, is itself an important step in recognising the potential hazards of unfettered consumption, whether at an individual, national or global level.

7 HOW FAR CAN SOCIAL, POLITICAL AND ECONOMIC FACTORS INFLUENCE DRINKING?

Social control is an unpopular – even sinister – concept, particularly to those of a liberal persuasion. Those who seek to restrict the drinking habits of others are liable to be labelled as ascetic prohibitionists or meddlesome do-gooders interfering with the freedom of the individual to drink as much as he pleases when and wherever he chooses. Alcohol controls are often associated with bureaucratic interference, unacceptable intrusions into what is seen as essentially private behaviour. In many developing countries, they are also associated with former laws imposed by a governing colonial power which commonly prohibited the indigenous population from consuming imported alcohol, particularly spirits (Pan 1975). It is therefore hardly surprising that many social and political strategies have focussed in recent years on more generally acceptable strategies concerned with the individual problem drinker rather than alcohol as such. Emphasis has been given to early recognition, treatment and education. More recently still, however, doubts about the effectiveness of these politically comfortable approaches have caused a number of policy makers to look afresh at alcohol controls and view them as a necessary part of any plan for the prevention of alcohol related problems. Although few would now suggest that controls alone form a sufficient or feasible response, it is necessary to demonstrate how educational and control policies can be interdependent, the one preparing the ground for and enhancing the other.

The traditional liberal stance on the rights of the individual in relation to the community is J.S. Mills' often-quoted assertion that the only justification for interfering with the 'liberty of action' of another person is self-protection. 'His own good, either physical or moral is not a sufficient warrant. He cannot rightfully be compelled to do or forbear because it will be better for him to do so, because it will make him happier, because in the opinions of others to do so would be wise, or even right. The only part of the conduct of anyone, for which he is answerable to society, is that which concerns others . . . Over his own body and mind, the individual is sovereign.'

In reality the interdependence of individuals, whether in the state or the family, make controls of various kinds part of everyday life. Yet when it comes to drinking there is a widespread belief that 'a man's drinking is his own concern and no concern of the community's'. In a recent study, half of a sample of adults in the Lothian Region of Scotland agreed with this view and in a similar survey in Mexico and Zambia the agreement was even higher (WHO 1983).

Some controls over alcohol use are more politically acceptable than others. Probably the simplest example is drinking and driving, since most citizens now accept the idea that there should be legal restrictions limiting the blood alcohol level above which an individual is allowed to drive. Here indeed Mills' requirement of 'the protection of others' operates and provides justification. When, however, controls extend to limiting the availability of alcohol, the effects become more uncertain and the assertion that the right of the individual drinker is being eroded becomes more clamorous.

Those who favour alcohol control policies argue that the individuals who drink most heavily are those who are most at risk to a range of alcohol related problems, which include not only alcohol dependence, but social and physical crises, such as child neglect, wife beating, industrial injuries and liver disease. They further observe that there is a relationship between mean *per capita* consumption in the population and the number of excessive drinkers. The conclusion of this line of thinking is that controls which reduce the *per capita* consumption in the population will reduce the number of excessive drinkers and thereby the number of problem drinkers.

Many authors (Duffy 1977) have warned against the uncritical acceptance of this equation in such simple terms but very few would dispute the general truth which it contains. It may well prove that the association between consumption level and harm is clearest for liver cirrhosis, while some of the other social and interpersonal problems associated with excessive drinking are more dependent on *patterns* of alcohol use. Thus, an individual may have a very low annual consumption of alcohol, but if his intake is confined to three monumental binges in which his dunkenness wreaks havoc in the neighbourhood, his pattern of drinking causes very real problems. Others have pointed out that consumption varies considerably within a country (Plant & Pirrie 1979) and that a global approach based on consumption figures for a whole population may be too crude and misleading a measure for the fine tuning of relevant and acceptable planning. The assumptions underlying the relationship between consumption and harm have obvious implications for prevention and will be touched upon frequently in this book, especially in relation to Chapters 13 and 15.

The feasibility and character of alcohol control policies are highly dependent on the cultural-political setting in which they are implemented. Governments which rely on concensus or electoral support for their actions have a very different task from those in which there is a high degree of central control with less public accountability. The pressure groups involved in influencing decisions about alcohol controls will look different in a capitalist economy from those based on socialist or communist principles. It is important that we avoid making assumptions about the extent to which ideas and policies can easily travel across cultural and geographic boundaries. Alcohol control policies are mostly concerned with reducing or restricting availability. They often fail to specify their objectives with sufficient accuracy, but those which are most basic among a range of alternatives are '(a) reduction of the amount of alcohol consumed, and (b) change in the pattern of alcohol use in order to avoid inappropriate settings or inappropriate times' (WHO 1980). Many diverse techniques have been adopted in an attempt to limit alcohol consumption. These were usefully reviewed by Bruun and others in 1975. Some of the widespread strategies are briefly discussed below and will be considered in Chapters 12, 13, 14 and 15.

In many countries the supply of alcohol is governed by regulations specifying the number and form of outlets and the times at which drinks may be purchased. This 'control of access' approach is discussed in more detail in Chapter 14.

The number of bars and other points of sale is often restricted by licensing authorities who endeavour to limit the density of outlets and have some influence on their character. The state authority has the economic sanction of withdrawing a licence if the publican fails to maintain certain standards. The effectiveness of this form of control has rarely been tested and enforcement of regulations, such as those limiting under age drinking, is extremely difficult. There is some evidence that an increased density of points of sale is associated with increased consumption, but the studies which have suggested this come from rather exceptional rural Nordic settings. It could also prove, for example, that while consumption of beer increased when it became more readily available, there was a concomitant decline in home brewing and distilling.

Rules governing the character of pubs and taverns are very varied and tend to reflect prevailing social habits. For instance, in some states of the USA, drink must be taken with food even if it is only a sandwich; in some places you must sit down when drinking, while in others you must stand. It has been argued that bars should be positively uncongenial in order to discourage customers and equally that their windows should be frosted over, so that the unseemly habit will be concealed from public view. A contrary view would seek to make pubs more comfortable and welcoming, so that families might drink together in a civilised way. This latter philosophy was espoused by the Clayson Committee in Scotland, who felt that improved comfort and the provision of alternative non-alcoholic beverages would make drinking a less frenetic and single-minded pursuit than it often seems to be in Scottish pubs. The impact of any of these measures on consumption and drinking patterns is unknown, but the character of the outlet has been shown to influence the purchasing of alcohol. Shoppers have been shown to purchase and consume more alcohol when buying from an open counter supermarket than they did when having to order over the counter from the shop assistant (Smart 1974).

Restricting hours of opening is a common measure of control which was originally introduced to ensure that workers were fit to return to work during the day. It has also been used to limit nocturnal carousing. Recent modest extensions to hours of opening in Scotland do not seem to have provided any increase in drunkenness or alcohol consumption overall although the pattern of drinking has changed somewhat (Bruce 1980) and young men did seem to be drinking more (Knight & Wilson 1980). Age restrictions in purchasing and drinking alcohol in public are common but difficult to enforce, particularly in countries where there is no universal system of identification. Where age limits have been lowered, there has been some observed increase in alcohol related road traffic accidents amongst young people but others have argued that the presence of an age limit labels drinking as an 'adult activity', thereby making it particularly attractive to the young.

Even a cursory glance at controls of this kind shows the variety of contradictory views that exist. Most controls have been implemented without any plans for evaluation and their efficacy is therefore unknown. Regulations governing sale are often introduced for reasons of trade, without a thought to their possible public health consequences. Thus, the sale of alcohol in supermarkets was introduced without detailed consideration of the consequences which such ease of access might bring. Yet this move is often quoted as a factor which made it much easier for women to purchase alcohol and may therefore indirectly have contributed to the growth of their alcohol problems. Even if the answers to such questions are far from clear, it is obvious that because alcohol is a drug it cannot be viewed simply as a commodity available on the free market like any other. Its sale and distribution are indeed the concern of a wide constituency of health, social work and law enforcement agencies.

Although some countries, such as Finland and Norway, have endeavoured to remove the profit motive from the manufacture of alcohol and limit production, in most parts of the world manufacture is controlled by market forces. As it is relatively easy to make, breweries are often one of the first new industries to move into a developing country, particularly since the beer produced can then be heavily taxed to the government's interest. None the less, this practice is now being increasingly questioned as is clear from the vigorous debate which forms Chapter 13 of this book.

Evidence suggests that people quickly acquire new drinking habits, but do not so readily abandon the old. This may not be true when an African villager abandons his traditional home brewed drink for commercial beer, but it is certainly the case amongst the growing number of tourists who import drinking customs from other countries. These informal imports of drinking customs become more prevalent as the world shrinks through tourism and they are reinforced by the internationalisation of the trade in alcohol. Who, one wonders, will eventually drink the European wine lake? It is interesting that the illicit trade in drugs such as cannabis attracts so much intense and costly interest, while the regulation of the flow of alcohol into countries unused to drink has received comparatively little attention so that even simple data about the movement of alcohol between countries scarcely exists.

Advertising is banned in countries such as Poland and the USSR, while in others it is restricted to point of sale or is subject to regulations governing its form and content. Those who advocate further control of advertising point to its apparent effect on overall levels of consumption (McGuinness 1979) and are often particularly concerned about its potential for influencing young people by fostering the belief that drinking enhances sophistication and social competence. Others argue that it simply influences brand choice, noting that, for example, Poland has a growing alcohol problem without any advertisements. Some also fear that, deprived of advertising competition, the more successful companies would engage in price cutting wars, which might promote further sales. The argument will be continued in Chapter 12, but the rather pusillanimous approach of government in this country to alcohol advertising contrasts with its growing stringency towards tobacco.

Governments almost universally levy a tax on alcohol and this income is an important part of revenue. Revenue to the government from customs and excise duty and VAT on alcoholic beverages in Britain now runs at well over £2,000,000,000 each year. So important is the income thus generated that it is thought to outweigh the social cost of alcohol problems in some countries (Walsh 1980). The use of taxation as a technique for controlling consumption is a relatively new concept, recognised by few governments outside Scandinavia. As long as the Treasury continues to regard alcohol as a source of income, it will come into conflict with those who wish to effect a reduction in overall consumption to the level where the revenue also drops. Economic arguments around the cost of alcohol further illustrate the competing claims of various interest groups — not least the drinker himself who will look askance at further rises in the cost of drink. The drink trade already speaks of recession with consequent unemployment in certain key areas; the tourist industry will be concerned about the effect on trade and travel; the trade unions, noting not only the threat to employment, but also the rise in the cost of living engendered by the new tax, may incorporate the rise in the next season's round of wage demands and so forth.

Despite the complexity of the issue and the uncertainty of the effects there is evidence that the relative cost of alcohol does influence the overall level of consumption. There is ample historical evidence that *per capita* consumption of alcohol fluctuates in accordance with its relative cost and on those occasions when there has been a massive rise in cost there has been a concomitant drop in the consumption of that particular beverage. Most of the cost of a bottle of whisky or a pint of beer lies in tax. This makes alcohol a commodity which is less vulnerable to inflation and it rapidly falls behind other goods in relative cost, unless government intervenes. Governments are naturally reluctant to impose massive rises in the cost of drinks since this is rarely a popular policy but those concerned with alcohol problems have recommended that they use the power of fiscal controls to ensure at least that the relative cost of alcohol does not slip any further behind other commodities. The issues involved in fiscal changes are discussed in greater detail in Chapter 15.

Evaluating the impact of price changes and other controls is extremely difficult. Much of the evidence has accumulated from an historical perspective. At first glance, it may seem that cost is the crucial factor, but what about the social climate that caused or allowed such changes? The same questions arise even more forcefully in relation to prohibitionist and liberalising trends — were they cause or consequence? The example of Prohibition in the USA, where the decline in alcohol problems was balanced by a rise in bootlegging and other crime, has been discussed already in Chapter 3. At present we do not know which sector of the drinking public will be most influenced by a steep price rise. The rich will presumably continue drinking, but will the poorer heavy drinkers relinquish the habit or will they become ill-nourished and neglect their families? Recent research suggests that the heavy, even dependent, drinker does reduce consumption in response to economic pressures (Kendell *et al* 1983).

Controls of the kinds outlined above are rarely popular and it is fruitless trying to impose laws, restrictions and taxes on a totally unwilling public. The laws will not be enforced, the regulations will be ignored and the disapproval of the taxes will be registered at the next election, unless the changes are linked to a programme of education aimed at making these controls both acceptable and understandable. Thus it is educational and control policies which need to be part of an integrated preventive plan of action.

8 WHAT STATE OF WHICH ART?

When an area of intellectual inquiry, social policy or scientific research is undergoing a process of rapid development which makes it difficult to point to an established and irreducible body of basic knowledge, there is often an attempt to draw together an overview of the best available evidence, drawing upon traditional theoretical models from the past and pointing towards promising directions for the future. Such an overview is frequently described as presenting the current state-of-the-art. Nobody can doubt that the prevention of alcohol problems (combining, as it does, social policy, intellectual inquiry and scientific research) is far from being a static area at the present time. Competing analytic models, strategic plans, views of costs, benefits, effects, effectiveness and efficiency all vie with one other. Education is locked in a hand to hand struggle with control policies. The individual perspective resonates with and rebounds against the sociopolitical perspective. The vested interests of different government departments are in direct conflict with each other, as are the agendas of different international bodies. The ultimate objective of all this effort (the elimination of alcohol or the elimination of problems) is itself the subject of fundamental dispute. In such a maelstrom of conflicting activity, it is reasonable for the reader to hold up hands of horror and to ask, the simplest question often being the most difficult to answer: what state of which art?

What we have attempted to do in this introductory section is to outline the context within which an integrated preventive approach to alcohol problems will have to be developed. We have tried to highlight the need to achieve a balance between the various competing views (individual versus sociopolitical, disease versus control of consumption, and so on) in the hope that essential common elements will have been shaken into prominence during that process. In using the life of the individual as an organising principle, from conception through childhood and adolescence to full adult participation in the affairs of society, we have tried to indicate how ubiquitous are the opportunities for developing preventive tactics and how essential it is that each tactical advance is seen in terms of a larger strategic plan.

What emerges is the variety of different social factors involved in determining and interpreting policy. Politicians, statesmen, educators, health professionals, media professionals, lawyers, the beverage trade, the advertising trade, the taxman, the scientist, the town planner, the publican, the policeman, the drinker and the drunk: all have a part to play in influencing the way in which prevention succeeds or fails. It would clearly be unrealistic to expect that such a diverse group of actors could be marshalled together within the confines of a single script. They are all acting in their own dramas, pursuing their own particular scripts. Sometimes, almost by chance it seems, these scripts interact or even run in parallel for a few scenes. But then, just as suddenly, they are off again, moving at different speeds towards different objectives. And the scripts themselves are far from quiescent. They all involve conflict, disagreement, acrimony and competing systems of values. It is, therefore, little wonder that there is no such thing as an integrated preventive policy, however attractive it might seem in principle and however loud the voices raised in its support. Integration is something which it is impossible not to agree upon in principle but which is notoriously difficult to achieve in practice.

In preparing this book, therefore, we were faced with an interesting dilemma. Having provided an introductory section as a context for the real issues that were to follow, how could these issues be presented in a way which did justice to their rigour and excitement without sacrific- in the very heterogeneity which contributes so much to the sense we had, and still have, that the debate about preventing alcohol problems has reached an important watershed? Our solution lay in our definition of the problem. If there really is, as we suggest, a debate, then actually to present that debate might be the best way to illuminate the salient issues. Further, since there is not just one debate, but several, it can be argued that the current state-of-the-art is marked less by consensus about anything than by a series of heated debates, none of which has as yet reached a state of resolution and all of which are, in turn, in lively debate with one other.

The remainder of this book consists of an attempt to catch the flavour of the most important of these debates. What we have attempted to do is to stimulate and focus them so that the central issues are laid bare. We have not, generally, chosen to solicit contributions from individuals who are known to be traditionally antagonistic to each other. Rather, we have selected contributors for the originality and persuasiveness of their thinking and tried to set in juxtaposition points of view sufficiently diverse to make the range of reasonable alternatives clear to the reader.

As part of our wish to retain the special flavour of each debate, we have chosen to adopt a modified epistolary approach to each section, rather than just to seek a series of short scholarly papers from our contributors. Although the technique and the results vary somewhat from debate to debate, the way we prepared the ground was broadly similar in each case. What we did was to identify a cluster of three or four questions that seemed central to the topic of the debate. We then wrote to one contributor, outlining the overall shape of the book, and asking him to initiate the debate on his particular topic by responding to the questions we had asked. His response was then sent on to another contributor with the request that he react to the points which had already been made. Sometimes we sent that reaction back to the first respondent and sometimes we sent both the initial response and the reaction on to a third contributor, who was asked to comment upon both. Finally, we tried to collate all the material, eliminating overlap, repetition, personal endearments, expressions of outrage and libellous remarks. Not every debate achieved all we had hoped, but some far exceeded our expectations.

Time, no doubt, will be the judge as to which voices turn out to be the strongest and which debates turn out to be the arenas in which policies are really thrashed out. The purpose of this book is less to give the reader a sense that preventive policy has developed to some kind of maturity than to demonstrate just how diverse, confused, even contradictory much thinking about these issues still remains today. There is not, and there never will be, one single answer to the alcohol problem, if only because there is no single problem. There are a multitude of different alcohol problems and there are probably multiple solutions to that multitude of problems. Yet some sense of integration, of direction, of basing present experiment upon past experience is a heartfelt need amongst workers at local, national and global level. If nothing else, what this book seeks to do is to set the terms for the voting which must take place if the debates are to be resolved.

9 THE SCHOOLS EDUCATION DEBATE

Introduction

The current popularity of educational approaches intended to minimise alcohol problems could hardly be more widespread. As we have already seen, 1981 saw the publication of the Department of Health and Social Security's 'Prevention and Heath: Drinking Sensibly' (DHSS 1981), the Brewers' Society's 'A Strategy for the Prevention of Problem Drinking' (Brewers' Society 1981) and the announcement by the United Kingdom Temperance Alliance of a new national educational campaign. That three such disparate, even in many ways opposing bodies should be united in a common call for more alcohol education is remarkable in itself. Even more remarkable is the extent to which they agree that the primary focus for educational effort should be upon young people.

This is hardly an isolated phenomenon. In the United States of America before the turn of the century, virtually every state required by law that instruction about alcohol be included in the public school curriculum. The earliest of these laws was passed in 1858 and legislative activity was continued this century when several state laws were revised in the 1930s following the repeal of Prohibition. Roe's review (Roe 1942) of these regulations and her subsequent survey (Roe 1943) of the content of textbooks in use in the United States at that time confirm the seriousness with which school-based alcohol education was being invested. More recently, Milgram's series of annotated bibliographies (Milgram 1975; Milgram & Page 1979, 1980) of alcohol education materials demonstrates overwhelmingly just how massive the proliferation of alcohol education initiatives directed towards young people has been during the last decade.

This proliferation of youth-targeted material, most of it intended for use within the school system, includes a considerable heterogeneity of approaches, using different styles to approach different objectives. If there is one salient trend, however, which is revealed by taking a broad overview of the evidence it seems to be a shift away from education concentrating only upon the increase of knowledge towards education intended also to make impact upon attitudes towards drinking. In view of this trend, we wrote to Martin Evans (Director of the Teachers' Advisory Council on Alcohol and Drug

Education, Manchester, UK) asking him whether in his view, attitude change was an appropriate aim for school-based alcohol education.

Attitude Formation

The areas of attitude formation, reinforcement and change have for some time been of interest to education in general and health education in particular. Health education has often identified itself with appropriate behaviour change and psychology has shown us that attitudes play an important part in behavioural responses. The work of Fishbein (1967) has been of importance here. Unfortunately many health educationalists have applied a somewhat superficial interpretation of this and have proceeded on the basis that their educational responsibility has been simply to pour relevant information into one end of the student conveyor belt in the expectation that this would, as a matter of course, be transformed into the appropriate attitudes which, in turn, would produce the anticipated behaviour. These assumptions are often made when health educationalists, of whatever profession, have broad, fairly undefined goals of prevention for their health education programmes (Davidson & Jaccard 1975).

Experience has shown us that this strategy is doomed to a high degree of failure. Indeed, this failure is compounded by the fact that there seems as strong a case for behaviour change precipitating attitude change as vice versa.

However, it should not be assumed, on the lines of the above argument, that work on attitudes has no place in a health education context. There is a powerful school of thought which sees the role of health education not merely to modify behaviour or to bring about appropriate behavioural responses, but to build up a body of knowledge and skills which the individual can utilise in the choice of appropriate behaviours for himself. Within this context, attitude and value clarification find an acceptable home, since these exercises are part of the process by which the individual assumes responsibility for, and control of, his own life.

We are next confronted by the problem of what we actually mean by an attitude. Robert Gagne (1975) has given us one definition: 'An attitude is an acquired internal state that influences the choice of personal action.' It can be seen this owes much to the behaviourists; a slightly more rounded definition has been put forward by Fishbein (1975): 'An attitude is a learned predisposition to respond in a consistently favourable or unfavourable manner with respect to a given object.' Thus, it becomes clear that when we are considering educational strategies related to attitudes our very first task is to clarify which particular attitude(s) we are concerned with. Quite often attitudes seem to have been left intentionally vague and, have, as such, played the role of the scapegoat. 'Oh,' we say 'their attitude is all wrong' or 'you can tell what he thinks by his attitude' as if this was explanation enough.

Alcohol education provides fertile ground to illustrate this point. Many have blamed the apparent increase in young people's drinking on the attitudes of society in general, or of the young people themselves or even that of publicans or parents. We are left no wiser by these observations on how to plan our relevant attitude education. There have, however, been some attempts to be more specific. Some have suggested that young people's drinking is some form of 'adolescent rebellion' (Hancock 1970) against parents and authority in general — teenagers pay less attention to what they are told to do and more attention to what might be disapproved of by adults. Again, Davies and Stacey (1972) have coined the 'alcohol myth' which suggests that young people drink either to appear tough or more mature or alternatively, they drink in order not to appear weak in their peer group.

We have here, then, something to build on. If it can be shown that, for example, the attitude reflected in the 'alcohol myth', something like 'a real man can hold his drink', is present in young drinkers, then we can design an appropriate educational programme to help clarify or modify this attitude on the assumption that, from the point of view of increasing the individual's control of his life or being concerned for his behaviour, such an attitude is not likely to be helpful in the long run.

Drug education research can give us some guidelines about the possible effectiveness of alcohol education programmes, given the scarcity of empirical evidence of the effects of alcohol education alone. A review of the literature shows that the effects of education about drugs are mixed in that there are some positive and some negative effects. For example, attitudes to drugs may change one way, whilst at the same time attitudes to drug-takers may change the other way (de Haes & Schuurman 1975). Related to alcohol education, one of the main reasons for this we would suggest, is that teaching programmes usually have an overall goal of prevention and are expected to have an influence on the level of knowledge, the attitude to drink, drinkers and drunkenness as well as the behaviour of the pupils. In a review of drug research Goodstadt (1973) concluded that knowledge about drugs is relatively easy to change, attitude change not too difficult but behaviour difficult. It has therefore been suggested that teaching might be more effective if, instead of having a broad goal of prevention, a narrower, more specific goal was selected (Dorn, Swift and Thompson 1974) so that the effect can be better assessed. It therefore follows that a programme should be aimed at a favourable change in knowledge, attitude or behaviour, but not in them all. Dorn (1972) in fact concludes that the priority goal should be 'what particular aspect of knowledge, attitude or behaviour we consider most important, and for whom'.

Martin Evans

Developing Effective Strategies

Taking into account the theoretical relationship between knowledge, attitudes and behaviour, and noting the burden of the empirical evidence supporting a sceptical view of any single consecutive causal relationship, the need to develop strategies for alcohol education which did not rely upon a wholly cognitive approach was clearly of considerable importance. Yet, it could be argued, the traditional approach of schools has been to provide information. We therefore asked Martin Evans whether specific techniques had been developed which were known to be particularly effective. Having already bemoaned the scarcity of good experimental work, he told us about a pilot research project undertaken by Keith Eades (1978) a colleague of his at TACADE.

Eades' study was an attempt to use some of the recommendations from previous research and evaluation studies done mainly in the field of drug education in general and to relate them specifically to alcohol education. To this end it was decided that an evaluation would be carried out on a programme of alcohol education designed to change a particular attitude in a positive direction so that if the attitude was already positive, that attitude would be reinforced.

It has been suggested that one of the main reasons that young people drink alcohol is to appear more mature. The attitude selected therefore as a goal for this research project was: 'THAT YOUNG PEOPLE WHO DRINK ALCOHOL AND PARTICULARLY IN LARGE QUANTITIES ARE MORE MATURE THAN THOSE WHO DO NOT DRINK ALCOHOL.'

Eades devised a teaching programme which consisted of two lessons of factual information and two lessons based on five imaginary situations, in work-card form, to be used as stimulus material for class discussions. This approach was used since attitudes, although well developed, may be ill-informed at this stage, and any alcohol education of this type would provide the pupils with the opportunity to examine their own attitudes and ideas about alcohol and the way it is used. The purpose of this section was, therefore, to allow the pupils to use the group discussion techniques to examine freely their own, and the rest of the group's attitude towards alcohol. It was hoped that, by enabling them to ventilate their feelings, discussion would assist them to recognise myths and, in developing new attitudes based on correct information, indicate to pupils biases of which they had previously been unaware.

The programme was tested in three schools in one Local Authority with a total sample of 181 fourth year (14 to 15 year old) pupils. Time does not allow me to go into the methodological and statistical problems of the study and the attempts to overcome these. Nevertheless, the results were extremely encouraging. The main objective of the programme, that of changing or reinforcing the particular attitude in question, was successfully achieved. The change in attitude of the experimental groups was statistically significant at the 5 per cent level of probability whilst the change in the control group was not statistically significant. The change in attitude was measured using the five-point Likert scale on pre and post course questionnaires. Increases in knowledge were also measured and again, in overall terms, the increase in the experimental group was statistically significant whereas the control, again, was not. Although the course was designed to increase knowledge and affect one particular attitude, it was felt appropriate to attempt to measure some aspects of drinking behaviour before and after the course. The number of the experimental group who had had too much to drink (using a range of criteria) in the month prior to the questionnaire actually increased between pre and post test. This by itself would be a very depressing result. It is qualified, however, by the fact that this increase was not anything like as significant as the increase in the control group, which does suggest that the course may have had some influence in moderating the behaviour of the experimental group.

Although these results are tentative and, to a degree, speculative, they do seem to reinforce the main conclusions of previous research in alcohol and drug education. These are the need to specify objectives and to develop materials closely matched to these objectives in teaching programmes. Again, there is the need to specify objectives within the three broad educational domains, the cognitive, affective and behavioural, and not to expect increases in one area necessarily to involve increases in the others. Finally, there is the need to evaluate and monitor teaching programmes as closely as possible as a way of finding out whether objectives are being achieved and as a way of checking that aims and objectives are not too broad.

One final point about teaching techniques needs to be mentioned. If schools attempt to work explicitly within the area of affective development, then this has definite implications for teaching techniques employed. Most initial teacher training is aimed at developing teaching skills within the cognitive area and, by their own admission, most teachers feel insecure with what are seen as the 'newer' methods, such as the use of structured discussion in large groups, role play and simulation. There seems an increasing need for in-service teacher training in these areas to develop the appropriate teaching skills and also to help the teacher to think through many of the very difficult moral and social questions raised by teaching within the area of values, attitudes, emotions and relationships.

Martin Evans

Values 'Clarification or Values' Modification

We asked Sally 'Casswell (Director of the Alcohol Research Unit, Department of Community Health, University of Auckland, New Zealand) to comment upon Martin Evans' views on attitude formation and upon the implications which he drew from Eades' study.

The idea that one's behaviour does not necessarily and inevitably change following a change in one's attitude has gained considerable currency among academic researchers (Fishbein 1967). Fishbein's analysis and subsequent empirical work (Ajzen 1971; Davidson and Jaccard 1975) locates the impulse to action in a variety of sources other than simply attitude toward the object. A close correlation can be demonstrated between a specific action and the individual's attitude towards the performance of this specific action but, as Evans points out, this relationship could theoretically be a justification of one's past behaviour rather than a causal factor in subsequent behaviour. The causal links between attitude and behaviour cannot be revealed by the typical cross-sectional study and, given the measurement problems inherent in using self-reported data, are difficult to assess in longitudinal studies. There are therefore problems in assuming a simple model of an immediate change in behaviour following a change in attitude and these call into question the goal of attitude change as an aim for alcohol education.

It is perhaps not only the lack of theoretical justification for attitude change as a goal for alcohol education, but also a growing dissatisfaction with the results of such education, which has encouraged a questioning of previous attempts. And the increases in the liberalization of controls on alcohol experienced by many western industrialized countries has meant that the content of previous attitude change alcohol education became out of step with the wider attitudes of society. The replacement emphasis in the area of teaching 'drinking skills' and 'moderate drinking' practices is more in keeping with liberalized opinion.

Despite some questioning of old style attitude change education the role of attitudes continues to be assumed to be important by many educationalists and the current trend within school based education is a focus on more specific beliefs. Evans cites as an example of this Eades' (1978) work which dealt with the belief that drinking alcohol makes one mature. It is interesting that his description of Eades' work is an illustration of a values' *clarification* technique being portrayed as synonymous with the *modification* of values; it is assumed that the provision of factual information leads to a 'clarification' of values which is implicitly assumed to be equivalent to a modification of belief. (Given the evidence that alcohol functions as a marker of adult status in many societies it is difficult to be sure that this will follow.)

The values' clarification process may function as a vehicle for attitude change but not just through the provision of factual information. There is also ample room for the values' clarification process to include those techniques which research has shown to be efficacious in changing beliefs. These include communications from credible sources (one's peers) and the opportunity to hear two sided communications as well as opportunity to make public one's own stance (Hovland, *et al* 1963). In so far as the values' clarification situation allows for modelling of social responses appropriate to a particular attitude this may also affect both behaviour and attitude (Evans, *et al* 1970).

The examples of Eades' (1978) work deals with a specific belief about alcohol but still retains the implicit assumption that a change in belief will directly change the individual's behaviour. An alternative approach for alcohol educationalists is to persist in attempting to modify, or at least reinforce, attitudes towards alcohol but without the assumption that such change will result in an immediate, direct and measurable change in the individual's behaviour. (Considering the high level of exchange of attitudes concerning alcohol in most societies in which it is used the involvement of alcohol educationalists in the debate is almost inevitable.)

Attitudes can be conceptualized as collective explanations for existing situations and patterns of behaviour but these are not, of course, uniform within a society, nor over time. If one accepts that changes in behaviour depend largely on changes in the relevant structure of society (how available and cheap alcohol is, for example) rather than changes in an individual's attitude, it is still likely that the expression of these attitudes has an influence on the structure, in other words that the process is a two-way one. The changes in society's structure will also reflect increasing support for certain attitudes, or an increasing intensity of support.

Given the available evidence that alcohol consumption and related problems depend on the ready availability of alcohol at cheap cost, and on the image of the user, built up in part by the promotion of the product, there is an obvious need for discussion of these social policies to be part of alcohol education. The necessary explanation concerning the need for such controls will inevitably deal with the adverse consequences for society of increased alcohol consumption. Such education would therefore bear a resemblance to that of the temperance-orientated alcohol education of the past. The objectives would also bear some resemblance since the temperance movement also sought not only to affect the individual's behaviour but the wider issues of availability.

The value of this attitude change goal for alcohol education will still depend upon the relationship between the attitudes, but at a less individual level than have the goals of attitude change in recent alcohol education. The behaviour change objectives would not be changes in individual drinking patterns towards moderation but instead range from verbal expressions of concern through to participation in action groups for or against alcohol policy.

Sally Casswell

Decision-Making Skills

Much of the debate on attitudes and values hinges upon how they relate to behaviour. One area of increasing attention has been the possibilities provided by education which focuses upon the development of specific decision-making skills. We asked Martin Evans whether he thought such an approach was likely to yield better results than some of the more traditional approaches, which concentrated exclusively upon knowledge or upon attitudes.

The case for teaching decision-making skills would appear to be a clear one. As Watts (1975) has stated, 'Students and adults in our society are faced with more and more choices: the growing pace and complexity of social life makes this inevitable. At each choice point they are faced with more and more options, the process of 'product differentiation' means that consumers are faced with ever greater ranges of cars, washing powders, etc., from which to choose; society imposes fewer proscriptions on moral choices than it used to; greater geographical and social mobility allows much more freedom of choice in such major life style decisions as the choice of occupation or the choice of whom one will marry. Moreover, there is an ideological assumption in our society that extending choice is 'good': that it offers greater scope for individual autonomy and increases the likelihood that individuals with different personalities and needs will find the options that suit them best.'

We make decisions all the time. Some are of major importance to us and have a significant influence on our lives, most are less so. And yet we have little formal training in the processes and influences involved in all this decision-making. Some teachers may feel that they do help children to make decisions, but giving the class some information and then asking Johnny what he would do in such and such a situation is not teaching decision-making skills, because Johnny is being forced into thinking about a situation in which he appreciates little of the pressures and influences that would be at work on him.

What then, is the process of 'good' decision-making? In relation to the formal teaching situation, it has been popularly expressed in the following way:—

Encounter problem → find as much information as possible about problem → clarify values related to it → write down all available alternatives → predict outcomes of the alternatives, weighing up each outcome in relation to value structure → try out a course of action → accept consequences → learn from and build on the success or failure of the decision.

According to this model, then, the important part of the process is the ability to weigh up alternative courses of action in relation to the value placed upon them by the individual. This is given an extra dimension by Dorn in his work on decision-making skills in drug education (Dorn 1977) when he states that, 'the way the pupil values things and the decisions he reaches whilst sitting in the classroom, may well differ from the way he would value them if actually faced with an offer of a drug'. Thus, the pupil practising decision-making has both to anticipate the choice-situation and then think about how he would value and balance up the various kinds of facts when in that situation (Dorn & Thompson 1976).

This is accomplished by presenting the pupils with a series of 'imagine' situations into which they are asked to project themselves. each situation involves the offer of a specific substance.

They are given an opportunity to consider future circumstances in which they might regret their decision, and how far back they would have to go to set off on a more satisfactory sequence of decisions. Interestingly, the evaluation (Dorn 1977) of these materials showed that decision-making about drugs increased much more significantly.

This model, of course, assumes that what is being outlined is the process of decision-making, that the value-clarification/rational response model is the one true style of decision-making. Some recent work by Arroba (1977) questions this assumption. From a study of 523 decisions of various kinds made by 64 men and women, she isolates six basic styles of decision-making. 'Style' is defined as a way of approaching, responding to and acting in a decision-making situation, that is, it is the overall manner in which the decision is made. The six styles were labelled as logical, emotional, intuitive, no thought, hesitant and compliant. It was found that the majority of the sample possessed a repertoire of styles. Further, the study showed that, depending on circumstances such as the level of control a person had over a decision or how important a decision was to the decision-maker, certain styles were employed more or less than others. For example, in relation to the level of control experienced by the decision-maker, if a decision was seen as entirely voluntary then the 'no thought' style was used more while the 'compliant' style was used less. The use of the other styles was not affected by this criteria. This point certainly reinforces Dorn's observation of the necessity of taking into account not only the person, but also the person in the situation, in terms of what the situation means subjectively.

Given that people operate different styles of decision-making and vary their use according to circumstance, the next step on from Arroba's work is to ask with which styles people are most satisfied. At present, we are continuing with the assumption that the value clarification/rational response model is the most satisfactory style. This is in many ways an uncomfortable assumption with which to live. For example, one point is that this process is inevitably so complicated that it might actually make decisions more difficult — a person surrounded by a whole welter of values, information and strategies etc., might feel utterly paralysed. Again, there is little help given within this model for the split-second decision where the person, without warning, has to make up his mind about something.

Of a more theoretical nature, there have been questions raised (Cowley 1978) about the actual feasibility of teaching decision-making skills to school children. Cowley cites research from the areas of cognitive and moral development to suggest that some of the teaching programmes being operated may be inappropriate to the level of development of the children the programmes are aimed at. He does make some positive suggestions for modifying these programmes to bring them in line with cognitive and moral development.

Finally, it is commonly accepted that helping the decision-maker to be satisfied with his decisions is one of the basic aims of teaching decision-making skills. This is fundamental when one of the foremost tasks is clarification of values which are inevitably subjectively defined. As Watts and Elsom (1974) state, 'Considering values removes the implication that there are 'right' answers or outcomes, emphasising instead the effective use of a process to produce consequences that satisfy the individual concerned . . . With decision-making two individuals faced with a similar choice may make widely differing decisions which are equally valid in terms of their own value-systems. It is the individual who determines the 'rightness' of decisions.' Health education has traditionally seen itself as being inextricably tied up with behaviour modification and change, and 'skill' based objectives certainly would appear to be philosophically at odds with such a tradition. The fear then is, given that it is difficult for a leopard to change its spots, all that is happening with these new approaches is that we are dressing up the old baby in new clothes! We need to ask ourselves whether, as health educators we are really prepared to accept a situation where those whom we are educating might, as a result of the skills we impart to them, choose to live out a life-style which may well be at odds with what we may consider to be healthy or responsible.

Martin Evans

In her response to this communication, Sally Casswell chose to con-centrate upon the extent to which even the decision-making approach to alcohol education permits some control policy views to be side-stepped.

Public Policy and Individual Lifestyle

Evans questions whether school children are developmentally able to learn decision-making skills and whether the values' clarification/ rational decision-making style is the only, or always appropriate, style of decision-making in alcohol related situations. I think these questions are valid and important ones. It seems likely to me that many 'decisions', including those related to alcohol use, are made without mental weighing of the pros and cons of a specific action. It is note-worthy that the attempts to change attitudes and behaviour made by the commercial world do not, by and large, assume a rational, decision-making approach. The function of tobacco and alcohol advertising has been compared to a modern day myth; it acts to reduce anxiety and it creates an immediate impression (Egger 1979). It does not matter if one is later allowed to see through the myth, its action is assumed to be stronger than the rational explanations which later belie it (Barthes 1972). It is likely that a young person's drinking behaviour is in large part determined by his or her image of an alcohol user and the social situation in which he/she is rather than a rational process of decision-making, a weighing up of the pros and cons of alcohol use.

One of the major values of Nick Dorn's decision-making programme for drug education (Dorn 1977) is the focus on the social situation in which use takes place. The work of Evans *et al* (1978) in the cigarette smoking field in the United States has developed this focus beyond the decision-making approach; they concentrate on role play in which students rehearse how they will translate into verbal behaviour the decision to refuse a cigarette. Information about the adverse conse-quences of cigarette smoking is given but the emphasis is not on the decision-making stage of the process but the translation of the decision into action.

Despite the lack of an adequate theoretical base for the decision-making/values' clarification approach it has assumed considerable pop-ularity and I think this is because the approach answered certain critical needs which school-based alcohol education had, particularly in the 1970s. These needs arose out of an increasing awareness that giving facts about the physiological effects of alcohol consumption was not successful in preventing alcohol use. An uncompromising statement to children that alcohol was a dangerous substance to be avoided was also out of step with the increasing liberalization of alcohol use within the wider society at this time. The decision-making/values' clarification approach answered the needs of school-based education particularly well. Since it assumes a rational, thinking person, it continues to provide an avenue for imparting information about the effects of alcohol, and, perhaps most importantly of all, obviates the need to make clear what the expected outcome of the education is in behavioural terms.

This latter point, which Evans believes puts the decision-making approach at odds with traditional health education, is the one which I believe, explains its popularity. He suggests that the traditional goal of health education has been 'inextricably tied up with behaviour modification and change'; on the contrary it seems to me that traditional health education has frequently been confined to giving information about signs of sickness and the behaviourally based goals have been limited to visits to medical personnel and vaccinations.

This is understandable since recommendations for specific changes in lifestyle or public policy must be made in simple (some would say simplistic) terms and are easily open to criticism. Such criticism can be and is made on grounds of lacking 'scientific' evidence (is high cholesterol really a risk factor for heart disease; does advertising increase alcohol-related problems?), and infringement of individual freedom (should people be forced to wear seatbelts or crash helmets?). Such specific recommendations may also come in conflict with powerful vested interests. It is far more comfortable to stick to an information-giving, awareness-raising style of health education and this the decision-making approach does very well.

Incidentally, it is also very acceptable to the age group at whom it is aimed, many of whom are thoroughly tired of being told by authority what they should and should not do. In the programme we developed for use with 12-14 year old students (Casswell 1982) we found that the non-directive veneer of the decision-making approach was a useful avenue to present not only information about drug effects but also more subtle cues about images. In our video-tape presentations in which social situations were illustrated some of the students were shown making 'appropriate' decisions and taking 'appropriate' courses of action and attention was paid to creating a positive image for these role models. The difficulty we had in deciding what would be appropriate behaviour in alcohol-related situations contrasts with the comfort of the traditional decision-making approach in which no specific, appropriate behaviour has to be illustrated.

The dilemma of school-based alcohol education is the dilemma of much alcohol education — what precisely are the problems one is trying to prevent? In the school population one has the added disadvantage that many alcohol-related problems develop only after prolonged drinking and the relationship between early drinking patterns and later ones is not well understood. So the issue becomes one of recommending a specific way of handling alcohol which can be scientifically shown to relate to minimization of alcohol problems, does not outrage those who believe that children should be taught abstinence nor those who feel their own pattern of drinking is being criticized and which, at the same time, still seems relevant to the children. It is not surprising that the clarification of values has become a popular approach.

Sally Casswell

Conclusions

It may be that the crucial question in this debate is one which is common to other areas of health education as well, namely whether the educational process is seen as being directed primarily towards the goal of individual behaviour change or whether a larger, more ambitious agenda is being considered, in which education is seen essentially as an instrument of social change (Partanen 1982). Here the Report on the Technical Discussions at the 1982 World Health Assembly (WHO 1982) is illuminating. 'It was appreciated,' it states, 'that education meant a great deal more than simply providing reasonably accurate information. In fact, it has to do with the creation of social awareness. If the political will of the people is to be stimulated, then education must play a central part in that process.'

Thus, at an individual level, there may be a need to turn attention away from persistent consideration of the damaging effects of excessive drinking, particularly when these effects are predominately of a chronic nature and when the target of the educational programmes is young people who perceive such effects as irrelevant to their lives. There are, after all, well-documented accounts of those situational and inter-personal factors which exert the strongest influence upon young people's attitudes and behaviour with respect to alcohol. Family and peer influence have been carefully analysed by a number of researchers (O'Connor 1978; Davies & Stacey 1972; Strickland 1982a), who have related their conclusions to stages in emotional and educational development and to society's explicit and implicit values regarding drinking, intoxication and marketing practice. Similarly, the role of media stereotyping (Cook & Lewington 1979) and of advertising (Grant 1982a; Strickland 1983) have been assessed. What emerges certainly in societies like Britain, Ireland, the United States and other northern industrialised nations is that despite the ambivalence of the value system, despite the pluralistic nature of the social networks, learning to drink is one important demonstration of the ritual passage from childhood into adulthood. Although occasionally this passage is associated with rebellion, with experimentation and with repeated excessive consumption, far more frequently it is sanctioned, even encouraged, by the adult population (Aitkin & Leathar 1981). Many children, probably the majority in all the countries listed above, are given their first drink by their parents. Later, perhaps, peer influences become more important determinants of drinking behaviour than parental models, but, as things stand currently, most youth-targeted alcohol education programmes take little account of either parents or peers.

They focus instead upon the consequential damage of excessive consumption, a lesson which, to judge from the pre-test evaluations examined by Grant (1982b) is already quite well internalised by the young people towards whom these programmes are directed. It comes as no surprise to them to learn that drunk people crash their cars or that alcoholics die of liver cirrhosis. More to the point, perhaps, would be an educational approach which dealt with the influences (parents, peers, the media) upon young people's drinking, rather than one which, taking these influences for granted, concentrates upon what may well be perceived as depersonalised effects.

If, indeed, education is an instrument of social change, then it is more likely to resonate when the interests of society and the interests of the individual are seen to be in harmony. This may well speak for a narrowing of the aims of some alcohol education programmes, if narrowing means focussing more precisely upon those issues and influences which are perceived as relevant by the recipients. If, however, as is likely, some of those issues (such as youth employment) and some of those influences (such as relationships with parents) turn out to be far wider than the alcohol field itself, then that will test the centrality of what it is that is being communicated. Alcohol education may become less popular with the Department of Health and Social Security, with the Brewers' Society and with the UK Temperance Alliance, but it may become a lot more popular with young people themselves.

10 THE HEALTH EDUCATION DEBATE

Introduction

It is one of health education's greatest burdens that people's expectations of it run so high. It is, and maybe it always will be, more acceptable to plan to educate the population rather than to seek to control it. Education seems to land us on one side of John Stuart Mill's dictum ('each is the proper guardian of his own health, whether bodily, or mental and spiritual') whilst controls take us firmly away from those principles of individual liberty which appear so fundamental to our view of the relationship between the individual and society. It is, therefore, the sense of health education as almost too good to be true which leads to a hope, often pious, always misplaced, that it can by itself exert a powerful influence upon the behaviour of those sections of the population most likely to cause themselves damage. The notion that it might also influence those in some way responsible for causing the damage is a much less common presumption.

Recognising the gap between expectations and performance, and aware how easy it is for educators to start talking about 'should' and 'must' instead of relying upon empirical data, we decided that it would be most fruitful to begin this debate by looking at how a national plan of alcohol education might be developed. Accordingly, we asked David Player (at that time Director of the Scottish Health Education Group, now Director General of the Health Education Council in London) to tell us about the way in which he and his colleagues had decided to tackle the legendary problem of Scotland's alcohol abuse problem. In the hope that attention might be focussed upon specific key issues, we asked him to respond specifically to five separate questions.

The Scottish Response to Alcohol Problems

1. What are the priority groups towards which you direct health education about alcohol?

Originally attention was focused on alcoholism at the extreme end of the abuse spectrum. Alcoholics and their families were given priority. From 1974, an annual mass media campaign was run to alert the general public to the signs and symptoms of alcoholism and to indicate relevant helping agencies for alcoholics. The aim was to increase the level of awareness in the population, reduce stigma and thereby reach and encourage alcoholics to come forward for treatment.

At the same time professional workers were seen as secondary targets. Funds were provided for the training of alcoholism counsellors, for promotion of annual schools on alcoholism and for periodic seminars on specific topics. In the industrial field, attempts were made to stimulate the formation of employee counselling schemes for potential alcoholics. Management and personnel staff were seen as targets here.

More recently the emphasis on alcoholism has been dropped. For one thing there is now a relatively high level of knowledge about alcoholism in the population. More importantly it is recognised that the issue needs to be tackled at a much earlier stage, before harmful drinking patterns have become deeply entrenched. The Scottish Health Education Group (SHEG), believes that a concerted effort is needed not only to change individual drinking behaviour but also to affect attitudes to drink and drunkenness in society as a whole, so that moderate drinking is encouraged.

To this end present strategy focuses on the young, ranging from broad educational programmes for children at school, to a self-monitoring approach for young regular drinkers. Additionally an attack is made on the tough, manly image of heavy drinking in the media and the social acceptance of drunkenness. Since 1980 SHEG has had responsibility for the in-service training of professionals concerned with health education. Where a need arises, courses on aspects of alcohol education are devised for professional groups, such as teachers, health visitors and GP's.

At a different level, local and national policy-makers are seen as legitimate targets for education. Advice is given to statutory bodies on the role of health education within a comprehensive alcohol control policy and SHEG is represented on a number of related committees and working groups.

Increasingly the use of alcohol is seen in the wider context of life-style and its effects on health. For example alcohol education is only one component of an experimental cartoon programme aimed at social classes III, IV and V, which also covers smoking, family planning and fitness. Likewise SHEG's positive health promotions aimed at the general public, touch on the use of alcohol but are more concerned to show people the positive actions and alternatives available for a healthy enjoyable lifestyle.

2. *How do you achieve an optimum relationship between message content and the audience?*

SHEG employs a variety of methods to match up the message and the target. Firstly, from a *review of the literature*, information can be collected on the known characteristics of the target group, as well as on the results of previous attempts at health education in a similar area. The data can act as a basis for ideas on how to present the topic to the target. However, often the review shows up areas which have not been adequately researched and in which there is a lack of information. In some cases, SHEG can *sponsor basic research* to help fill in the gaps in knowledge concerning the target groups. For example, SHEG sponsored a three-part study into the attitudes and behaviour of Scottish children in relation to alcohol (Jahoda & Crammond 1972; Davies & Stacey 1972; Aitken 1978). The results of these surveys were used in the making of three films on alcohol aimed at school children. A follow-up study published in 1981, looked at adults' attitudes to drinking and smoking in young people (Aitken & Leathar 1981). Turning to the adult population in Scotland, a survey of Scottish drinking habits was funded by SHEG (Dight 1976). This gave a general view of the use of alcohol in Scotland in terms of age, sex, social class, etc. The study provided a profile of the heavy drinkers in the population as well as information on the general circumstances surrounding drinking.

Pre-testing of publicity material on a sample of the target audience usually follows. Checks are made that the message is understood, the tone of the advert is correct, and that the images created are favourable and relevant to the audience. From results of the pre-testing, material can be continually refined, and improved until it is ready for release. Since 1979 SHEG has funded an Advertising Research Unit at Strathclyde University which undertakes research of this nature on major mass media programmes. The unit has developed a comprehensive cycle of research covering each step in programme development from problem definition to evaluation once the programme gets underway.

In addition, *Intervention studies* are sponsored from time to time. In a test-area a health education project is developed, evaluated and adapted while another area acts as control. These are often long-term projects employing a variety of techniques. A current one sponsored by SHEG is concerned with health promotion among deprived families in the Edinburgh area. In this the 'consumers' are being surveyed at the beginning to find out not only what they *need* but also what they *want* in terms of health education. Any programmes developed should therefore be suited to the community and sensitive to living conditions there.

3. *With smoking the message is 'don't', with alcohol it seems to be one of moderation. Is that more difficult to convey?*
The whole question of alcohol is not as clear-cut as smoking. There are virtually no positive health reasons for smoking and a great deal of research evidence against it, so the 'Don't smoke' message is on firm ground. The effects of smoking, although often long-term, can be seen in the form of physical illness such as coughs, bronchitis, shortness of breath, and finally cancer and coronary heart disease.

With alcohol the adverse effects are often mental or social as well as physical and thus harder to pin-point as due to a single cause. For example, alcohol may contribute to family breakdown, inefficiency at work, and violence towards friends. It is more difficult to get over the message of alcohol abuse when the results are so diffuse.

When promoting moderation, there is always the problem of 'what is moderate drinking?' There is no clear evidence on what a safe level of consumption is since it will vary from person to person. If SHEG were to define a maximum limit of consumption, as other countries have done, then it runs the risk of people drinking up to that limit because they believe it to be safe. One way round that problem is to define the limit of safe drinking in social and mental health terms and this is the approach SHEG is taking.

Moderation as a message is easier to convey in some areas, particularly that of primary health education. Such programmes are aimed at the healthy individual who has not started drinking or who drinks moderately anyway. It is easier to use a calm, non-threatening approach, discussing both sides of the question of the use of alcohol than a negative 'Don't Drink' approach which might alienate the audience.

4. *What is your answer to critics who say that health education is of untested value? How do you evaluate the effects of a health education campaign?*
The field of health education is so vast that generalisations of this nature have no real meaning. Of course, some health education programmes have not been tested in the past and some still go untested, but an increasing number do have rigorous evaluation built-in at the planning stage. Of these, some have proved successful while others have not.

It is useful to put the statement into perspective. Tones (1977) points out that much of curative medicine goes untested or has inadequate testing. However, it carries such prestige and authority that the same challenge for justification rarely arises. Health education on the other hand has low credibility, little prestige, and so is frequently called upon to prove its worth. The situation becomes even more interesting when the vast resources poured into curative medicine are considered, compared with the relatively minor amounts allocated to health education. Despite the discrepancy, the major improvements in health in this century have had less to do with medical treatment and more to do with environmental change including advances in public health medicine. Taking this long-term perspective, many preventive measures have already proved their worth.

In practice it is often very difficult to evaluate the effects of health education programmes. It is not as simple as doing controlled experiments in a laboratory. The control population in a health education experiment cannot be shielded from outside interference. In addition direct proof of prevention is often not available – the individual who has been prevented from becoming an alcoholic might not have become one anyway.

As far as SHEG is concerned, 10 per cent of the budget is allocated for evaluation studies. We try to set realistic measurable objectives for campaigns so that at least an evaluation is possible. For this reason any evaluation should be planned right at the beginning when the programme is being devised. Then if a base-line study is required the *right* questions will be asked and can be compared with measurements taken after the programme has taken place.

5. What considerations dictate your choice of medium in conveying information about alcohol?

The choice of medium open to health educators is very wide indeed – for instance television, press and other mass media advertising; group discussion; one-to-one counselling; lectures and conferences. In addition the target can be reached indirectly by providing professional workers with the training or the teaching aids to carry out health education themselves. In reality the range of choice is narrowed considerably when manpower, cost and target characterstics are taken into account. The final decision is usually based on a combination of these factors. A number of questions are relevant:

i.   What are the aims of the programme? How complex is the message? If the aim is to give simple information to a large number of people, the mass media might be used. We also tend to use the mass media to create images and atmosphere related to changing social attitudes. If we need to present two sides of an argument or if we are aiming at a bigger shift in behaviour, other media would be more appropriate – like group discussion/counselling to help individuals reduce heavy drinking or stop smoking.

ii.   What are the characteristics of the target group? What do they do? Where do they go? What media do they come in contact with? The medium chosen must relate as closely as possible to the habits of the target group.

iii.   Have we got the workforce to use the medium effectively? In some cases the answer is no, particularly where personal contact is required. However, there are ways of getting round the problem. SHEG has been working on increasing the number of people in Scotland actively involved in personal health education. Doctors, nurses, social workers, teachers and other professionals are seen as valuable potential health educators in their day-to-day work. Through the funding of lectureships in Scottish Universities, and the provision of in-service training courses, professionals are encouraged to recognise their role as health educators and are given the necessary training to carry out the work.

iv.   Last but not least, how much will it cost? Television advertising has the potential to reach a large audience but is so expensive that it can only be used in selected areas. With tobacco and alcohol manufacturers spending fifty times as much on advertising as health educators, there is a danger that the health message will get swamped by opposing messages. Other channels have to be investigated. At the moment we are experimenting with two alternatives. The first is the sponsorship of sport (Docherty 1981) – a technique used successfully already by many alcohol manufacturers. They manage to get plenty of free publicity and link alcohol with popular events through sponsorship. We saw the opportunity to do the same in our health promotion programmes. The main aim was to boost healthy activities and forge an association between health education and enjoyment in the minds of the public. To date SHEG has sponsored such events as Health Race '81 and '82 (two international cycle races around Scotland with associated 'Health Weeks'), the 1982 Fun Run and the Scottish Football Team for the 1982 World Cup. In terms of media coverage and spinoff activities the events have already proved cost-effective.

The second experiment involves promoting health education in standard television and radio programmes like plays, serials and documentaries, and in drama productions taken round schools. Certain health issues can be discussed in greater detail than is possible in 30-second commercials. It may also be a way of making rather negative health messages less threatening to the target audience.

David Player and Margaret Whitehead

The description of the national strategy of the SHEG was originally written in 1979 and then revised in 1982, to take account of developments which had occurred since the first draft. It was, in fact, that first draft which we sent to Michael Goodstadt of the Addiction Research Foundation in Toronto. We asked him to comment not so much upon the specifics of SHEG's programmes as upon the extent to which he felt their solutions to common health education problems reflected important trends in alcohol education. He was at pains to point out that his comments were not intended as criticism of SHEG in particular. He also recognised the problems inherent in focusing the debate upon the questions which we had asked, questions which might limit as well as focus SHEG's ability to present a coherent case. Our questions, indeed, came in for increasing criticism as this debate developed. Maybe, of course, they were inappropriate questions. Or maybe health educators are not accustomed to providing answers.

I would like to begin by highlighting some issues which I consider to be central to effective health education. My first concern is not only with the definition of 'health education' but, more importantly, with the context in which this form of influence is seen to exist. To what extent is education considered to stand alone? Is it viewed as one element in a matrix of direct and/or indirect influences on awareness and/or behaviour? What is alcohol education's relationship, for example, to alcohol policies? Is any attempt made to integrate, or render compatible, these two or other approaches to dealing with alcohol problems?

Extending the same enquiry in a slightly different direction, is any consideration given to the relationships between alcohol use and other behaviours (particular or general)? What are the general and the particular characteristics of alcohol use/abuse? How do the latter fit into a matrix of other behaviours and values? What are the positive and negative alternatives to alcohol abuse? How effectively can one influence alcohol-related behaviours without at the same time influencing non-alcohol behaviours. To what extent can the problems of alcohol use be addressed only through the promotion of health in general and positive alternatives in particular?

The first task faced by SHEG, or any similar group, is the specific-ation of the nature, extent and origin of the problems associated with alcohol. Its early research seems to have identified a set of problems associated with 'alcoholism' and 'alcoholics', problems of significant dimensions. This, implicitly or explicitly, narrowed the focus of SHEG's initial efforts and it is interesting to compare its early ideas with later, more broadly-based interventions. When the problem was defined differently, for example, in terms of alcohol use or 'healthful lifestyle' rather than alcoholism a very different set of preventive out-comes emerged.

One of the next steps involved a decision regarding the priority of these problems. Player and Whitehead say they addressed the problem of alcoholism 'originally at the extreme end . . . alcoholics and their families'. This decision raises several issues. Firstly, the prioritizing of problems, especially as measured by their size, does not necessarily indicate the order or manner in which these problems should be addressed — radical surgery, for example, may be too late, inappro-priate, less effective than alternatives and unrelated to future events.

Examples of a reversal of the order of addressing the problem is to be found in efforts by Scandinavian countries (and now Canada) to foster a generation of non-smokers. Previous mass influence efforts with respect to alcohol problems seems to have favoured the 'alcoholism-alcoholics' approach. One can ask, however, (1) how effec-tive have such programmes been in identifying alcoholics? (2) Are resources available, adequate and effective to meet the needs of the large number of alcoholics? And, (3) what has been done to stem the flow of new alcoholics? To judge from the information it provides about its later efforts, SHEG is coming to share this view of its appointed task.

Having identified problems, and decided on the order in which these would be addressed, SHEG appears initially to have adopted mass media campaigns, supported by professional training, messages targeted to opinion leaders, etc. Responses to the fifth question, regarding the choice of medium, indicate that they are well aware of the cost-effective-ness limitations inherent in the use of the mass media.

The mass media tend frequently to be favoured by those wishing to influence large segments of the general population. With few excep-tions, the mass media have not, however, been effective in influencing significant behaviours to a significant extent. Why do we continue to be enamoured by the mass media? What are the alternatives? Answers to the first question include our belief in the mass media's overwhelming influence in all aspects of daily life — we are especially prone to believe that most other people are manipulated by the media. The mass media also appeal because they suggest an easy answer to our problems; by definition, they will channel our messages and hence influence masses of people, thus 'guaranteeing' that we will successfully influence a countable number of people. Mass media programmes are also appealing for those involved in their production and dissemination; one readily feels like a military general developing strategies, marshalling and deploying forces, and delighting in the sense of accomplishment once 'D-day' arrives. Unfortunately, the effectiveness of one's health education labours is rarely as apparent as in a military context.

Alternatives to the electronic non-personal mass media approach are not as appealing to the 'health general'; they are less 'sexy', involve a great deal more planning and organisation, and do not foster a 'D-day' mentality. Examples include the use of an army of volunteer workers (e.g. employed by the Cancer Societies) whose task is to knock on doors and help spread the word by personal conact. Another technique is to use a panel of speakers (e.g. employed by the Manchester Regional Committee for Cancer Education) who, over an extended period of time, talk to a larger number of small groups, resulting in ultimate contact and re-contact with a very large number of individuals, perhaps even more effectively than via more traditional mass media techniques. Again, to judge from descriptions of its more recent work, SHEG appears to be shouldering this more complex and less immediately gratifying burden.

SHEG, perhaps wisely, considers the use of mass media inadequate for producing behavioural change. I sometimes wonder, however, whether we are not selling the mass media short in this regard. Could they not be successfully used to promote behavioural change through (1) identifying the sequence of behavioural steps required for change (e.g. reducing tobacco or alcohol consumption), and (2) reinforcing this sequence as it occurs in the target audience? A third issue involves one of my major concerns: what measures are taken to ensure that the target audience (e.g. young heavy drinking males) are, in fact, being reached by the media? If, as I suspect, such a group is reached in this way only with great difficulty, alternative media or intermediaries would be required.

A further step in planning of health education occurs at some point prior to or in association with selection of media, namely goals and objectives. A distinction is sometimes made between longer term goals and shorter term objectives, but in any case both the longer and shorter time frame objectives require specification.

SHEG's long range goals might seem ambiguous. Is it concerned to reduce alcoholism prevalence or incidence; to reduce social, economic, or personal costs associated with alcoholism; to cure alcoholics? Its original aims were 'to increase the level of awareness (regarding "the signs and symptoms of alcoholism and the helping agencies available") in the population, reduce stigma, and thereby reach and encourage alcoholics to come forward for treatment'. But even these objectives involve a variety of assumptions both with respect to their relationship to some overall goal involving alcoholism, and with respect to their attainability. What is known about current levels of awareness? How is it inadequate? What evidence is there that increasing the population's level of awareness will lead to the identification and treatment of alcoholics? Why would reduction of stigma be expected to encourage the seeking of help? Is this not also likely to shift the balance of responsibility from the individual to external forces and, thereby, remove a potent source of internal control? How are alcoholics expected to be 'reached and encouraged' — directly (questionable) or indirectly through significant others (more feasible)?

All this suggests a need among health educators for a more elaborate and solid conceptual exposition of the problem, its etiology, its alleviation and its prevention. It is interesting to note how SHEG has modified its original aims and objectives between 1979 and 1982, indicating the application of cumulative experience in programme development. This is something worth stressing, lest it seem that some of my comments about SHEG are unreasonably critical. Its 1982 modifications make it clear how well aware it is of its involvement in a dynamic process, rather than in the business of providing final solutions.

SHEG's comparison between alcohol and tobacco messages was, I felt, succinctly on the mark. It struck me, however, that this question raised one of the most troublesome of issues — one which I believe those in the alcohol field will have to face squarely in the very near future. How can we make statements about the positive (health as well as social and economic) value of alcohol use without encouraging its use, raising *per capita* consumption and perhaps also increasing the prevalence of its associated problems? The evidence regarding tobacco, as pointed out, is less ambiguously negative. It is for this reason that one may have to search for a way to incorporate alcohol use into a broader framework that embraces the positive use of food, stress and relaxation, exercise, other drugs, etc.

Justification for our continuing in the field of health education must include the recognition that the overwhelming proportion of health education programmes are of unknown value, principally due to an absence of evaluation. Of the remainder, the overwhelming majority are of zero or mixed value. The more effective ones are probably those which have clear, limited, attainable objectives, are well planned and executed, are of sufficient duration, and include follow-up efforts. I am concerned, however, that recent successes (e.g. Stanford Heart Disease Prevention Program) and other less clearly successful projects (e.g. North Kerelia Project) are leading us to inappropriate conclusions. It is being put about and/or accepted that (1) mass media programmes are effective in reducing smoking and cardio-vascular risk and, therefore, (2) that other health problems are equally amenable to amelioration through the same means. Such a conclusion is inappropriate because it fails to take account of differences in: (1) the nature and extent of the problems, (2) the prior cumulative efforts made to deal with the problems, and (3) the supportive role of social norms for desired behavioural change. The conclusions that can be validly drawn from previous successful experiences are those suggested above, namely successful health education is more likely to result from programmes that (1) have a sound conceptual foundation, (2) are well planned and developed and (3) extremely well implemented. These principles are not new; nor do I believe that we have progressed much in developing a scientific discipline of health education. Perhaps in the 1980s, we are being obliged to apply more rigorously the scientific and other principles'long available, as a result of the pressures to reduce the economic burden being placed on our health and social services, and to do so cost-effectively.

In summary, SHEG's responses to your questions provided me, and I hope your readers, with an opportunity to examine our own soul and professional shop. My major concern is with our (collective) need to be more precise in our conceptual analysis of both the presenting problems and the alternative strategies to address these questions.

Michael Goodstadt

Our second commentator, Lawrence Wallack of the Prevention Research Group, Medical Research Institute, Berkeley, was altogether less satisfied, both with the questions we had originally asked and with the responses which we had received.

I read with interest SHEG's responses to your questions and the subsequent comments of Michael Goodstadt. I found myself in general agreement with Goodstadt's thoughts but felt that the overall thrust of this debate was quite predictable and lacked sufficient critical assessment of the central issues in health education. This fault lies at least as much with the questions as the responses. Your questions to SHEG invited a response that saw the problems addressed by health education (such as alcohol) eventually dissolving as target populations are better defined and described, and the message type and channel is more effectively and efficiently matched with the audience. In other words, it seems that regardless of the problem, health education can be successful given the right combination of social marketing techniques and rigorous scientific methods of programme planning and evaluation. The questions presupposed health education as a process that is focused on the individual and the responses reflected this narrow view. Perhaps more challenging questions could have been asked about the role of health education as it relates to broader issues of social policy concerning alcohol (a point suggested by Goodstadt) or how health education could be used to empower people and communities to address alcohol-related problems through organisational or collective approaches. Community organisation, after all, is as much an integral part of health education as is mass media or the overhead projector.

My main concern is that the alcohol education of SHEG (as I interpret its responses), and alcohol education in general, is not unlike much health promotion activity that attempts to alter the lifestyle of the individual by essentially appealing to increased self-control. The underlying assumption here is that individuals freely choose their lifestyle and thereby, to a large extent, choose their health status. The aim of health education or alcohol education is presumably to facilitate 'good' choices by providing the right information to the right people in the right way at the right time. Successful health education, it seems, results from filling in the equation implied above. This seems to be the primary conceptual framework on which health educators draw and it is certainly evident in your original questions and in the responses in the SHEG paper.

Perhaps the most popular illustrative story regarding prevention is the upstream/downstream one. This story tells about a health worker who keeps pulling people out of a river. Just as the worker revives one person another cry for help is heard, so in jumps the health worker to pull out another casualty. Finally, the person realises that he/she is so busy pulling people out of the water that there is no time to look upstream and find out how all these people are falling, or being pushed, into the river. The task of prevention is to look upstream and focus on factors that influence the conditions that form an important part of the environment in which the problem exists. These conditions and the forces that sustain them are an important part of the problem and cannot be ignored. The focus on upstream factors does not mean that we abandon downstream efforts. It means that the downstream problem needs to be seen as a manifestation of a larger system that is producing disease. Thus, the downstream problem must be defined in the context of the larger system.

It is clear that, as a society, we have taken a primarily downstream approach to human needs; we wait for people to develop problems that have serious adverse effects and then invest enormous resources in attempts to rescue them. These people are then sent back into the same system that was the source of their problems in the first place. The decision to work 'upstream' means that we have to broaden our perspective to include a range of variables outside the individual. The more general social arrangements that in large part set the climate in which problematic behaviours take place, which to date have been largely ignored, must be considered in addressing public health problems. In most instances of public health and health education practice, this will require a redefinition of the problem being addressed.

The implications of how a problem is defined is clearly seen in the alcohol problem area. The typical definition of alcohol problems as a function only of the individual encourages individual-focused informational or coercive approaches that seek to motivate the individual to consume less alcohol. When problems are defined as a function of a broader system of which the individual is one part, a host of other strategies becomes possible. In addition to looking at individuals' drinking habits it is possible to focus on situations or settings in which drinking takes place, and upon the larger context of informal rules, laws and regulations that define the setting. The broader view also allows the problem *per se* to be selected as the focus of attention; for example, traffic crashes rather than drunk drivers might become the starting point of a problem analysis. The 'problem-specific' approach considers the role of alcohol as only one of a number of factors involved in the problem. This approach also encourages parties whose interests may be outside the alcohol area to bring their expertise to bear on the problem and thus enfranchises a variety of groups in analysing and addressing the problem. It also allows communities to select for attention those problems that are of special local concern.

Because social/public health problems are inherent in systems and not just individuals, it is important that the prevention of such problems addresses the various levels of the system. This has not been the case in the alcohol field, or in the health field in general, where prevention efforts have been consistently confined to attempts to change individual behaviour. This is not an improper goal if such efforts are supported by efforts on other levels of the system that seek to create an overall environment that is consistent with the goal of prevention. For example, it makes little sense to educate school children about alcohol when the messages they receive from the larger environment (eg mass media, family, community) contradict what they are being taught. Unless the moderation message, and the message that abstinence is an equally acceptable behaviour, is consistent throughout the entire system, educational efforts and other activities done in isolation have little chance of success. An important aim of prevention initiatives is to work for consistency in messages across all levels for an agreed upon purpose: to minimise the adverse personal and societal consequences of alcohol use.

The health educator must therefore work toward consistency of purpose and action across the entire system. This can only happen when the problem of concern is redefined as part of a larger social context. We must also consider the ethical issues inherent in a problem definition that puts the sole responsibility for problems on the individual. This emphasis on 'self-regulation', a throw-back to the early nineteenth-century view of social problems (Levine 1978) shields the broader society, and particularly the producers who benefit from alcohol, tobacco and drug use or poor dietary practices, from assuming their rightful part of the prevention burden. In thinking about the public health problems we address, we have to accept that these problems can be defined in a variety of ways. Different definitions benefit different groups but, as Caplan and Nelson (1973) conclude: 'Person-blame interpretations are in everyone's interests except those subjected to the analysis.' Public health educators have an important ethical responsibility to challenge definitions that benefit the advantaged at the expense of the less advantaged.

Public education is an activity that has long been a major role of health educators. This is vital and it is important that it continue with increasing levels of vigour. Once the problems of alcohol, or other life-style and safety problems are redefined as properties of systems and not individuals, a massive education effort to support this redefinition is necessary. As part of this education process I support the suggestions of Terris (1981) who predicts a central position for health education in the public health movement. He sees health education addressing two major aspects: first, education of the public about the scientific basis for new public health programmes, particularly concerning the systemic nature of public health problems; and second, he suggests that health educators must continue to encourage individuals to change their own behaviour. He recognises, however, that this latter task is unlikely to succeed unless the anti-health education that takes place through advertising, and I would add television programming, is substantially curbed. Terris has long opposed the separation of the individual from the social context and has acknowledged that vested economic interests affect the choices that individuals make concerning their health behaviour. Health educators need to focus specifically on the fallacy of choice in health behaviour, which is currently the implicit basis for many health education programmes. The consequence of the health promotion movement, whether or not by intent, has been to create the impression that poor health is a function of an individual's choice concerning lifestyle (Labonte & Penfold 1981).

C. Arden Miller (1976) in his Presidential Address to the 103rd Annual Meeting of the American Public Health Association, criticised this increasing emphasis on the rhetoric of individual choice: 'For the vast majority of people in our society the life circumstances leading to poor health are not adopted as a matter of personal choice, but are thrust upon people by the social and economic circumstances into which they are born.'

To base public health programmes on an assumption of freedom of choice is misleading and deflects attention from important forces in the social and economic environment that limit and determine our range of choices. The first task of health eduction should be to increase consciousness about the fallacy of choice. Amos Hawley's (1973) comments are illustrative of the restricted choice that individuals have in making decisions: 'Individuals may expound at length on the reasons for their having a given number of children, for migrating from one place to another, or for engaging in any other kind of activity, but only a few are perceptive enough to recognise that the degrees of freedom in their decision-making are fixed in the structure of society.'

Advertising is one way in which the choices we make are influenced so that the concept of free choice is violated. Ironically, the justification for advertising is that it facilitates choice by providing necessary consumer information. Yet little accurate consumer information is provided in alcohol or tobacco advertisements that associate product use with valued social and health benefits. As Neubauer and Pratt (1981) note, advertising exploits the fundamental American value of individualism in promoting products. The outcome is always in the interests of the producer and only rarely in the interests of the consumer: 'Examination of the advertiser's message reveals that the objective of selling outweighs, to the point of defrauding, the objective of providing information. Consumers are left to make empty choices. They cannot know enough to make substantive distinction between apparent options. We have the illusion of information and the reality of people making psuedo-choices. Those pseudo-choices often lead consumers to act against their own interests.' The heavy reliance of advertising on a 'freedom of choice' image fits well into a model of public health and health education that sees the individual as the sole arbiter of his or her health. Advertising represents a freedom for manufacturers to compete and freedom for consumers to choose. Unfortunately, as Goldsen (1980) points out, such demonstrations of free choice are rigged so that the producer usually wins and the consumer usually loses.

Health educators, in doing the organising that is so central to their task, need to get people involved in the advertising issue and pose the following questions:

(1)   Whose interests are *supposed* to be served by the regulation of alcoholic beverage advertising?
(2)   Whose interests are *actually* served by the regulation of alcoholic beverage advertising?
(3)   What are, and who bears, the social and financial costs of this arrangement?
(4)   What are, and who reaps, the benefits of this arrangement?
Currently there is no programmatic or policy model for taking action in this area. Some groups like Action for Children's Television, Action on Smoking and Health, and the Center for Science in the Public Interest have tackled various advertising issues. Yet health educators, to my knowledge, have not played a major role in confronting the anti-health dimension of advertising.

It is my assumption that once the public is educated about the contradictions in public policy there will be increasing pressure placed on corporate interests and government regulatory bodies to respond to public health and safety issues. Although many think it is worthless to work with the various industries, it is for the above reason that I think health educators need to focus attention on educating the industry. It is unlikely that producers will decide voluntarily to forsake the pursuit of profits in the interests of public health, but it may be that some flexibility is built into the system. Some marketing firms, for example, refuse to accept cigarette accounts (Robertson 1976). As a matter of economy of effort it seems that health educators cannot continue to focus on changing the behaviour only of victims but must focus also on changing the behaviour of those whose decisions contribute to increased hazards and unsafe situations. As Robertson explains: 'Some producers and suppliers of hazards are unaware of the consequences and will withdraw or change products when so informed. Even if the decisions are not changed as a result of the education, the decision-maker cannot plead ignorance and, in many cases, may be legally liable for knowingly contributing to or allowing hazardous conditions.'

Health educators should, however, start from the assumption that corporations are more interested in profits than in public health. Indeed, many cases have shown that regulators and corporate interests show a blatant disregard for public health and safety issues (eg O'Malley 1979; Drinkhall 1981; Savoy 1981). There should be no mistake about this, nor any surprise that it is so. Historically, public health has always existed in an economic environment that was hostile to health and safety issues. Despite this, health educators should not be reluctant to engage in debates that facilitate the uncovering of these basic value differences. On the contrary, they should encourage such debates with the expectation that underlying assumptions will be made more explicit and issues clarified. Also, health educators should not be reluctant to engage in the regulatory arena. Recently the Bureau of Alcohol, Tobacco and Firearms (the US government body that regulates advertising in this area) held hearings in San Francisco on proposed reforms in alcoholic beverage advertising regulations. Although the alcoholic beverage industry was well represented, there were no social scientists, and no health educators, save for myself and one colleague. It is little wonder that regulators discharge their responsibility in the interests of those being regulated rather than the general public, for it is the regulated that tutor the regulators.

In addressing the issue of health-related content of television programming, health educators should closely examine the model put forth by Warren Breed and James De Foe (1982) who have been successful in working with television writers and also the comic book industry. They have developed a technique called co-operative consultation. This procedure is based on the assumption, like Robertson's comments above, that industries will be willing to correct a problem when it is convincingly brought to their attention; in other words, some corporations are seen as simply ignorant of the high-risk quality of some of their products, television writers as not aware of the inaccurate alcohol education they are providing on a daily basis.

Breed and De Foe's experience in working with television writers bears out this 'ignorance' assumption They developed a four-part process of co-operative consultation that started with extensive research. They conducted detailed content analysis of drinking on television over a period of several years, researched television production methods so they would be able to frame thier findings and suggestions in an acceptable way, and became well-informed concerning issues related to alcohol problems and alcoholism. From research the process moved to general education of the industry (in this case all those involved in the many stages of television production). This included a series of presentations to the Standards and Practices Offices of two of the three networks, extensive personal contacts with writers, and the development of a newsletter on alcohol topics that was widely distributed to industry people. The next stage was specific education. This happened when an industry person requested further information, which often took the form of requests for help on specific problems related to scripts addressing alcohol issues. To meet these requests De Foe, a member of the Writers Guild, offered a series of alternatives that served the purpose of moving the script along but not at a cost of inaccurate alcohol information being used. The final part of the process was feedback from the industry (Breed & De Foe 1982).

In a sense, the apparent success of Breed and De Foe is in part due to the way that they have developed their project as a resource that serves the needs of the industry. In this case both the industry and the viewer benefit. The process of research, general and specific education, and feedback fits well with a health education view of the world, yet according to Breed (1982) no health educators were involved in their work nor has he come upon any literature in health education that addresses this topic. This may be a model that health educators could benefit from, and deserves a close look. In calling for education of the industry we should not be naive. There are, perhaps, only a few places where health educators and the people served by them could benefit from co-operation with the industry. We should not, however, lose sight of these areas no matter how few.

Lawrence Wallack

Because of the length of time between the writing of the different contributions to this debate and particularly because David Player had in the meantime moved from the Scottish Health Education Group to the Health Education Council, we asked Sam Docherty of SHEG to provide us with a brief postscript, updating SHEG's position on these important issues.

I read the comments of Goodstadt and Wallack with interest, but with a growing sense of exasperation. I felt that the limit of the questions and the time lapse between responses probably did disguise the fact that all the contributors were in basic agreement about the direction in which alcohol education should be going.

The general consensus seemed to be that:—

— alcohol education should be seen as only one component of a more comprehensive policy encompassing legal and fiscal measures;

— focussing on alcoholism was too narrow a perspective. There should be a move towards looking at the use of alcohol in society and its links with other factors of lifestyle;

— health educators should not lay the blame for abuse solely at the feet of the individual, but should tackle social and community influences as well;

— less reliance should be placed on mass media advertising and more research carried out on effective methods of reaching the target audience.

In a way these points are not in dispute. Certainly if you look closely at the work of SHEG you will see these policies emerging in the current programmes.

What I felt was missing from the debate was some political realism. We can spend all day every day devising perfect strategies to solve the nation's problems, but sometime we have to come down to earth and face reality. Health educators are constrained by and answerable to the people who hold the purse strings. They are not absolutely free to tackle the job in the way they think best. Alcoholism is a very obvious and socially unacceptable consequence of alcohol use. In purely public relations terms it is useful for politicians and the alcohol industry alike to be seen trying to do something about the situation. It is therefore relatively easy to gain approval and resources for 'pulling people out of the river' even if only as a token gesture. However it is a very different story when health educators want to deal with the more fundamental and less immediate causes of alcohol abuse. Then any progress with policy-makers seems painfully slow and can be opposed by powerful anti-health lobbies. Even when projects do get off the ground they may be so underfinanced that they are almost bound to fail from the outset.

If we at least acknowledge that these constraints exist then we can explore ways of coping with the political arena we find ourselves in. Perhaps we have spent enough time working out *what* should be happening. Now is the time to sit down and work out *how* to make it happen.

Sam Docherty

Clearly, running through all the contributions to this debate is the question of whether health education is, in any real sense, expected to take on the beverage alcohol trade in some kind of open conflict. It is interesting to note that alcohol producers and health educators alike are calling for educational programmes which encourage moderation. There remain doubts as to whether both parties mean the same thing by that term and what price they may be prepared to pay to achieve it. Nevertheless, the most serious question posed by this debate is whether more is likely to be achieved through consultation or through confront- ation. In their different ways, all the contributors to this debate are asking for some kind of redefinition of the problem. The question which that raises is, of course, in whose terms it will be redefined.

11 THE MEDIA DEBATE

Introduction

Although the relationship between any behaviour and the portrayal of that behaviour on film and television is complex, there is a growing recognition that popular entertainment media do exercise a powerful influence over the value systems which society uses to judge the behaviour in question. Whether that influence is exercised through a reflective or causative process remains open to examination from a number of points of view. Nevertheless, where a pattern of behaviour, such as drinking, is both widespread in the community and is frequently portrayed on television, and where that behaviour can, in certain circumstances, lead to social and health damage which could be avoided, the opportunities abound for a vigorous debate about the potentially harmful effects of unfettered media exploitation of an area of human weakness.

Media portrayals of drinking and, sometimes, of alcohol problems can produce a cumulative value system which resonates with popular views of drinking in the culture which receives the media portrayals. Meanwhile, health education is attempting to influence attitudes and drinking behaviour with a view to minimising the scale and severity of alcohol problems. An understanding of the media processes, both from a historical and from a psycho-social point of view, could enable preventive planning to proceed from firmer ground regarding the expectations of its target audience.

Portrayals of drinking, of drunkenness, of alcoholism and of the boundaries between these three phenomena are all susceptible to investigation. An understanding of how these boundaries are defined in media terms will go a long way towards providing the ground rules for specific health strategies within different communities. In order to focus our debate upon the question of the influence of the media, we wrote first to Peggy Gray of the Centre for Mass Communications Research at the University of Leicester, UK, to ask her what she saw as the major issues which required clarification.

Searching for Dominant Images

Recent years have witnessed a growing concern about the medical and social consequences of excessive drinking and of alcohol related problems. In Britain, this concern has been accompanied by the development of various pressure groups and lobbies seeking to regulate alcohol consumption by socio-economic means and by the control of advertising.

The debate usually seems to be based upon the assumption, supported by the Royal College of Psychiatrists, that the level of problem drinking in society is directly related to the level of total consumption and, therefore, the aim of all policy makers should be to reduce total consumption, thereby inevitably bringing about a reduction in the incidence of alcohol related problems in society. The real danger, as I see it, is that controls may be imposed, regulations and policies formulated and legislation enacted without adequate knowledge of the real nature of alcohol related problems or the complex interaction of the many factors which may contribute to the development of such problems.

Differences in styles and patterns of drinking behaviour exist among different groups of people and in different localities. If policies are to be soundly based it is important to recognise these differences and to understand the ways in which they have been developed, maintained, reinforced or changed from time to time. In the past, few questions have been asked about the factors that impinge upon these processes. It is only now when a crisis appears to exist and policy makers are seeking to bring about a reduction in total consumption that attention has been drawn to the need to identify possible sources of influence. The mass media have been recognised as one such source.

There are two overt ways in which the mass media are employed with the direct intention of influencing the use of alcohol. On the one hand, the drinks industry employs the mass media through commerical advertising to promote the sale of alcoholic beverages; while on the other hand health education media campaigns are designed to make people aware of the potentially harmful effects of the consumption of alcohol, the dangers of excessive and inappropriate drinking, the early recognition of symptoms of alcohol related problems and the services available when such problems are suspected or detected.

Much of the debate about the role of the mass media only takes into account these deliberate attempts to stimulate a particular course of action, impart knowledge or influence attitudes. Very often the discussion is centred on the direct power of advertising or shock and emotional reactions to documentary programmes about the dire consequences to health, family and lifestyle of those suffering from the results of alcohol abuse. Such discussions often assume a 'hypodermic needle' effect whereby the media message is thought to have an immediate and direct affect on the knowledge, attitudes and even behaviour of 'the audience'. In fact, as we know, communication research has shown that the influence of the mass media is much more subtle.

Different groups in society use the media in vastly different ways. There is not one audience, but many audiences. People select from what the media offer according to their own predispositions based upon their social and cultural background and experience. We know that even when people see the same programme or read the same newspaper they will selectively recall and interpret the messages and images and construct meanings according to their own prejudices and to satisfy their own needs. Their existing beliefs are likely to be reinforced rather than modified or challenged. Since this is the case, it seems to me that claims about the effects on drinking behaviour of both advertising and health education may be exaggerated.

On the other hand, whatever the intentions of the drinks industry, I think it would be naive not to recognise the potential of alcohol advertising to encourage drinking generally and, therefore, to increase overall consumption, introduce young people to drinking and in some cases foster harmful styles and patterns of consumption. Equally, in relation to the use of media for health education, a recent study of the Alcohol Education Campaign in the North East of England undertaken by myself and colleagues at the Leicester Centre for Mass Communication Research, has shown that over a period of eight years many lessons have been learned. Among these lessons is that to be successful it is necessary to make media presentations speak directly to the styles of drinking of the locality and to be presented in such a way as to enable the audience to identify with the message or at least to recognise others who fit into the pattern.

So far I have only written about the two aspects of media alcohol presentation which form the basis of most discussions. However, my real concern is to suggest that the way in which alcohol and alcohol related issues are portrayed in prime time television is the issue which is of most vital importance.

Since learning through the media is a 'process which is often incidental unplanned and unconscious for the receiver, and almost always unintentional on the part of the sender' (McQuail 1977) the patterns, values and perspectives most consistently presented in entertainment programmes are likely to play a large part in the process of social learning. The audience may accept the version of social reality offered by the media and may be led to adapt its own attitudes and behaviour accordingly. Communication research indicates that the media influence people's ideas and beliefs about lifestyles and norms both directly and indirectly. The portrayal of alcohol consumption and related lifestyles in entertainment programmes may well contribute to the overall 'climate of opinion' and so influence the way in which drinking patterns develop and advertising and health education messages are received.

What, then, are the dominant images presented in prime time television? Many people suggest that regular drinking is presented as the norm and is seen as an integral part of and contributory factor to success in all walks of life, and as a symbol of achievement. There has been little systematic or significant research in Britain to provide baseline information on this matter, or to indicate how important a part is played by mass media in alcohol socialisation.

Many people comment on the frequency with which alcohol is used in television programmes and the infrequency with which any ill effects or socially unacceptable consequences are shown or even mentioned. There are numerous instances in which beautiful successful people are seen drinking either as a routine relaxation, a relief of stress, to celebrate a happy or successful event, promotion or improvement in status, to escape from problems or to facilitate business discussions or romance. Where drunkenness is shown it seems to me that it most usually receives humorous treatment so that excessive drinking is seen as a matter for laughter rather than as a serious problem. As far as I can see, little is shown which is likely to discourage the use of alcohol or warn of the possible long term ill effects or dangers of excessive drinking or the development of styles and patterns of drinking which may lead to dependency or ill health. Of course there are some instances in which negative short or long term effects are portrayed, but these are relatively few and the surrounding attitudes and ideas need to be studied.

Indeed, a great deal of research is needed to provide baseline information on the way in which the use of alcohol and related issues is portrayed in prime time television. Systematic studies of content will supply a great deal of valuable information. Then it will be necessary to study the 'images in the minds' of various sections of the audience in different localities where there are known to be differing styles and patterns of drinking behaviour, in order to compare images portrayed in television with those held in the community.

I know that some work on content analysis has been undertaken in the USA and that it has been suggested that the 'world of prime time network programming is a world saturated with alcohol' (Lowry 1981). I feel that it is important to examine the situation in Britain in order that policy makers here may be well informed about the possible influence of the media on the development of patterns of alcohol use and related issues.

The crucial questions seem to me to be: are the styles and patterns of drinking behaviour and the social facilitation functions and attitudes towards alcohol use most usually presented on television, accepted as the norm by the audience or sections of it? How far are existing stereotypes of the drinker sustained or challenged by media portrayals? We can all speculate about these issues, but they can only be usefully handled by those in positions of authority if we researchers can offer well researched data on which to develop policies.

Some people believe it is right to implement legal controls on alcohol advertisements, sales operations, etc., without waiting for more information about the development and operation of social controls in this field. I believe the role of the media may be so crucial to the reception and effectiveness of other influences on alcohol use and abuse and therefore the 'climate of opinion' within which all other influences operate, that study of this area should take high priority.

Peggy Gray

The concern which Peggy Gray raises regarding the need for more research on how alcohol is portrayed in prime time television is echoed from the other side of the Atlantic. Commenting on the issues she raised, Denise Herd of the Alcohol Research Group, Medical Research Institute, Berkeley, California, concentrates upon the interaction of various societal forces that play key roles in shaping media images of drinking and drunkenness.

Images of Drinking: Distortion or Re-creation?

Media studies on the content of drinking portrayals were initiated in the United States as early as the 1930s. They were initiated in response to what government officials and social scientists perceived as the deleterious effects of motion pictures on young people. This research employed a rudimentary form of content analysis which helped establish the overall level or 'prevalence' of drinking in films, its distribution among character types, and behavioural consequences. Unfortunately, contemporary studies of the mass media and drinking behaviour have made few substantive advances relative to this earlier research. Studies from both eras concluded that alcohol consumption is far heavier and more favourably regarded on movie and television screens than among ordinary citizens in everyday life. The studies provoked concern by policy-makers about decency and morals in the earlier period, and adverse health consequences in recent years. As a result, various forms of censorship and intervention have been proposed with, at best, only modest success.

Because of the strict focus on the objective 'content' and presumed *effects* of the media, researchers have ignored some of the pressing theoretical dimensions of this problem. They have failed to provide critical insight into *why* the drinking behaviour in the world of the movies and prime time television is so radically different from the social reality. Social scientists have not looked at what factors in the society itself or what factors pertaining to the media help create and sustain such skewed presentations of drinking values and behaviour. They have seldom addressed how the general values and perceived functions of the media — such as the premium on entertainment and 'escape' — affect the presentation of drinking. Similarly, there is little known about media technology and its effect on drinking portrayals. Finally, there has been virtually no analysis of how the vast array of social forces, such as the alcohol treatment system; beer, wine, and spirits industries; cultural attitudes toward alcohol; and legal statutes regarding alcohol consumption affect depictions of alcohol behaviour in the mass media. Theoretical grounding in these and related issues seems of pre-eminent importance for any real understanding of the media's role in creating or reinforcing social attitudes about alcohol use.

My comments will share some of the ideas that are emerging as we begin to explore the complex relationship between drinking, society, and the mass media. Through a recent public film series and related research we have been looking at the portrayal of drinking in American films since the turn of the century. Our underlying assumption suggests that changing images of drinking reflect the dynamic interplay between changes in the social context and changes in the film institution. In one sense, we regard films as barometers of social values regarding drinking.

On the other hand we recognise that films and their portraits of
drinking are symbolic representations that are created by a highly cen-
tralised, and technologically complex film industry.

We have identified several areas of research which seem critical for
understanding how filmed portrayals of drinking are created, how they
relate to the social context, and how they function in the media. In
taking this approach, we are trying to analyse the interaction of various
societal forces that appear to play a key role in shaping movie images of
drinking and drunkenness and are less concerned with drawing conclusions about the direct 'effects' of the movies on the social climate of
drinking.

First of all we recognise that films draw in part upon common sense
reality and everyday experience in creating an aura of realism and
believability. At this level, they are likely to incorporate popular conceptions about drinking and drunkenness. The body of these conceptions which collectively denotes a *folklore of drinking practices*
includes ideas about the powers of alcohol as a mind and mood altering
substance, styles of drunken comportment, and the various rituals (eg
seduction, solidarity, sacredness) that are associated with drinking.

Secondly, the *alcohol control structure and alcohol treatment
system* may directly or indirectly affect portrayals of drinking. In
America, the enactment and repeal of the national prohibition amend-
ment, the rise of Alcoholics Anonymous and the development of a
major alcoholism treatment bureaucracy appeared to have far-reaching
implications for the movies. For example, the political pressure wielded
by temperance groups led to strict limitations on the use of liquor in
films of the 1920s. During the same period, prohibition served as a
backdrop for many films which used bootlegging, liquor smuggling, and
illegal nightclubs as major plot devices. Alcoholics Anonymous has
become directly involved in later films depicting alcoholism. They
have served as consultants on scripts involving alcoholism; and AA
groups are often dramatised as a standard part of many films about
alcoholics.

Thirdly, the *ideology of alcohol problems* may affect the models
of drinking behaviour portrayed in film. The recent shift in ideas on
alcoholism from a moral and socially defined problem to a problem of
individualised predispositions — both biological and psychological —
may account in part for the emphasis on Freudian and psychoanalytic
themes in contemporary movie characterisations of alcoholism and
alcoholics.

Fourthly, *issues of social domination and conflict* can influence how drinking is portrayed. During the early decades, American films were noted for their strong anti-alcohol messages. These temperance messages reflected the values of native-born Protestants who often saw themselves in conflict with foreigners from different ethnic and religious backgrounds. In later years, the development of a 'mass culture' blurred ethnic distinctions and mitigated gaping class cleavages. Films of this period reflected these changing social mores – various class and ethnic groups socialised, drank and got drunk together in nightclub and speakeasy settings.

Along with major shifts in the social context of drinking practices and the handling of alcohol problems, depictions of drinking reflect important changes in the film institution and its relationship to society. For example, the *social role and functions* attributed to the movies in American society has undergone major changes at various time periods. At the turn of the century, 'respectable' Protestant groups viewed movie theatres as a nexus of vice and immorality in lower-class immigrants. Several years later these same groups reversed their position and hailed motion pictures as the most attractive 'substitute' ever devised for the saloon. Movies, they argued, strengthened the family, enhanced education, and safely channeled dangerous 'passions'. With the expansion of the movies to the middle classes, films became much 'drier', promoting temperance and anti-saloon melodramas. In contemporary times, American film audiences are growing smaller and more specialised so that the movies are less subject to general public concern and scrutiny. The result is a more liberal attitude towards 'moral' issues such as sexuality, drug and alcohol use.

The history of public regulation and censorship does seem to parallel the changing social function and class composition of movie audiences. During certain periods, these codes apparently had a major impact on how liquor was portrayed in films. The tight anti-liquor policies of the New York Censorship Board in the early part of the century and the 1925 Hays Code resulted in films where drinking was rarely shown – when necessary to the plot, liquor was consumed off-screen, with the back to the movie audience or merely implied. The 1934 Breen Code sponsored by the Catholic Legion of Decency had a similar effect – it seemed effectively to tone down the wave of heavy drinking, crime, and sex films that emerged during the Depression. By the 1940s, the Code was rarely applied to drinking situations in the movies, with casual alcohol use accepted as common and even desirable. The Code was abandoned in the 1950s and recent years have witnessed the rise of a major soft-pornographic film industry accompanied by a wave of

sexually explicit films featuring heavy drug and alcohol use.
The *ideology of the film institution* exerts a similar influence on
how alcohol issues are portrayed. During the political struggles for
prohibition, the movies were viewed as vehicles for preaching
middle-class morality and promoting mild social reforms. This was
the heyday of films which encouraged total abstinence and viewed
alcohol as the 'Bottled Demon.' By the mid 1920s, the film industry
had switched from its emphasis on social and political reform to a pre-
occupation with romance, crime, and luxury. Films of this period were
considerably 'wetter' with heroes and heroines shown in approved
drinking situations several times more frequently than the villains and
villainesses. As American films have become solidly grounded as a pure
entertainment medium, alcohol is most often associated with glamour
and pleasure, with little or no emphasis given to the negative consequences of overdrinking.

Economic factors appear to play a paramount role in shaping film
content. Film producers are under constant pressure to maintain large
film viewing audiences to ensure adequate profits. In times of declining
popularity, filmmakers have resorted to sensationalist themes — sex,
violence, and heavy drug and alcohol use — to recapture public interest.
Film content is also subject to pressure from outside financial interests.
In the United States, 'product sampling', whereby corporations provide
film studios with free products to use as props is becoming a common
practice. Through the route of 'product sampling', named brand alcohol
products frequently make their way into motion pictures.

> In *Making Love*, a bottle of Johnny Walker Scotch was used to
> represent an expensive, high-quality gift. And in the scenes filmed on
> location in a West Hollywood bar, the filmmakers left hundreds of
> cases of Miller Lite beer stacked against the walls where the bar
> always keeps them.
>
> (*Wall Street Journal*, 24.5.82, p. 1)

In 'product sampling', film audiences are not only continually
exposed to scenes showing named brand alcoholic drinks, but brewery
and spirits companies are careful to make sure their products are
presented in the best possible manner:

> The nation's largest brewer has become AFP's (Associated Film
> Promotions) most lucrative client. 'By having Hollywood contacts,'
> says Mr. Brandon, 'we're usually successful in making sure our

products aren't used in disparaging ways such as in bar-room brawls, teenage drinking or drinking-and-driving scenes.' After AFP reviews a script that might involve an Anheuser-Busch beer, the script is examined by legal, marketing and public relations officials. 'Sometimes we mark areas of concern,' Mr. Brandon adds, 'and often producers will accept our suggestions to change things slightly.' In return, Anheuser-Busch will supply historically accurate advertising material and bottles — and perhaps 50 cases of beer for a thirsty cast and crew.

(*Wall Street Journal*, 24.5.82, p. 1)

Along with political and social factors, the film institution draws upon a *set of literary, dramatic and photographic codes* which seem to influence greatly the presentation of drinking. Themes from the nineteenth century theatre and contemporary novels permeate many films portraying heavy drinking and alcoholic characters. For example, the modern alcoholism film has its roots in the nineteenth century temperance play and primitive morality film. From these earlier forms, modern films have inherited a stock set of themes and conventions to portray the alcoholic — a convincing case of the delirium tremens, stereotyped forms of dress and demeanor, and strong overtones of romantic tragedy.

Twentieth century novelists made a similar impact on drinking characterisations in American films. The group of 'Lost Generation' writers, including, Hemingway and F. Scott Fitzgerald, who in the 1920s drank and wrote their way through Paris, eventually went on to Hollywood. On the one hand they contributed to the cosmopolitan wetness that pervaded films such as *The Sun Also Rises*; on the other hand, they helped to shape the new alcoholism film genre as a result of their drinking problems. For example, *The Lost Weekend* (1945) was based on Charles Jackson's autobiographical novel which depicted the writer's own struggle with alcoholism. Another novelist, Dorothy Parker worked on *Smash Up* (1947) also with the hope of overcoming her own drinking problems.

From their literary and dramatic roots, depictions of alcohol have acquired symbolic and metaphorical usages which are further expanded in the film medium. Liquor is associated with psychological and behavioural states ranging from anger to passivity and depression, euphoria, and sensuality. Film makers often exploit these qualities to heighten dramatic and emotional effects in movies. As an example, the film critic Thomas Elsaesser highlights the rich symbolism associated with alcoholism in contemporary family melodramas:

> *Written on the Wind* is perhaps the movie that most consistently builds on the metaphoric possibilities of alcohol (liquidity, potency, the phallic shape of the bottles) . . . It . . . has Robert Stack compensate for his sexual impotence and childhood guilt feelings by hugging a bottle of raw corn every time he feels suicidal, which he proceeds to smash in disgust against the paternal mansion. In the same movie, Stack is making an unmistakable gesture with an empty Martini bottle in the direction of his wife, and an unconsummated relationship is visually underscored when two brimful glasses remain untouched on the table, as Dorothy Malone does her best to seduce an unresponsive Rock Hudson at the family party, having previously poured her whiskey into the flower vase of her rival, Lauren Bacall.
> (from *Tales of Sound and Fury: Observations on the Family Melodrama*)

Written on the Wind is a single example among many Hollywood films where drinking and alcohol problems are used to symbolize moral and emotional relationships. Although these characterisations add texture and colour to movies, they often distort the portrayal of drinking practices and problems. In *Images of Alcoholism*, Bruce Ritson vividly recounts the twisted portrayals of clinical alcoholism: 'My own memory of treatment episodes in alcoholism films becomes a blur of needles, burly attendants, locked doors and terrifying screams. Delirium tremens is thought to occur in approximately 5 per cent of alcoholics – the films show delirium and hallucinations as part of most alcoholics' experiences. The reason for this distortion presumably is the dramatic appeal of the symptoms and their horrifying quality.' The association of alcohol problems with prostitution, nymphomania, and homosexuality in films of the 1960s illustrates another aspect of the same exploitative trend.

The distortion of drinking behaviour and alcohol problems often takes a more subtle form. The implicit structure of many popular films restricts how alcohol problems can be portrayed. For example, most American films depict a very slanted world view – one that revolves around romantic love and materialistic pursuits among wealthier social groups. Within these films alcohol is usually portrayed as a symbol of glamour and pleasure. On the infrequent occasions that problem drinking is shown, it is generally interpreted in highly personal and psychological terms. Few films explore the social issues associated with alcohol problems or deal with problems relevant to the working class.

In sum, structural issues of this type seem to exert a great influence on how alcohol behaviour is created and maintained in films. Our initial research suggests that drinking portrayals arise from a number of factors in the socio-cultural context — drinking practices and social sentiments, the alcohol control structure and alcohol treatment system, sociological aspects of the film institution, as well as literary and dramatic conventions. Images of drinking thus appear to be interwoven with and deeply embedded in the socio-cultural fabric. The way alcohol is used in films seems to be a reflection of the society itself; not only how it drinks and how it feels about alcohol, but what it sees as the social function of movies, its political and economic structure, and its ideology. If we are critical of the way drinking is managed in film and other forms of visual media, then it seems imperative that we also look critically at the social institutions that sustain these portrayals.

This approach entails a degree of theoretical rigour which is notably absent in many conventional studies of media content and which may argue against their generally short-range intervention goals. We may have to examine whether the structural features of the media, the power of special interest groups, and the weight of the socio-cultural trends go against any true reform of the way alcohol is portrayed in the media. Real change may be possible only with a truly radical shift in the social function and values underlying the media. Short of this we will have to be aware of the limitations of traditional health education programmes and recognise the challenge of addressing the larger economic, socio-political, and cultural forces that imprison us in distorted images of drinking and alcohol problems.

Denise Herd

12 THE ADVERTISING DEBATE

There is a vigorous debate about the extent to which alcohol advertising should be controlled. Some advocate a total ban while others would argue any measure of that kind was unjustified. Advertisements for alcoholic drinks are subject to the general provisions of the British Code of Advertising Practice in precisely the same way as advertisements for any other task or product. This Code is reviewed approximately every five years. Drink advertising also has to conform to a series of special rules which are drawn up by representatives of the drinks business and under the aegis of the Incorporated Society of British Advertising. These are:—

1. Young People

Advertisements should not be directed at young people or in any way encourage them to start drinking. Anyone shown drinking must appear to be over 21. Children should not be depicted in advertisements except where it would be usual for them to appear (eg in a family scene or in background crowds) but they should never be shown drinking alcoholic beverages nor should it be implied that they are.

2. Challenge

Advertisements should not be based on a dare nor impute any failing to those who do not accept the challenge of a particular drink.

3. Health

Advertisements should not emphasise the stimulant, sedative or tranquillising effects of any drink or imply that it can improve physical performance. However, references to the refreshing attributes of drink are permissable.

4. Strength

Advertisements should not give the general impression of being inducements to prefer a drink because of its higher alcohol content or intoxicating effect. Factual information for the guidance of drinkers about such alcoholic strength may, however, be included.

5. Social Success

Advertisements may emphasise the pleasures of companionship and social communication associated with the consumption of alcoholic drinks, but it should never be implied that drinking is necessary to social or business success or distinction, nor that those who do not drink are less likely to be acceptable or successful than those who do. Advertisements should neither claim nor suggest that any drink can contribute towards sexual success or make the drinker more attractive to the opposite sex.

6. Drinking and Machinery

Advertisements should not associate drink with driving or dangerous machinery. Specific warnings of the dangers of drinking in these circumstances may, however, be used.

7. Excessive Drinking

Advertisements should not encourage or appear to condone over-indulgence. Repeated buying of large rounds should not be implied.
(*British Code of Advertising Practice*, April 1979)

> *The code is concerned with advertisements and not with labels and packages, price tickets and the like, though it does cover trade as well as consumer advertising.*
>
> *There is also a separate sales promotion code which contains restrictions essentially on the technique rather than the content of such promotions. Responding to criticisms of the code on the grounds that it is self-regulatory, the Director General of the Advertising Standards Authority (Peter Thomson) noted:*

Our system cannot in practice or theory compete with systems of control which are legally based, *but* the proof of the pudding was in the eating. It is true that sanctions (notably withdrawal of advertising space or time by media) can only be effective where those in the advertising business, and especially media are prepared in the short term to forego some part of their freedom of action (in their own long term interest and that of the advertising business in general). There are, of course, around the fringe of the business, those who are not prepared to make this commitment, with the result we can find ourselves in a weak position to compel compliance with the Code. However, the quantity of advertising which is thus out of reach of any sanctions except public criticism and exposure is in fact small. We would argue that over the great mass of advertisements, where a pre-publication approval system would simply be unworkable, the evidence shows that the voluntary support which is necessary to make self-regulation work is in fact forth- coming. This has the result that the theoretical imperfections of the system are less important than its practical strength particularly given the complementary fact that the mere passage of legislation does not ensure its effective enforcement.

The Scotch Whisky Association Alcohol Research and Education Committee stated that it regarded the Code as 'strict but reasonable', further adding that:

The objectives of advertising are to influence consumers to buy a particular product or brand of product and thus to maintain a share or secure a larger share of an existing market. To the best of our know-ledge there is no scientific evidence that advertising of alcoholic beverages has ever led to an increase in total alcohol consumption. Indeed, in countries where there are embargoes or restrictions on such advertising, for example, Poland, France and Canada, not only is there a high *per capita* consumption of alcohol but a high incidence of alcohol related problems.

Clearly, the relationship between aggregate levels of advertising and aggregate levels of consumption form an important strand in this debate. Although many of the issues involved are of a rather technical nature, the principles which lie behind it are discussed by both the other con-tributors to this chapter.

We were, however, particularly interested in the question of the 'youth market', with its huge spending power, its pressing need to be fashion-able and its as yet unpledged brand loyalties. We therefore spoke to a number of advertising men about this question. What emerged was the clear sense that this youth market is indeed a prime target group for many product categories (such as cosmetics, clothing, electronic equipment) and that alcoholic drinks were certainly no exception.

Since many drinkers remain loyal throughout their lives to the brands which they begin drinking when young, it is, from an advertising point of view, important to do everything possible to ensure that, when they do start drinking, it is your brand rather than your rival's that they choose. Those fighting to gain larger market shares in the adult market have to contend with what are often virtually irreversible brand loyalties. In the case of young people, however, their only loyalty may be a negative one, in the sense that they might not wish to identify with their parents' favourite beverage.

At the same time, they are desperately seeking the approval of their peers (male and female) and are highly sensitive to the ebb and flow of fashion. They are therefore also highly desirable as consumers (even if rather dangerous because so volatile). That is why the argument that each brand is genuinely only fighting for a bigger slice of the total cake is at best ingenuous and certainly highly questionable. Make your cake look attractive enough and those who are just reaching cake-eating age are certainly likely to want to join the table to have a taste of it.

It is indeed curious that this proposition – so obvious and, indeed, not necessarily so reprehensible – should be considered so controversial. Nor is this the only issue on which feelings run high. We asked M.J. Waterson of the Advertising Association to support the proposition that there is no justification for imposing future controls on alcohol advertising.

As you are no doubt aware many of the experts most closely involved with the problem of alcohol abuse do not believe that advertising has anything to do with the problems arising from excessive drinking in the UK. However, there is clearly a small body of serious opinion which does believe that advertising is a contributory cause of alcohol abuse. This criticism must be considered.

The main theme of critics of alcohol advertising is quite simply that advertising increases total drink consumption and any *per capita* increase in drink consumption increases the number of problem drinkers. Thus drink advertising partly 'causes' problem drinking.

The first point that must be made very clear is that advertising is not the all-powerful persuasive activity that it is sometimes claimed to be. Advertising may possibly over certain periods of time persuade drinkers to drink more or petrol buyers to buy more petrol (ie change consumer purchasing patterns from already existing ones), but the limited amount of national income available obviously means advertising cannot continually persuade everyone to buy more of everything.

Given that no drink advertisements nowadays attempt to sell 'drinking' as opposed to one particular brand of drink, that drink advertising is more tightly regulated than is the case for most other products, that spirit advertising cannot appear on the most powerful medium – television – at all, and that alcoholic drink advertising levels are relatively small (in advertising per unit of sale terms) compared with many other product groups, it would in fact be rather surprising if drink advertisements could increase total sales of drink at the expense of other product groups. There is a great deal of competition for the consumer's pound. To suggest that advertising *must* have the effect of increasing total drink sales is obviously nonsense.

This basic fact – that drink advertising may or may not influence the amount of drink sold, but is unlikely to have more than very minor impact – is sometimes viewed with incredulity by critics of advertising. Why then do they bother to advertise? is a common question. Such statements can only come from people who have never experienced at first hand the intense competition by manufacturers for market share that exists in most consumer markets. Some companies win, and others necessarily lose the battle, but it is the competitive process of striving for market share that is at the heart of our economic system. As someone said many years ago, 'the Russians have fantastic athletes because they compete, and awful cars and fashions because they don't'.

A slightly more sophisticated version of the critics' claim that advertising increases total drink consumption, centres on the belief that whilst advertising may not stimulate total drink consumption in a general sense, it does contribute to the overall level of drink consumption by recruiting into the ranks of existing drinkers people who would not otherwise have become drinkers. The two segments of the population usually singled out in this context are young people and women.

It is of course impossible to prove that advertising never recruits drinkers who would otherwise never have become drinkers. However, it is possible to show that the argument is essentially little different from the basic proposition that advertising increases drink consumption in total. Firstly, it is clear that both young people and women are just as subject to competing attempts to persuade them to buy a huge variety of products as are adult men. Every young person and woman knows about the existence and desirability of cars, stereos, clothes, foreign holidays, cosmetics and so on. To suggest that drink advertisers are uniquely competent at marketing their wares in the context of these two particular groups is just as silly as it is in the general context. A significant proportion of advertising is directed at young people simply because they have for many years formed a very large segment of the total drink market. Most people tend to drink more between the ages of 18 and 25 than they do subsequently. They go out more to places where they can meet people –pubs, dance halls or discos, clubs, etc., – they have fewer responsibilities, particularly of a financial nature and therefore more disposable income than a comparable 30 year old with a mortgage and family and so on.

The *increase* over the past twenty years in alcohol consumption among young adults has moved roughly in step with the increase in consumption of many other products, and reflects more than any other single factor the general increase in income levels. To suggest that this increase in wealth might have been saved or spent in more 'desirable' ways than in expenditure on drink, had drink advertising not existed, is naive in the extreme, as is so graphically illustrated by the massive growth of the (non-advertised) multi-million pound (although illegal) soft drug industry over the post war period.

Perhaps the clearest illustration of the negligible role drink advertising plays in forming attitudes to drink has been shown recently by the growth of the wine bar. Virtually non existent ten years ago, almost all towns in Southern England now have at least one. Is this phenomenon a reflection of the powers of advertising? Clearly not, since neither wine nor wine bars are heavily advertised – certainly not the latter which are hardly advertised at all. The rapid spread of the wine bar owes everything to those entrepreneurs who realised many people – particularly women – would prefer a rather different style of meeting place to the traditional pub. The rise in wine bar going, and at the same time, drink consumption, among women does not reflect their advertising induced craving for drink; it reflects the rapid change in the role of women in society in recent years. Those who believe that women should somehow not be allowed to drink alcohol, or should be denied the pleasures of the wine bar, should not attempt to confuse the issue with misleading statements about advertising pressures. As Paul Johnson wrote in The Spectator recently, 'Women are paying a heavy price for 'liberation': more and more of them are committing felonies, going to jail, dying of lung cancer and cirrhosis, having illegitimate babies, getting raped and getting divorced. The part that advertising plays in this revolution is pretty small.' Curiously, women's organisations of all descriptions have implicitly backed up the last part of this statement. They now form a major segment of critics of advertising.

Their complaint? That advertisements portray only an out-of-date stereotype woman – the good little housewife!

So much for the arguments. Arguments themselves, however presented, are obviously open to doubt. Fortunately on the question of the impact of advertising there is a considerable body of evidence which backs up the general lines of argument I have advanced.

For example: Smart and Cutler (1976) in a review of the data deriving from the total ban on alcohol advertising in British Columbia concluded: 'the data presented led little support for the view that the British Columbian advertising ban reduced alcohol consumption. Both the yearly and monthly analysis of beer, wine or liquor show no substantial effect of the ban.'

Ogbourne and Smart (1980) considered the effects of restrictions on alcohol advertising in Manitoba, Canada, and in the USA using statistical data on alcohol consumption. They concluded: 'it is considered unlikely that restrictions on advertising will reduce consumption'.

Another illustration of the ineffectiveness of banning advertising comes from France, where the advertising of whisky has been prohibited since 1957. In that year imports of Scotch whisky were 157,000 proof gallons. In 1979 they totalled 6,294,000 proof gallons. Whatever it was that caused the increase it certainly wasn't advertising.

Further evidence comes from Eastern Europe – where *per capita* alcohol consumption has risen over the past 30 years at the same rate as in Western Europe – without, of course, the benefit of advertising. In Russia particularly, alcohol abuse is considered a very big problem. A recent report by the Times Moscow correspondent stated bluntly: 'In spite of an unrelenting campaign against alcohol, stricter laws on the sale of drink, daily temperence propaganda in the press, at school and on the factory floor, the Russians appear powerless against the waves of vodka and wine now washing over the country.'

A variety of econometric studies show that advertising appears to have little impact on national expenditure, or on large sectors of consumers' expenditure in a variety of different markets. One of the most extensive surveys was done by Lambin (1976), covering 108 brands and 16 classes of products in 25 markets. The author concluded that advertising seldom increases the primary demand for a class of products. A number of other major studies, for example, by Ashley, Gramper and Schmalensee (1980), Grabowski (1976), Sturgess (1982) and Kyle (1982) have arrived at similar conclusions. Some studies have found that advertising did effect sales of some commodities but these tended to be intensive commodities such as toiletries and detergents.

No significant study has found a close relationship between alcoholic drink advertising and alcoholic drink sales in the UK. For example, a study by McGuiness (1983) covering the years 1950-75 found no link between total drink advertising and total drink sales or between the advertising of the main types of drink and sales of drink type. McGuinness concluded that changes in the level of real advertising of alcohol do not have much of an effect on alcohol consumption.

Other econometric studies in the UK confirm these results. For example, Waterson and Hagan (1980), in a detailed review of 20 years data covering 1959-78 concluded: 'The results from the analysis strongly suggest that advertising has no measureable effect on total (alcohol) consumption, and therefore that it has not been a factor in the alcohol market growth of the past two decades.'

Duffy (1982) in another detailed econometric exercise covering the factors affecting demand for beer, spirits and wine in the UK found that 'there is nothing in either the results of our statistical research or in those of other investigations in this area which could cause any one to predict with even a modest degree of confidence that a reduction in drink advertising would produce anything more than the most marginal reduction in *per capita* consumption of drink in this country.'

Schweitzer, Intriligator and Salehi (1983) in an econometric model covering American data found that 'a prohibition of advertising would lead not to a general reduction in alcoholic beverage consumption, but rather to a shift from beer consumption to spirits consumption'.

Another type of evidence derives from regional variations in the UK in drinking patterns. The General Household Survey (OPCS 1978) and the latest DHSS/OPCS (Wilson 1980) study to name but two indicate that the incidence of both drinking and 'heavy' drinking varies between regions. Advertising intensity and spending do not show similar variations.

It is also true that research studies have not found a link between young people's drinking habits and advertising. For example, Hawker (1978) found that 'there is not a great deal of evidence that advertising alcoholic drink starts anyone drinking'. On the other hand, several studies, for example, by O'Connor (1978), have shown the great importance of parental and peer group behaviour in forming young people's attitudes towards alcoholic drink.

Strickland (1983), using a rather sophisticated methodology, found 'advertising was shown to have meagre effects on the level of consumption, and these effects rarely translated into effects on alcohol problem . . . In contrast to the advertising effects, a set of interpersonal influences, especially differential peer association, was shown to have significant impact on both consumption levels and alcoholic abuse behaviour . . . virtually no impact on the prevalence or severity of alcohol problems among teenagers . . . suggests that advertising restrictions will be even less likely to influence abusive drinking behaviour in the general population.'

Finally, it is worth noting that a variety of academics have independently summarised the research evidence available concerning the impact of advertising on alcoholic drink consumption. For example, Pittman and Lambert (1978) in a massive review of available literature and evidence concluded that advertising has not been found to have any significant impact on the behaviour of either youths or adults *vis-à-vis* drinking behaviour. On the other hand, they did find evidence that advertising influences the brand preferences of those who are already beer drinkers. They quote a 43 per cent gain in barrelage of one brewer in 1976 — in a year of extremely small growth in the US beer market.

Walsh (1980) found that 'restrictions on publicity and advertising are not judged likely to have a major impact on drinking or even on the recruitment of young people to the drinking population'. Van Iwaarden (1983) concluded 'a ban on commercials will not have any direct impact on the overall use of alcohol. Even in the long run the effects probably would be hardly substantial.'

Chiplin, Sturgess and Dunning (1981), in the most recent of all studies, concluded 'the causal relationship between advertising and aggregate demand is still a matter of considerable controversy, but the latest careful research using sophisticated estimation procedures does tend to suggest that any causal effect is rather weak. Thus it seems to remain unproven that advertising has led to any marked increase in aggregate demand in general, or in the demand for either tobacco or alcohol products . . . It must be recognised that advertising could well be the wrong target in seeking to curtail consumption of products such as alcohol . . . it does appear that so far there is little convincing support for the argument that changes in total consumption of these products are caused by advertising. Indeed, advertising appears to have surprisingly little effect on the total consumption of alcohol.'

To conclude, I believe that there is no evidence to suggest that drink advertising has any impact at all on levels of alcohol abuse in the UK. There is therefore no reason for any change in the current restrictions which are placed on alcohol advertisers.

M.J. Waterson

Dr. Martin A. Plant, sociologist with the Alcohol Research Group in Edinburgh formed very different opinions about where the evidence seemed to lead.

Available evidence shows fairly clearly that there is an association between the general level of alcohol consumption in a society and the level of alcohol-related problems. This does not imply, as Ledermann and his 'orthodox' adherents have imputed, that a precise neat mathematical reationship exists between consumption and harm. The world is a more whimsical and complicated place than that. Even so, the level of alcohol-related problems is usually, but not necessarily, always greater in a country with a high level of consumption than in one where consumption is low. Similarly, when *per capita* alcohol consumption fluctuates, broadly comparable changes in the level of various forms of alcohol-related harm are to be expected.

Many different factors influence patterns of alcohol use and misuse. As recently reviewed by Peck (1982), these include the price and availability of alcohol, genetic predisposition, family, peer group, occupation, age, sex, religion, income, personality and life events.

Alcohol is a commodity and as such is subject to the usual economic influence. The demand for alcohol is rather more inelastic (resilient) than is that for some other commodities but, nevertheless, alcohol consumption is influenced by price and income, as demonstrated by the fall in alcohol consumption during the recent recession.

The alcohol manufacturers currently spend large sums of money on advertising their products. From the preceding correspondence, it appears that there is no dissent from the view that a major, if not the major, reason for this expenditure is concern to capture the largest possible share of the market. Controversy centres around whether or not alcohol advertising increases the general level of alcohol consumption. Strangely very little 'hard evidence' on this subject exists. Only a handful of relevant studies appear to have been conducted on the entire surface of the planet. Most of these indicate that advertising has little or no discernible influence on the overall level of alcohol consumption. It must be noted that existing studies have been extremely limited in their scope. If they have employed apparently sophisticated statistical techniques, such methods have been applied to a selective range of sometimes extremely dubious data. In addition, the few genuine examples of the effects of an alcohol advertising ban having been evaluated, such as those in Manitoba and British Columbia, were greatly weakened. This is because in neither province was the population quarantined from advertising (including television advertising) coming in from elsewhere in Canada and the USA. In consequence these evaluations related to a reduction in, rather than to a ban on, such propaganda.

The precise role of alcohol advertising remains strangely unclear. Some investigators (eg McGuinness 1983; Schweitzer et al, 1983) have identified a tangible effect upon alcohol consumption. Others have not (eg Strickland 1983; van Iwaarden 1983). These conclusions remain the subject of a debate far too esoteric for the comprehension of all but a few highly numerate cognoscenti. This debate will probably rumble on until future studies produce evidence supporting one side or the other. In the meantime, while academics dispute, livers are cirrhosed and alcohol-related tragedies proliferate, curbed probably only by mass unemployment and the world recession.

It does not follow that because little evidence exists to link alcohol advertising with alcohol consumption that no case exists to further curb or even ban such advertising. Before this line can be pursued further an important practical point must be noted. Professor Alan Williams of the Department of Economics and Related Studies at the University of York, recently commented that advertising being expensive, may have the effect of raising the price of alcohol and in consequence of depresing consumption. It is a possibility that a ban on alcohol advertising would lead not to a fall, but to a rise, in alcohol consumption since the manufacturers could pass on their enforced savings to the consumer (Williams 1981).

Who would suffer from an advertising ban? Probably not the drink trade. As indicated by the correspondence from both the Scotch Whisky Association and the Advertising Association, there is general acceptance that advertising does not increase total alcohol sales or consumption. If this is so, then banning advertising would hardly be expected to lead to a fall in consumption and as noted above the drink trade would save a lot of money. The disadvantages would be felt by up-and-coming manufacturers who might have enlarged their future market share at the expense of the larger and more established producers. In other words, the current division of the market might be 'frozen' or at least made less resilient. Presumably such a situation would be widely welcomed by some manufacturers, even if detested by others.

It can be expected that if ever a ban on alcohol advertising was seriously proposed or appeared probable, the advertising industry, having most to lose, might oppose such a strategy most vehemently. Other losers from a reduction of alcohol advertising would be all those who currently receive revenue through this activity. These include commercial radio and television companies, newspaper and magazine publishers, printers, the owners of billboards, the people who paste up the posters and many others. It is doubtful, especially during hard times, whether other forms of advertising would rush in to fill the vacuum so created. People would lose their jobs.

People might also lose their lives. If, as Professor Williams speculated, prices fell following the absence or diminution of alcohol advertising, some people might drink more and thereby face a marginally greater risk of experiencing alcohol-related harm. Without alcohol advertising, the world would become a duller place. Sundays would cease to be enlivened by shapely females water-skiing behind Scottish plesiosaurs or by humming birds sipping nectar.

Who would gain from an advertising ban? The most obvious beneficiaries would be the health educationalists. At present even the relatively large amounts spent on alcohol education campaigns pale into triviality in comparison with those spent on alcohol advertising. It must be noted that most alcohol educational activities appear to be both ineffective and conducted with a blithe disregard for whether or not they do produce tangible effects. Such activities are often, sadly, symbolic, mere tokens. Possibly such activities are simply a waste of money. Even so it is reasonable to conclude that if the public is to be persuaded by a propaganda war then an advertising ban might be a reasonable precondition to clear the field for some future productive education campaign. Such a campaign, incidentally, might well be supported if not actually initiated by the drink trade which has already demonstrated a capacity to produce material of a far higher quality than that often generated by government funded bodies. In any event, a dramatic improvement is warrented in the scientific credibility of alcohol education which in future must be directed towards specific realistic goals and which must always be evaluated.

As indicated by Professor Williams, a reduction or elimination of advertising might benefit moderate drinkers whose favourite tipple might become cheaper. Large established alcohol producers might have their dominant positions reinforced.

Most economists appear to take the view that it is a naive futile exercise to attempt to weigh the costs and benefits of alcohol use and misuse (Grant, Plant and Williams 1983). Many of the key factors pleasure, injury and death — are intangible, since few would agree upon their value in purely monetary terms. What amount of pleasure justifies or balances even a single diseased liver or life lost?

One important practical consideration is relevant. Two recent UK public opinion polls have indicated that while there is a high level of general support for some strategies such as penalising drunken drivers or implementing health education, approximately three-quarters of the adult population appear to oppose the imposition of a full ban on alcohol advertising (MORI 1981). The way needs to be paved for any future draconian control policies by the creation of a receptive climate of opinion. At present, there is little evidence of political enthusiasm for any policy viewed at one extreme as an interference with free market forces or at the other as an onslaught on the working man's pint.

At this point, an almost overwhelming urge arises to turn to the nearest fence and sit upon it. Such intellectual cowardice is reluctantly repelled. There are, it is clear, two opposing viewpoints, both of which have much to commend them. There are far more uncertainties than certainties in this debate but a fairly clear general conclusion does appear to be justified. To adopt the phraseology of the foreperson of a Scottish jury, the case against alcohol advertising remains 'not proven'. It is far from clear what the effects of advertising are upon *per capita* alcohol consumption and probable that these effects, if not non-existent (which is possible) are at best trivial. It is further possible that the harm caused by a ban of alcohol advertising might counter any possible gains. Research is all too often a substitute for making unpalatable decisions or enacting controversial or unpopular policies. In this particular area, further research does for once appear to be warranted. In the meantime, advertising executives may rest easy in their penthouses at night (unless, of course, they handle tobacco accounts).

Martin A. Plant

The debate therefore remains inconclusive. Advertising of alcoholic drinks may have some effect on overall consumption but does certainly have a significant effect on brand choice. It may also be important in subtly distilling and reinforcing the fantasy images of virility or sophistication which surround alcohol. Is advertising harmless fun, an attribute of the free market economy, which gives lucrative employment to some and brightens our television screens, or is the state colluding with the alcohol promoters by failing to curtail one of the factors in the upwards consumption spiral? A ban on advertising might be taken as a mark of the community's seriousness of intent as far as alcohol misuse is concerned, but this would be at a cost to individual freedom. We shall return to this basic question in Chapter 16. The issues here are part scientific and part moral; both require further clarification before we would be justified in coming to any final conclusion. For the time being, rational restriction rather than total prohibition seems the most appropriate and the most acceptable approach.

13 THE TRADE DEBATE

Introduction

It is obvious that the beverage alcohol trade is one of the most important forces in determining how people drink. Through the production, distribution and marketing of a wide range of different beverages, the trade not only responds to consumer demand, but plays a vital part in shaping future demand through the nature of current supply. At the same time, it is possible that some members of the public health lobby may tend to over estimate the extent to which the beverage trade is involved in a gigantic global conspiracy to maximise alcohol consumption wherever and however it can. As in the advertising debate, it is sometimes tempting to be able to find a bad guy to blame for the present state of affairs, if only to deflect attention from the inadequacies of other preventive measures.

None of this is to deny the potentially harmful consequences of unrestricted marketing of alcohol, particularly in naive and previously unexploited markets. What we wanted to do was to find out how justified fears of excesses were in terms of current practice and how far the beverage trade, in its attempts to show a responsible and responsive front, was prepared to recognise the legitimacy of a public health perspective which might include curbs upon marketing and, in turn, upon profits. Originally, therefore, we tried to create a debate which looked at a series of national and international controls over the production and distribution of beverage alcohol. In discussing how best to give this debate a sharp and non-technical focus, however, we found ourselves increasingly drawn to the role of transnational corporations as a key example of what it was that lay behind the other controls in which we were interested. A transnational corporation is any firm (industrial, agricultural, service, or any combination of these) which controls assets in two or more countries. There are approximately 18,000 around the world, led by the US firm Exxon, with 1980 sales of $110 billion.

Recognising that it was impossible in a short chapter to deal comprehensively with issues of nationalisation, antitrust legislation, prohibitive import tariffs, government aid schemes to industry and so on, we asked John Cavanagh (at that time a Technical Officer with the World

Health Organisation) to open the Trade Debate.

The Crucial Link

The rapid growth of transnational corporations (TNCs) across the full gamut of industries since World War II has not spared alcoholic beverages. Indeed, the beer and distilled spirits sectors in most countries are now dominated by a handful of giant TNCs whose marketing strategies have spread increasing quantities of alcoholic beverages to both national and international markets as well as to specific segments within those markets, notably women and youth. The wine sector in some countries is not far behind beer and distilled spirits corporations in these extensions.

What, it may be asked, have these developments to do with health? Previous studies have established a link between increased alcoholic beverage consumption and a rise in harmful effects (Bruun *et al* 1975; Skog 1982, Mäkelä *et al* 1981; WHO 1980). For the first time, WHO researchers have explored another crucial relationship, the link between corporate structures and the availability of, demand for, and consumption of alcoholic beverages. The overwhelming evidence is that the link is strong.

The relationship between availability and consumption is, however, rarely a simple one. While it is true that few available bottles of alcoholic beverages go unconsumed, what is far more revelatory is the specific income group breakdown of consumption. In developing countries, for example, the numerically small urban high income groups and expatriates consume the largest proportion of alcoholic beverages made available through imports. Indeed, their share of consumption is higher for wine and distilled spirits than beer. In sum, availability of specific alcoholic beverages in different countries has a highly differentiated impact on various consuming groups, an area ripe for future research.

An historical perspective is helpful here. For most of the post-war period, alcohol problems have been viewed primarily as individual problems. More recently, many researchers have highlighted factors related to the larger socio-economic environment that play a strong role in determining drinking levels, patterns and problems. The modern transnational corporation now controls the output, marketing and distribution of most of the world's alcoholic beverages. Central to the political economy of health is that the principal concern of the alcoholic beverage TNC is the joint maximization of profit and market share, often to the detriment of public health.

Impact of Concentration and Oligopoly[1]

At the onset of the twentieth century, alcoholic beverage output was largely under the control of small firms whose distributional reach was local and, in limited instances, regional. Over the ensuing decades, through accelerated capital accumulation within corporations, and waves of mergers between firms, large corporate units extended their distribution networks to a national plane. In many countries this vastly increased the availability and variety of alcoholic beverages, even in the remotest rural areas. To cite but one advanced case, San Miguel Corporation in the Philippines currently distributes its beer (via its own trucking, barge and shipping fleets) to over 125,000 retail outlets throughout the archipelago.

Increasing sophistication of distribution channels was to undergo another qualitative shift after World War II, with rapid strides in technologies for conquering distances, notably in shipping and telecommunications. These technical innovations coincided with the gradual deceleration of alcoholic beverage consumption in several developed countries. Just as the preceding developments could be considered as factors pushing alcohol on global markets, there were parallel developments that contributed to pull alcohol towards countries where consumption was traditionally low. Paramount among these pull factors in post-independence developing economies was the unprecedented migration from non-monetized rural areas to monetized urban aggregations. This was accompanied in many instances by a vast numerical increase in elites with high purchasing power and westernized consumption patterns. Related to these changes in several newly independent countries was the implementation of import substitution industrialization policies, which spurred the setting up of domestic breweries.

Especially in the 1960s and 1970s, large firms in the beer and distilled spirits sectors of many countries took advantage of this conjuncture of forces to extend their operations globally. Leaders in transnationalizing the beer sector included Heineken (Netherlands), United Breweries (Denmark) and Guinness (Ireland), each controlling over three-fifths of their national market by the late 1970s. Overseas forays by distilled spirits firms were spearheaded by the highly oligopolistic whisky sectors in the UK and North America, and the giant cognac

houses of France. More recently, the increasingly concentrated champagne sector in France and wine sectors in a few other countries have
also extended operations considerably in global markets. Only in rare
cases have governments applied antitrust legislation to slow the steady
drive toward concentration in alcoholic beverage sectors.

These overseas salients were made via three corporate mechanisms:
exports of goods, exports of capital and sales of licenses. The combined
impact of these three boosted significantly the availability, variety and
consumption of alcoholic beverages in developed market economies
and, even more markedly, in developing countries. Of over $10.1 billion
legal global alcohol beverage imports in 1980, more than $1.3 billion
was shipped into developing countries, the bulk of it distilled spirits.
The 1980 breakdown of developing country imports was: beer – $203
million; wine – $293 million; and distilled spirits – $812 million. For
beer and distilled spirits TNCs, another major avenue of expansion has
been the scaffolding of breweries and distilleries in developing countries, often in collaboration with members of the ruling oligarchies.
Leading the field, Nigeria has contracted with TNCs for the erection
of over ten breweries since 1978, with several more in the blueprint
stage. One other increasingly popular overseas expansion strategy,
spearheaded by Heineken and United Breweries, has been the TNC
sale of licenses to developing country entrepreneurs for construction of
breweries, wineries and distilleries.

That the combined impact of such overseas forays has contributed
to increased consumption is incontestable, particularly in the sectors
where concentration is most advanced, beer and distilled spirits. Out of
46 countries where beer output grew over 50 per cent from 1975 to
1980, 42 were developing countries, with the overwhelming bulk of
production consumed nationally. For distilled spirits, an indication of
the explosive impact of TNC expansion is that by 1977, 36 developing countries depended on imports for over a fifth of their recorded
distilled spirits consumption. Once again, rather than exercising
restraint on these overseas flows, governmental policies have often
augmented them through trade agreements favouring alcohol and state
aid to alcohol exporters.

Emergence of oligopoly in beer and spirits sectors has also exercised
an impact on consumption via other mechanisms. Control of a sector
by a small number of firms can lead, at times, to a panoply of collusive
practices between the oligopolists collectively. An informal geographical market sharing arrangement between the three largest Mexican
brewers has effectively carved the national market into three exclusive

spheres, offering each corporation reign over an area where promotional and distributional efforts are almost totally unhindered by competition.

Impact of Conglomeration

Concomitant with the dramatic rise of the TNC over the last two decades has been a related phenomenon: the growth of conglomerates.[2] Historically, an initial phase in conglomeration is often marked by corporate overspill into more than one alcoholic beverage sector, most notably distilled spirits companies entering the wine sector. In different countries, various combinations of such straddling operations can be seen, often involving extensions into soft drinks and other beverages. One of the important policy implications of this conglomerate movement is that it confers on these diverse sectors a unity which can be translated into enormous political leverage.

A second and no less important phase is an expansionary drive beyond the borders of alcohol. Of the 27 alcoholic beverage producing TNCs which registered sales of over $1 billion in 1980, almost all had extensive activities in industries outside the alcohol arena. These include such massive producers of alcoholic beverages as Philip Morris (through its Miller subsidiary), Coca Cola (through its Wine Spectrum subsidiary) and Lonhro (through a wide variety of alcoholic beverages), whose alcohol sales represent but a minor share of their total operations.

Such conglomerate extensions, often substantially under-written by large transnational banks, bear directly on consumption and health in two respects. Firstly, they create the conditions for widespread use of cross-subsidization,[3] whereby a firm can deploy profits from flourishing segments of its operations to subsidize losses in other lines. Philip Morris has historically been a pioneer practitioner of this technique, buying up a smaller regional brewer (Miller) in 1969 and massively subsidizing a promotional campaign to propel its brands nationally and even internationally. By 1980, it was the second largest (by output) brewer in the world. Invasion of new markets was often accelerated by underpricing competitors in new markets, with the low prices subsidized by other Philip Morris divisions, a practice actively stimulating consumption.

Secondly, conglomerate acquisition of alcohol interests has often been by firms which have already developed extensive international marketing networks for other consumer products. Alcohol, in these cases, simply flows into these existing channels, reaching far more consumers than if the company were beginning international distribution on its own. Significant in this respect have been extensive link-ups between alcohol corporations and four of the seven transnational tobacco conglomerates (UNCTAD 1978) that dominate world cigarette markets: Philip Morris (US) and Miller; R.J. Reynolds' (US) takeover of the distilled spirits and wine giant Heublein; the Imperial Group's (UK) takeover of Courage; and the Rembrandt/Rothmans Group (South Africa), which is a leading owner of its country's wine monopoly.

As producers and purveyors of one addictive commodity – cigarettes – they bring specialized expertise to the marketing of another – alcohol. All four have successfully deployed market segmentation, brand differentiation, sporting events sponsorship and other promotional techniques perfected in cigarette marketing to extend their alcohol products nationally and internationally. This has been of tremendous importance in developing countries where, along with soft drink TNCs, the tobacco conglomerates usually have the best developed marketing channels. These corporate tie-ups become even more serious in health terms as evidence surfaces that combined tobacco and alcohol consumption further enhances the incidence of certain harmful effects.

Corporate Marketing Strategies

The impact of concentrated corporate power on alcohol consumption can only be fully grasped by delving into the combined corporate marketing strategies deployed by the alcohol TNCs. Such a study reveals the mechanisms by which TNCs help create the images, desires and norms that stimulate drinking.

At the heart of alcohol marketing lies an estimated $2 billion dollars in global advertising campaigns (1981) that have launched new alcohol categories and brands, thereby stimulating new alcohol tastes and markets. Lavishly bankrolled marketing drives have helped alcoholic beverage TNCs compete much more effectively for the consumer's disposable income, thus also enlarging the alcohol market. Taking advantage of consumer heterogeneity in all societies by sex, age, ethnicity, income, and geographical groups, TNCs in all consumer product lines expand markets through product differentiation and brand proliferation. In recent years, alcoholic beverage TNCs have applied these techniques to new groups, females and adolescents, where alcohol consumption has traditionally been low in most societies. The consequences for health are ominous.

Alcoholic beverage TNCs targeting of women has involved two kinds of corporate strategy applicable to all forms of market segmentation: generating new brands and retargeting older ones, both backed up by large scale advertising in women's magazines and elsewhere. Particularly innovative in this realm has been Grand Metropolitan, which (through its IDV subsidiary) created the entirely new cream liqueur category aimed primarily at the female market. Such corporate strategies have become a prominent factor, in the growth of alcohol consumption and problems among women in several developed countries. Evidence of this is especially strong in the US, where advertising has been the most intense and pervasive. What makes these reports even more disturbing is the growing medical evidence that women may develop liver cirrhosis from alcohol consumption faster than men (Lake 1982) and that alcohol consumption by pregnant women is related to a range of fetal alcohol problems.

While women's importance as a consuming segment is unparalleled in size, the youth market assumes major importance for yet another reason. Due to laws against alcohol sales to adolescents in most developed counries, alcoholic beverage TNCs formulate strategies to win over consumers reaching the legal drinking age. This is critical for it is immensely easier to recruit a non-drinker to a specific brand than a consumer who is already locked into another brand.

Effectiveness of such multi-billion dollar advertising is further enhanced when coupled to a dazzling array of other promotional techniques, including free sampling, supporters clubs, sports promotion and logo merchandising, to name but a few. It is in this context that recent public utterances by several alcohol TNCs on the merits of drinking in moderation should be viewed. Even on the assumption that these corporate contentions are made in good faith, they are completely negated by the comprehensive integration of their global marketing strategies.

Conclusions

In delineating these corporate currents, it is clearly not my intent to document the serious social, economic and medical impact of different levels of alcohol consumption. This has been, and is being, comprehensively carried out by doctors, sociologists and other social scientists elsewhere. Nor is it contended that corporate factors are the sole forces behind alcohol consumption. Obviously, alcoholic beverage consumption existed in many developing countries before the intrusion of TNCs, and exists in centrally planned economies in the absence of capitalist corporate entities.

Rather, I would suggest, on the basis of historical analysis, that transnational corporate structures and marketing strategies in the alcoholic beverage industry have exercised a strong impact on the availability of, and demand for, alcoholic beverages in both developed and developing countries. Attempts to increase awareness about the prevalence of alcohol problems should take this into account, as should any prevention oriented policy considerations to limit the supply or demand of alcoholic beverages. In the history of debate on alcoholic beverage control, considerations of this nature are long overdue.

John Cavanagh[4]

Such a sweeping attack upon the marketing practices of TNCs required an equally spirited rejoinder. In seeking a response from Tim Ambler, Group Marketing Director of International Distillers and Vintners, we deliberately chose an individual who both represented one of the TNCs that John Cavanagh had been attacking and who was also noted for his conspicuous involvement in various UK trade committees concerned with alcohol education, research and policy. We asked him not to produce a piece of bland and polished copy, with all its rough edges smoothed away by the egregious efforts of professional PR men, but rather to respond to the challenge directly and with vigour. The result certainly makes the trade debate one of the most lively and, therefore, the most useful exchanges in this whole book.

A Personal Prologue

It seems that I am one of the villains of Mr. Cavanagh's piece. I work for International Distillers and Vintners Ltd., which is in profit terms about the fourth or fifth largest such company in the world league of wine and spirit companies. This paper is, however, my own and does not necessarily represent the views of IDV or colleagues. In accepting the invitation to respond to Mr. Cavanagh's challenge, I recognise that what he says is both personal and fundamental. He implies that we are doing more harm than good to mankind. Also that in pursuit of profits, we are less than honest. In short, a personal challenge deserves a personal response.

The Central Theme

The World Health Organisation is concerned with nutrition as a key part of health. Its skirmish with TNCs over packaged baby foods, whatever the rights or wrongs of that case, has left it with understandable attitudes to TNCs in general. The relative marketing strengths of such companies in different commodity markets are, however, totally different. Whilst a few leading packaged baby food manufacturers have a very large share of their market, the top ten wine and spirit producers have less than 10 per cent of the world market.

In other words, drink companies have nowhere near the market dominance of packaged baby foods, or breakfast cereals or any highly technological food producer. The reason is simple: making wines and spirits is relatively easy. We have been doing it for thousands of years. The costs of market entry are low and, indeed, quite a few of my colleagues have over the years left to start their own businesses in competition with IDV. Our commercial objectives do not include any reference to market share (which made the figures above rather hard to come by).

Curiously, the pursuit of profits which is itself (as any economist can show) a benefit to mankind, is consistent with this policy not to set out to sell the most alcohol to the most people. Mr. Cavanagh points to the proliferation of brands as an example of TNCs 'taking advantage of consumer heterogeneity in all societies'. He really cannot have it both ways. If we had the power he ascribes to us, we would limit the number of brands and thereby maximise our profits. Contrary to Mr. Cavanagh's assertion that the Scotch Whisky Market is 'highly oligopolistic', there are reputed to be over 1,500 brands, widely owned. The vast majority of these are only marginally, if at all, profitable for their owners. Furthermore, their existence detracts from the profitability of the successful ones.

We discovered long ago that there was little or no profit in making alcohol or growing vines. Our profits come from supplying 'brands'. Brands are distinguished from their generic categories by their higher quality, better presentation, higher prices and genuine consumer demand. Why else would consumers pay the higher price? The world marketplace is littered with rejected brands which failed to give the consumer what he wanted. It is worth noting, too, that the alcoholic strength, which for spirits has to be declared on the label, is often less for advertised brands than other equivalent commodities. Smirnoff in the UK is less alcoholic than gin. Baileys Irish Cream is less alcoholic than most other liqueurs. We are therefore interested in the quality of our brands and how this quality is seen by our consumers. We are not trying to maximise the quantity of alcohol sold.

Alcohol Good or Bad?

Road accidents are not caused by cars but by their makers, drivers or service mechanics. The great improvements in car safety in the last thirty years have resulted from co-operation between the parties concerned. A scientist once told me that there was no such thing as a 'poison' since poison was only a matter of degree. Curare is used in medicine. Excessive milk consumption can be fatal. Alcohol in moderation is good; in excess it is bad. It is astonishing that such a normal and obvious fact of life is so widely ignored. The problems resulting from the abuse of alcohol are increasingly reported and rightly so. It is high time that more was done to combat them. Whilst health lobbyists direct their attack on the industry and vice versa, too few people are working together constructively.

Alcohol is produced from sugar and supplies human energy needs in much the same way. It improves circulation, which is why brandy is traditionally administered to those brought into the warm from the cold. Spirits were used as an antiseptic before some orderly discovered they were also nice to drink. In the current very proper concern with abuse, the benefits from correct use may be forgotten. Because of its easy ingestion, alcohol is a valuable energy source for the elderly, besides assisting the digestion for many other people. This may contribute to the fact that moderate consumers tend to outlive teetotallers, although a medical explanation for this phenomenon has yet to be found. Moderate consumption has been shown to reduce the incidence of heart disease. If doctors continued with their traditional practice of prescribing a little whisky or brandy in place of the more modern (and more expensive) relaxants, national health costs could be greatly reduced. The world might also be a healthier and happier place.

The prime benefit of alcohol is as the catalyst to improving human relationships. Whether it be at a party, or a family Christmas, or the drink that goes with shaking hands over an agreement, alcohol has always been part of breaking down barriers of shyness or formality or hospitality. Better a glass in the hand than a gun.

Of course we must recognise and act on the problems of excessive use to the individuals, to their families and to third parties. Drunk driving is of outstanding concern. The research evidence so far is that the particular problems need particular solutions. Time spent in search of a general, simplistic solution is, perhaps, time wasted.

The most popular solution endorsed by Mr. Cavanagh, is that supply of alcohol be curtailed. Clearly if there was no alcohol there could be no abuse of it. Dr. Ledermann gave this theory academic respectability when he demonstrated a relationship between average consumption and alcohol related problems. Unfortunately for Mr. Cavanagh, there is no longer the unquestioning and unanimous acceptance of Ledermann's work which he implies. Increasingly, it is being challenged as logically and statistically flawed. Even if the relationship did exist, however, it would be counter-productive drastically to limit supply. I have already noted that alcohol is easy to make. It is even easier to make badly. Prohibition in India has produced uncounted health problems following drinking home-made alcohol. In one incident alone, in Kerala, 300 died. Most Indian states now permit sales of alcoholic products again. Bathtub gin during the US prohibition was not the joke it seems today.

Even more persuasive, however, is the simple fact that despite its abuse, alcohol provides a net benefit to mankind. It is accepted by most researchers that alcohol, in moderation, is good for you.

Mr. Cavanagh's Propositions

Having marked out what will become, hopefully, common ground, let me now attempt to relate this to Mr. Cavanagh's specific propositions. These are not easy to extract fairly from the flow of his salient and persuasive article, but I shall try to look in turn at each of his central assertions.

That beer, wine and distilled spirits markets are dominated by a handful of TNCs. It is true that TNCs have significantly expanded their operations. Greater travel, improved communications and many other features of a changing world are making it possible to market brands in similar ways in markets old and new. The top ten represent about 9 per cent of the world's wine and spirit market. The leading ten beer producers perhaps 25 per cent. This may increase further but there is no prospect of 'domination' by TNCs.

Mr. Cavanagh alludes to 'a panoply of collusive practices between the oligopolists collectively'. I would have been interested to learn more about this. My own experience indicates a remarkable inability of the leading firms even to agree those things they are supposed to agree. The US and EEC's antitrust provisions are formidable and much feared by the larger companies, especially in the drinks business. They would also, no doubt, be delighted to have any evidence Mr. Cavanagh may possess on 'collusive practices'.

That TNCs are concerned with profit and market share. As these go up, public health goes down. It is true that TNCs are concerned with profit but less so with market share. What is incorrect is the seesaw model which indicates that public health is negatively correlated with TNC profits and market share. For the reasons of quality indicated previously, it is more likely that these are positively correlated. It is more likely still that they are totally independent variables.

Mr. Cavanagh's arguments seem occasionally to contradict one another. If profits are as important as they are, why do we indulge in 'cross subsidisation whereby a firm can deploy profits from flourishing segments of its operation to subsidise losses in other lines'? Apart from the perfectly normal business practice whereby investment precedes profits so that a new project may well make losses in early years, losses are generally a symptom of management error, not subtle strategy. TNCs are invariably anxious to terminate losses as soon as possible, not to grow through their use.

Similarly, Mr. Cavanagh finds it reprehensible that Philip Morris should attract custom in new markets by offering lower prices whilst simultaneously deploring the 'collusive practices' of the oligopolists presumably in relation to fixing prices and rigging markets.

At the end of the day the major drink companies know full well that their future profits will not come from customers whose alcohol excesses have led to death, injury or sickness. They have a clear interest vested in health.

That TNCs through scale, corporate structure, use of parallel distribution channels (eg tobacco) can achieve much greater availability of alcohol. The availability of alcohol is a function of retail outlets. These are rarely controlled by TNCs. In the USA, drink producers are, with minor exceptions, banned from retail interests. Similar moves are planned in South Africa. The UK is exceptional in that large numbers of retail outlets are owned by the large brewing companies of which only Grand Metropolitan could truly be considered a TNC. But these outlets have been losing market share as magistrates have freely (arguably too freely) issued licences to supermarkets, wine bars and other new outlets. The reality is that TNCs have very little involvement in determining the number of retail outlets, thus very little influence on availability.

The suggestion that conglomerates can use their other channels of distribution for drink, (he mentioned tobacco) is attractive but does not work. Reynolds has recently confirmed that the Heublein wines and spirits division will operate quite separately, indeed more separately than it did previously from its Kentucky Chicken Division. Imperial, Morris, and Rembrandt all totally separate their drink interests. There are close *financial* relationships between drink and other divisions in a TNC conglomerate but very few *operating* links.

That there is a strong causal relationship leading from availability to total consumption to harmful effects. The 'overwhelming evidence' of the strong link between corporate structures, availability and demand needs to be presented if it exists, not asserted. It is quite possible that there is some relationship between availability and demand. Excessive scarcity of availability is just as likely to increase demand as is excessive availability. For the latter reason, most countries use the judicial process to restrict retail drink licences. This sensible procedure is independent of the influence of TNCs.

The causal chain breaks down, however, when it relates *per capita* average consumption to harmful effects. Apart from the Ledermann fallacy, it is interesting that the most restrictive countries (Scandinavia, Eastern Europe) appear to have the greatest problems. It is hardly surprising that excessive restrictions act as a challenge to beat the system and binge excessively when one does. The US custom (now happily receding) of downing 100 proof cocktails in the early afternoon was born of prohibition. Ireland has a surprisingly low *per capita* average consumption but high incidence of problem drinking, whereas Italy seems to have high consumption coupled with relatively fewer problems.

TNCs are creating particular problems in developing countries. Finally, Mr. Cavanagh pinpoints developing countries as a particular focus of TNCs damaging health. Again he attempts to have it both ways. On the one hand, he alleges, we are taking advantage of developing countries by setting up joint domestic operations. On the other hand, we are taking advantage of them by 'shipping it in'. Mr. Cavanagh's figures for consumption of alcohol is these countries are inaccurate, and refer only to western style alcohol. Indeed the special conditions in West Africa and other developing countries make it almost impossible to obtain accurate estimates, since the figures exclude the traditional local beers and spirits.

In Nigeria for example palm wine is distilled to produce ogogoro (or kai kai) which is widely considered to be dangerous though as every

village in the south has its own still, quality varies considerably. Governments of non-Islamic developing countries believe in partnerships
between local and advanced western drink companies because of the
benefits to foreign exchange, local agriculture, tax revenue, reduction in
smuggling/graft, but especially health.

In its simplest terms is it not better that the local consumer spends
his free discretionary income on a small quantity of Gilbeys Gin made
locally, or yet a smaller quantity which is imported, than on a large
quantity of semi-lethal hooch at twice the strength? And where is the
harm in spending reasonable sums to persuade him to trade up to the
healthier option?

Conclusion

Mr. Cavanagh is welcome to visit our companies whether in Kenya or
Sri Lanka, in the USA, the UK or elsewhere, and see for himself that we
are reasonably honourable people (much like anyone else) trying to
achieve legitimate aims, and often failing.

We are open to criticism and much of it will be justified. But such
criticism will do nothing to solve the very real problems of alcohol
abuse. These problems need our joint and co-operative effort. The
World Health Organisation is currently reviewing its approach to this
area. We hope that greater common ground will result.

Tim Ambler

*Just as in the advertising debate and, to an extent, the health educa-
tion debate the question which is raised for the future is not so much:
who is right? It is rather, since the debate looks set to continue: how is
the best result to be achieved? Through consultation or through con-
frontation? Let us hope that this chapter has begun to set the terms for
the kind of dialogue which is often piously alluded to but so very
seldom actually takes place.*

Notes

1. Oligopoly defines a market dominated by a handful of firms whose corporate conduct is, at times, coordinated via such mechanisms as pricing policies
that deviate from those which might prevail under more competitive conditions;
various collusive practices; and a multiplicity of effective barriers against other
firms aspiring to enter the sector.

2. A conglomerate is a corporation consisting of subsidiaries engaged in

unrelated economic activities. Expansion of conglomerates takes place through mergers and takeovers.

3. Cross-subsidization is a familiar practice of conglomerates whereby profits from one product line are used to subsidize pricing another below the level of long-term total costs. This is an ideal/marketing device to enhance market shares in a given sector by underpricing competitors.

4. This essay was written while the author was a Technical Officer at the World Health Organisation, and most of the statistics cited are derived from WHO work in progress. The views expressed in the essay, however, are those of the author alone. The author wishes to express special thanks to Frederick F. Clairmonte of the United Nations Conference on Trade and Development, who participated equally in the formulation of the ideas presented here.

14 THE ENVIRONMENT DEBATE

Visitors to London who have not travelled on the underground for several years will now find that the great majority of the carriages are exclusively for non-smokers with perhaps a single densely polluted compartment left for a minority who are unable to relinquish their habit even for a half hour's train journey. Most people seem to have adapted readily to this environmental change and its influence on their drug taking. Similarly the style of many British pubs has been consciously manipulated to attract and retain female custom. Again a change in the environment in our own public house has influenced habits and clientele.

The importance of the drinking environment as a focus for preventive strategies is often overlooked because it is regarded as either irrelevant or immutable. We invited Friedner Wittman of the Alcohol Research Group in Berkeley to make the case for the importance of environmental influences and to demonstrate their susceptibility to local and national pressures.

The Environmental Debate

Settings are important for shaping, containing, and giving meanings to drinking occasions. People drink very differently in bars from the way they drink at home; they drink differently at the end of the day from the way they drink at lunch; they drink differently on weekends from the way they drink on weekdays; they drink differently in public and in private. People respond to the cues in the socio-physical environment they see about them. They drink as the situation requires, and often are guided in their drinking behavior by the expectations of the host, or by the standards of the management in the settings in which they drink. People drink as a gesture in response to the situations in which they find themselves: to be sociable and accommodating; to relieve embarrassment; as a gesture of defiance; to show they are 'in the know'. In bar settings, people can be made to behave as if they are drinking when they believe they are drinking, even if they are not actually consuming alcohol. Far from being passive elements in the drinking equation, drinking settings provide signals, cues and rewards to the individual drinker.

Drinking settings perform another function in the creation of drinking patterns: settings organize groups of people into groups of drinkers, creating social occasions predicated upon the use of alcohol. Bars in particular create social conditions in which the consumption of alcohol underlies all contacts between people. Homes, through the simple device of setting out bottles, putting up decorations, and playing music, are made to accomplish the same purpose for parties. Offices are made to do the same for celebrating the signing of that big contract, and for holidays. At the community level, the mix of 'watering holes' in relation to other places of entertainment, recreation, and civic activity, provides tangible evidence of the extent to which the town organizes its life around drinking. The mix of alcohol outlets in commercial retail activity provides an indication of the significance of alcohol in the community's economic life.

Characteristics of settings and kinds of drinking behavior often combine in problematic ways. Explorations of changes in the environmental mood of bars — the combination of lights, decor, music, furnishings — have been associated with increases in drinking rates and in aggressive behavior. Young men out on a toot can drink without problems in bar settings that cater to them, but encounter problems if they drink in settings used by older or more genteel people. Music and loud talking in neighborhood bars are O.K. in the early evening, but not late at night. Fast driving becomes especially dangerous when the driver has been drinking. In rapidly-developing communities, oldtimers and newcomers each acquire their own drinking settings; problems occur when the newcomer happens in to an oldtimer drinking establishment, and vice versa. Settings serve to insulate the experiences of one drinking group from another, and to protect the drinkers in a group from exposure to consequences in the outside world.

Drinking settings are also significant for the extent to which they expose their customary inhabitants to risk. Public authorities have long been concerned about permitting known alcoholics to drink in bars and taverns, and some countries forbid service of alcohol to publicly-identified inebriates. Restrictions on sales of alcohol to minors provide another example. These special cases point toward more general approaches to regulation that minimize inappropriate mixes of people and settings for the consumption of alcohol. The alcohol field presently pays little attention to questions of general regulation. It is left to workplaces to devise their own rules for drinking on the job, and to local zoning ordinances to establish patterns of availability at the community level. Virtually no general or community-level epidemiological studies have been done in this area to aid in the determination of rules for use or access to non-licensed settings where alcohol is consumed.

Given the power of settings to shape drinking experiences, and to hold implications for alcohol-related problems, a preventive perspective seems in order that inquires how settings might be shaped and regulated (a) to improve the ways in which alcohol is used and integrated into other daily activities and (b) to devise protections against problemmatic consequences of the uses of drinking settings. In other human services sectors, the design of settings for both therapeutic and protective purposes has received considerable attention in the US, notably in the areas of mental health, housing for the elderly, public housing, hazardous industry, and auto safety. It is somewhat surprising in comparison that the alcohol field has devoted little or no effort to health and welfare aspects of the design of drinking settings. Why not, and what are the prospects for increased attention to such design in the future?

At least three factors in developed Western countries, especially in the US, have inhibited interest in the regulation of drinking settings for the purposes of maintaining public health and reducing alcohol problems. These are factors of philosophy, ideology, and political utility.

Western philosophical traditions emphasize the freedom of the individual to exercise his or her talents and powers to the fullest in an environment rich with resources and opportunity. Individual mastery of one's life is taken to presuppose manipulation of the surrounding environment as the individual chooses. Restrictions on the availability of resources, and limitations on their use, have long been anathema to those who hold these views. Policy proposals which suggest restriction, limitation, and restriction of use or access to the environment are subject to harsh criticism, including charges that those who propose such policies are atheistic and unpatriotic.

Public health prevention policies are sensitive to this ethos. Despite the long-established link between cigarette smoking and cancer, cigarettes are still widely available, and restrictions on their use are limited to anti-smoking ordinances (often not well enforced) in a handful of communities. Prevention efforts instead focus on the education of individuals to emphasize personal decisions not to smoke despite the environment of extensive availability. The US track-record on the control of hazardous substances and pollutants, while effective in some respects, has been obtained only after hard-fought battles, and is in constant danger of being undone by those who are willing to trade off rises in health problems for economic-industrial development. Alcohol prevention programs have followed the personal education line, and continue to do so doggedly despite the lack of hoped-for results. Public health grounds for controls on the design and use of drinking settings are virtually absent in practice, despite the statements in alcohol beverage control agencies' charters requiring that such grounds be considered in licensing of outlets.

The alcohol field's ideology has operated firmly within this ethos over the past fifty years, since the rise of the alcoholism movement. With the end of Prohibition in the US, alcohol problems came to be seen as matters of individual alcoholism independent of the environment of consumption. Rapidly-emerging state controls over alcohol outlets in the 1930s placed a dual emphasis on the orderly control of the alcohol market (stimulated often by the active intervention of the alcoholic beverage industry in the drafting and interpretation of regulations), and upon preventing a reoccurrence of the social disorders that had been associated with the saloon. The controls were administered by newly-created alcohol beverage control agencies. Problems of alcoholism, on the other hand, became the province of state health agencies. Public attention to alcohol use moved into two bureaucracies, where it remains today, officially separating the regulation of availability from the treatment of problems of alcohol. The two bureaucracies presently have virtually nothing to do with each other.

Public sentiment generally follows the ideology of the alcohol field and the official guidance of the public agencies: alcohol availability and drinking settings are by and large seen to contribute little to the occurrence of alcohol problems.

Alcohol research activity has done little to challenge this view, in fact has been swept up in them for the most part. A few studies have been done on the relationships between settings and drinking in the context of bar studies; some note has been taken of the influence of settings in general population surveys of drinking practices; and only a scattered handful of studies have been done on fundamental issues in alcohol's presence in person-environment relationships.

The political utility of environmental control measures has yet to be demonstrated for its applicability to alcohol. Alcohol researchers' investigations into the control of environments for drinking and purchasing alcohol have not to date produced much confidence in the preventive benefit of restricting drinking settings and availability. Small-scale local experiments to design or to limit drinking settings have not resulted in notable drops in consumption, nor in diminutions of alcohol problems. People switch beverages, change purchasing habits, make their own alcohol, and alter drinking practices to maintain former levels of consumption. Controls on closing hours can shift the times at which traffic accidents occur, but not their prevalence. Short-term decreases in consumption and problems in response to local restrictions on supply return, after a time, to their former levels as people discover new forms of supply and create alternative drinking settings. Small scale environmental manipulation, in and of itself, seems to bring about little positive preventive result — not surprising, considering the modest levels of most small-scale environmental changes in the larger surrounding context of abundant availability.

Large scale changes in the environment of alcohol, on the other hand, do not occur in isolation. They are a part of broader economic, social, and political changes that are simultaneously afoot. It is tempting at this scale to view changes in the environment of alcohol availability as epiphenomenal to the 'real' forces at work: rises in *per capita* income; trends in political and social liberalism; marketing activity by the beverage industry — all seem to sweep along with them increased use, demand for, and creation of new drinking settings. To this view, little is to be gained by controlling alcohol environments *per se*.

Given these experiences, what, if anything, is to be done to take steps to design and regulate the environments of alcohol?

First, consider the present state of affairs. Absence of attention to alcohol environments by the polity and the alcohol field means that beverage producers and retailers are the principal arbiters of the emplacement and operation of alcohol outlets, and of the policies for creating new outlets. The industry has virtually unrestricted use of the environment of alcohol as a means for encouraging more consumption, and is free to encourage more drinking in more pleasant surroundings, regardless of the health or social consequences.

Second, inattention to the study of alcohol settings means that contributions made by settings to the occurrence of alcohol problems will be overlooked. Drinking and driving provide one example; the use of alcohol by train crews, even in trains carrying hazardous materials, is another. Nothing can be done to prevent such problems if they are not made visible.

Third, people's control over their own behavior depends to a large extent upon their abilities to manipulate the environments in which the behavior occurs. The affluent and powerful understand this well and have a strong interest in maintaining as much control as possible not only over their own environments but over other people's as well.

The environment of alcohol use is no exception. Absence of a public sector interest in the environments of alcohol hampers people's abilities to be attentive to the effects of the environments upon them, and eliminates challenges to the industry's efforts to create the environments, demand, conditions and meanings of consumption.

An approach to environmental regulation that addresses this state of affairs will look at a combination of macro- and micro-environment controls. Micro-level controls in a macro-environment of plentiful availability are ineffective and self-defeating and provoke anger on the public's part. It is silly to make alcohol attractive and cheap, then make it physically inconvenient to obtain. People will find their way round the restrictions, and will swear at the bureaucrats while they do it. Alternatively, it is not sensible to set macro-level restrictions without attending to the micro-environment. The US experience with Prohibition provides painful examples of this lesson. Further, it does not appear feasible to single out the environment of alcohol as the sole subject of alcohol control efforts, either at the micro- or the macro-levels without simultaneous attention to educational/attitudinal and social issues, and without engaging in a planning process that includes the participation of those who are the subjects of the regulatory effort.

Two things can be done in the near future to give the environment of alcohol the importance it deserves in the prevention of alcohol problems. First, the alcohol research and prevention fields can take seriously the significance of the relationship between environments, consumption, and alcohol-related problems. Studies of the environment of alcohol have not been exhausted by considering it epiphenomenal to other alcohol phenomena, or by the disappointing results of tiny, opportunistic experiments in regulation. Much can be learned about alcohol by considering the environment as an interactive, rather than as a dependent variable. The close correspondence between types of settings and kinds of drinking experiences is well known: it remains to document carefully the ways in which where people drinks affects how and with what consequences they drink. This information is essential to improve the quality, fairness, and effectiveness of the regulation of drinking settings.

Second, many local communities can take a greater part in the licensing and regulation of alcohol outlets in their midst. Wealthy communities, through their control over zoning ordinances and the greater mobility of their citizens, appear better able to control their alcohol environments than do poverty level communities. But many communities, no matter what the socio-economic status of their citizens, have only minor roles in regulating alcohol availability. In many states outlet operators, often key figures in the community, assume proprietary stances toward licenses which make difficult challenges to licensing of outlets and supervision over outlet operation. Officials often treat outlets in routine, *pro forma* ways. State licensing laws often make the removal of troublesome outlets an arduous and frustrating business. People's concerns and frustrations with outlets often go unvoiced or unattended. Yet the settings for alcohol use can be included in thinking and planning for the development of local programs for the prevention of alcohol problems; with only modest encouragement, people act vigorously to address the impact of alcohol upon community life and are willing to include review of the environments of alcohol on their planning agendas. People do not consider changing environments which they consider fixed and immutable; instead they try to live with them. But once people become aware of their powers to control the harmful influence of environments upon local health and welfare, they become creative and adept at designing and regulating those environments to obtain healthy, liveable settings.

Friedner D. Wittman

Commenting on this viewpoint, David Robinson and Philip Tether of the Institute for Health Studies of the University of Hull further emphasise the value and feasibility of local initiatives even in the face of national apathy or hostility.

In this short piece we outline some general points about the nature of the debate about alcohol prevention and pick up a familiar but unhelpful assertion in Wittman's contribution for further discussion. Our main aim is to draw attention to the fact that preventing alcohol problems is not just a matter for central governments and major institutions and to stress that there is enormous scope for action and impact at the local level.

Debates about identification, prevention and management have, by and large, been informed by three basic conceptions of the 'real' nature of the alcohol problem. Some see alcoholics as the main problem, others see it as contemporary society, its drinking 'culture' and attitudes while yet others see the problem as alcohol itself. Those who see alcoholics as the main problem are concerned about this minority of drinkers and emphasise the need to prevent them developing their condition. The aim is to get people to recognise the early signs of alcoholism in themselves and other people. Those who see the root of the 'alcohol problem' in the way alcohol is perceived and used in our society focus their attention upon the unhealthy and unhelpful influences, beliefs, practices, images and expectations which cumulatively create an unpropitious 'drinking culture'. Their aim is to find ways – through control of advertising, media presentation and education, to amend social behaviour in relation to alcohol and its use. Finally, those who see alcohol itself as the core issue draw attention to the links between levels of overall consumption in a society and the rates of various kinds of alcohol problems. Their concern is with the availability of alcohol and with a variety of controls over such things as the number and type of alcohol outlets and the contexts in which alcohol is purchased and consumed.

These differing approaches each offer a wide range of opportunities for action in relation to the prevention, identification and management of alcohol problems. Any overall alcohol prevention policy will need to accommodate or integrate all these approaches. 'Integration' is a word that is often used in connection with alcohol policy but seldom analysed. In essence, it means that the actions and messages rooted in different perspectives, concerns and objectives are compatible with each other, since different perspectives may suggest contradictory rather than complementary measures. For example, the sensible attempt to 'de-mystify' drink by making it more readily available as an accompaniment to normal routine occasions (a measure suggested by the socio-cultural approach) may conflict with another sensible attempt to regulate outlets and drinking occasions (a measure supported by those concerned to limit overall consumption). However, integration is more than just making sure that a variety of policy initiatives, rooted in a variety of perspectives, do not conflict. Policy initiatives must reinforce each other through the projection of common messages. To take a simple example: it would be extremely helpful for all major alcohol-related initiatives to acknowledge the same level of alcohol consumption as a 'safe level' or, if the idea of a safe level is anathema, to all agree that there is no safe level and that 'the more you drink the more difficulties you will get into'.

Friedner Wittman's contribution falls squarely into the third perspective on alcohol problems which has been outlined above. His concern is with the 'environment of alcohol'; the range, nature and location of alcohol outlets in a community and the kinds of 'drink settings' which they offer. This environment of alcohol should be controlled, he says, with restrictions on availability of addictive substances and limitations on their use. Clearly, any integrated 'alcohol prevention policy' would want to include measures concerned with the environment of alcohol. However, Wittners advocacy of the regulation and manipulation of outlets does contain one assertion that is particularly unhelpful and it is one which bedevils most debates on alcohol policy. He claims that 'micro-level' (i.e. local) controls on the environment of alcohol without macro-level (i.e. national) controls are 'ineffective and self-defeating'. Local action based on local resources, to regulate and manipulate the environment of alcohol will be doomed to failure, he says,without the largescale reinforcement, underpinning and backing of national action.

Most of the prevention policy options arising from the three main perspectives on the alcohol problem share a common characteristic: they seek, in one form or other, action by central policy-makers. Large-scale initiatives are demanded; such as major pieces of legislation, major commitments or the establishment of national bodies. These are usually seen as a necessary prerequisite to any effective response. National action is called for to restrict and control alcohol advertising. The drink-driving law, it is felt, should be amended to lower the permitted blood-alcohol level or the licensing law should be reformed. The price of alcohol, it is claimed, should be regulated through fiscal manipulation to stop it from becoming steadily cheaper in real terms. It is said that major funding should be pumped into health education programmes.

However, this excessive concentration upon the need for national policies, large scale commitments and allocation of resources is a mistake. Firstly, it diverts attention away from the wealth of (largely untapped) resources *at the local level* which could be mobilised in any co-ordinated prevention strategy. Secondly, it assumes that a complicated policy response to a complicated problem must require the action of central government. However, an alcohol policy package is more easily assembled at the local level away from the complications, inhibitions and difficulties surrounding national policy-making. Such a local 'policy package' would lack some dramatic ingredients. It could not, of course, change licensing laws, the retailing law, the drink-driving law or amend taxation policies. Nevertheless, it is entirely possible to do many effective and sensible things *at the local level* without the backing of legislation, massive funding or central government commitments. All that is required is careful identification and and cataloguing of resources, intervention by interested people, at the right time, through appropriate organisations to encourage, promote and co-ordinate minor but important changes in existing practices and procedures.

This emphasis on the significance of local resources and the scope for action they provide in no way reduces the need for an integrated and consistent *national* policy. However, those engaged in the identification, management and prevention of drinking problems should not be waiting for national initiatives, they should be creating policy at the periphery where the problems and many of the resources are located and where, moreover, developments serve as models for central policymakers. Good practice at the periphery is often, as any policy analyst knows, tomorrow's central policy.

What are these local resources which could underpin a local innovative 'alcohol policy'? They cover all the obvious services and the obvious groups of people; treatment units, halfway houses, day centres, counselling services, health and many other professionals and workers from a variety of non-statutory organisations. However, there is more to local resources than these obvious agencies and services. Local resources include all those institutions, groups, laws, regulations, policies, activities, interests and opportunities which could, if identified and mobilised, have something to contribute to a local prevention strategy. The list of potential resources in any locality is endless. Some, however, are briefly outlined below to convey an impression of the kind of activities that creative local policy-makers could and should be stimulating. The examples are taken from the United Kingdom, but the underlying principal 'to identify what is there at the local level and turn it to advantage in the attempt to prevent alcohol problems' is, of course universal.

'Alcohol and work' policies have long been recognised as a vital component of any co-ordinated response toward alcohol problems. The cost of alcohol abuse to industry in terms of accidents, absenteeism and low productivity is high. Moreover, the workplace provides an ideal opportunity to identify problems at an early stage of their development and to intervene with help. Nothing worth the name of a 'national initiative' has been seen in the United Kingdom. However, at the local level there is a whole web of organisations which could be mobilised to promote and put into effect alcohol and work policies or, at least, to assist in the spread of sensible practices in their locality. For example, there are the area offices of the Health and Safety Executive with functional branches serving different types of industry. The Health and Safety Executive is deeply concerned with matters affecting occupational health and safety and its inspectors are beginning to recognise the impact of alcohol problems at work. Then there are Environmental Health Departments based at local level, which have similar concerns in respect of their responsibilities under the Offices, Shops and Railway Premises

Act 1963. The Royal Society for the Prevention of Accidents has a loose national network of local occupational health and safety committees to which members affiliate. Occupational nurses have a well-developed structure of local groups which meet frequently to exchange information and to discuss topics of interest. Health and safety at work officers meet in the local branches of the Institute of Occupational Health and Safety. Personnel managers have a similar local organisational structure. Every locality has branches of the Confederation of British Industry and, of course, a web of trade union officers. A concerted attempt to educate and mobilise all of those groups would certainly have an impact in any locality.

Local branches of insurance companies could have a role to play in the promotion of 'alcohol and work' policies. Insurance companies could and should be made aware of the role of alcohol in accidents at work. If they could be brought to understand that 'alcohol and work' policies were important to employees' well-being and important as part of an industrial safety programme their pressure could help the development and spread of such policies. The existence of an alcohol and work policy coud perhaps be a condition of granting 'employers liability' insurance or qualify the insured firm for a lower premium.

The dangers of alcohol-related accidents in the home could be publicised by home safety committees which permissive legislation empowers local authorities to establish. They would provide perfect vehicles for an important 'alcohol issue'.

It is usually assumed that there is little which can be done locally about alcohol advertising and the presentation of alcohol in the media since these things are determined by codes of guidance and practice at the national level. However, if local groups were to monitor the acceptability of alcohol advertising and media presentation there is no reason why they could not, collectively, constitute an extremely effective lobby on these issues which will be difficult to ignore. But in order for local groups to do this effectively they will have to understand the often complex agreements, codes of guidance and codes of practice which govern alcohol advertising and media presentation. They would also have to understand how to form their response to meet the requirements of the advertising standard and other authorities and how to channel it appropriately.

However, in addition to this local pressure on national controls, regulations and bodies, there is a significant local control dimension to alcohol advertising and media presentation. Local newspapers are party to a specific code of practice setting advertising standards for the provincial press. Local TV and radio stations are also bound by codes of practice. All local radio stations are obliged to transmit a certain amount of 'public service' broadcasting. So there is scope for any local strategy to put pressure on local alcohol advertising and the media presentation of alcohol.

Moreover there is one very important lever within the reach of a local prevention strategy. Local authorities control the content of advertising on hoardings which are erected on their land. They also control the siting of the hoardings. Localities have it within their power to affect the presentation of 'drinking images'. This kind of national control is, as yet, nowhere in sight.

Road Safety Departments and Highways and Road Safety Advisory Committees are found inside local government. Their function is to advise local authorities on all aspects of road safety. Road Safety Departments also mount public education programmes and take the topic of road safety into schools. They are paying increasing attention to the role of alcohol in pedestrian and vehicle accidents and attempting to educate older children in what is involved in 'drinking sensibly'.

These bodies have an obvious role to play in local strategies aimed at tackling alcohol-related problems. Their understanding of alcohol issues, their teaching experience and educational materials constitute an important resource upon which a locality could draw. The potentially most interesting and as yet completely underdeveloped aspect of their work lies in their links with traffic planning inside local government. It is now well-established that crime can, to some extent, be 'planned out' of new estates when they are built. The same kind of 'planning for safety' could be developed in relation to road safety and alcohol. An awareness of alcohol and its relationship to road and pedestrian accidents could affect the siting of crossings, the placement of barriers and so on. In short, Road Safety Departments and Highways and Road Safety Advisory Committees have a body of knowledge and expertise which, if refocused, could be of significance to planners in particular and an overall community response to alcohol problems in general.

During the 1970s there was a move to de-criminalise certain kinds and types of drunkenness offence. The establishment of detoxification centres and the abolition of prison sentences for the offence of simple drunkenness were attempts to steer offenders away from the 'penal revolving door'. These efforts have not been successful. The number of drunkenness offenders now in prison has actually risen since 1977 thanks to the subsequent offence of defaulting on fines which were imposed as an alternative to prison!

In any locality local police forces need to be encouraged to develop a coherent consistent body of practice in relation to public drunkenness. It would, for instance, be helpful for them to develop routine assessment in relation to such questions as: Can the public drunk reach safe refuge? What is the level of inebriation? Is the behaviour boisterous or offensive or dangerous or criminal? Is the drunk in company or alone? and so on. At present police practice varies widely from place to place and time to time and in any locality needs codifying.

Similarly, court practice, particularly fining policy, has an important part to play in any local strategy aimed at decriminalising certain types of drunkenness offence. It is obvious that by setting fines at a nominal level the problem of subsequent jail sentences for non-payment of fines is avoided. This policy along with the changes in police practice, would, if it was thought desirable in any locality, keep the simple drunkenness offender out of jail.

Under-age drinking and associated problems are widespread. Once again, changes in local practice could have much to offer. For example, an experiment was conducted during the summer of 1978 in Torquay, England, which involved the police in making regular visits to public houses to 'remind' licencees of their obligations under the licensing laws and to constitute a 'presence' which could be noted by the clientele. Under-age drinking declined and there was a significant decrease in drunkenness, rowdyism and associated offences. The police clearly have a great deal to offer a local alcohol strategy and although they constitute a very visible resource, their contribution has, to date, been underrated.

The list of local resources, opportunities and activities is limitless. It could be extended to include, for example, the use of probation orders to promote counselling aid for drinking problems; staff training in off-sale retail outlets as a condition of the retail licence; insertion of specific material dealing with alcohol problems into housing departments' Codes of Guidance which supplement the legislation dealing with homelessness; training of local authority housing estate managers to recognise and respond to drink problems among tenants and so on and so on.

A carefully planned and co-ordinated local strategy would not only have an impact on a locality, it would cost little in extra effort to contact, inform and lobby the national groups, organisations and bodies which lie behind so many local resources and activities. In the area of 'alcohol and work' alone there are a number of professional organisations representing workers concerned with occupational health and safety, a course examination validating body, a training centre run by RoSPA, an academic study group and a variety of institutions of higher education offering courses in the subject. This web of hidden contact or pressure points above the local level but linked to it is found behind every local resource.

The ability to do something about the 'alcohol problem', complex though it is, does not lie exclusively with central government. There are some big levers in that particular cockpit but localities also have an impressive array of controls and there are fewer problems surrounding their manipulation.

David Robinson & Philip Tether

Although the viewpoints represented above differ in the weight they give to local vis-à-vis national influences, both are clear that individuals are not powerless to influence the drinking habits of their locality. In every part of the country there are many people with diverse reasons for being concerned about alcohol and its problems. If these individuals can be brought together in a neighbourhood they would represent an important force for change in that community. Their diversity is an asset because the range of experience they represent is likely to lead to innovative responses that are not restricted by the sometimes blinkered perceptions of health or social services. It is equally probable that the very specificity of their concerns will give rise to the kind of clearly focused intervention that is often most effective and easily evaluated.

15 THE FISCAL AND LEGISLATIVE DEBATE

Introduction

In choosing to combine fiscal and legislative considerations within the confines of a single chapter, we recognise here, as in so many other areas (genetics; health education) how far brevity imposes a tyranny of simplification upon our contributors. Yet there is, perhaps, no other area from which so many people seem to expect as much as they do from legal controls. Whether the Ledermann hypothesis is revered as having been written in letters of fire upon tablets of stone, whether it is grudgingly accepted as a worthwhile hypothesis with only marginally fewer flaws than its competitors, or whether it is rejected out of hand as neo-prohibitionist cant, there remains a surprising degree of unanimity regarding the potentially impressive impact that taxation and other legal measures would be likely to have in influencing patterns of alcohol consumption.

One difficulty, even more relevant here than in many other preventive strategies, is that the law can be perceived as operating through restrictions which are imposed as much upon the legitimate freedom of the normal drinker as they are upon those who are drinking excessively. Why, goes the cry, should the majority have to suffer in order to protect the minority? Part of the purpose of this chapter is to try to clarify just what suffering might be taken to mean in these circumstances and just how far freedom is in reality likely to be restricted for those who, in any case, have no wish to evade the law as it stands.

Rather than attempting to include all shades of opinion on the many complex economic and legal technicalities which season debates on law and on taxation we asked our next two contributors to present their own views of what the control issues were in the different areas which have formed the basis of previous attempts to establish social policy on alcohol. Taxation, the great leveller, or the great reinforcer of differentials, seemed to us very much at the core of thinking in this area in the past. Scandinavian countries press for higher and higher levels of purchase tax in order to make alcohol into a very special commodity indeed, whilst the alcohol-producing countries (especially those engaged in viticulture) actively campaign for government aid to wineries and the creation of tarrif arrangements designed to benefit their own interests and to protect their traditional or expanding markets.

Brendan Walsh, of the Department of Political Economy at University College, Dublin, undertook to give us his overview of the possible impact of fiscal measures on alcohol abuse.

Fiscal Measures and Alcohol Abuse

Economists are more involved in trying to determine the consequences of policies rather than prescribing what policies should be adopted. The typical question an economist tries to answer is 'how effective is this policy in attaining the objectives set for it'? But the dividing line between that type of question and questions such as 'should we try to attain these objectives in the first place'? is not hard and fast. This is nowhere more obvious than in regard to alcohol taxation. It is very hard to disentangle questions regarding the effectiveness of alcohol taxation in curbing alcohol-related problems from those concerned more with what we mean by 'abuse' and whether the state should try to curb these behaviours.

To undestand why economists tend to shift the argument to this more philosophical level, we must recall the strong influenceof a liberal political and moral philosophy on mainstream contemporary economies. A basic tenet of this view of human behaviour is that by and large individuals are the best judges of what contributes to their own happiness, and should be permitted to pursue this happiness in the maximum freedom consistent with other members of society doing the same.

The logic of this argument implies that if a solitary individual wishes to drink heavily, even to the point of premature death, that is his own business and the state is not justified in intervening. However, economists would concede a case for intervention if his drinking inflicts damage on others. The most important possibility is, of course, the tendency for heavy drinkers to make other members of their families bear much of the cost of their behaviour, but alcohol-related violence also spills over to the wider community. Heavy drinking, like smoking, also imposes costs on national health services and this gives the state a financial interest in altering these patterns of consumption. It could be argued that the state has a role to play in trying to avert behaviour that eventually becomes addictive because the typical young drinker may be unaware of the longer-run consequences of his present consumption patterns. One way in which the state could try to allow for the effects of these 'consumption externalities' is by the imposition of a tax on the offending commodity so as to bring the cost of acquiring it more closely into line with its total cost to society as distinct from the money costs of producing it.

This line of reasoning is certainly *not* why certain countries tax alcoholic beverages very heavily. The main reason for these heavy taxes, which are especially important in the United Kingdom, is the simple desire to raise revenue, and experience shows that taxing alcohol is an efficient way of doing so. In the late nineteenth century, the tax on beer, spirits, and tobacco provided the United Kingdom Exchequer with most of its peacetime revenue, a situation which led one MP to declare that the habitual drunkard was 'the sheet anchor of the British Constitution'! It is only in recent years that public health workers and those concerned with alcohol abuse have turned to taxation as a possible method of controlling the problems caused by excessive drinking.

If we accept the proposition that excessive drinking is a social problem in which the state has a legitimate involvement, two empirical issues arise before we should advocate higher taxes an as appropriate policy response. The first is, will the higher prices that follow heavier taxation lead to a reduction in total consumption? The second is, will the fall in total consumption, assuming it occurs, result in a drop in alcohol-related problems? Crucial to answering the first question is a knowledge of the 'elasticity of demand'. Studies of consumers' behaviour tend to show that in countries such as Britain higher beer prices do not result in a marked drop in beer consumption. Higher spirits prices have a more pronounced effect on consumption but the results are still not dramatic. If the price of a commodity that is 'inelastic' in this manner is raised, consumption does not fall proportionately, but expenditure on the commodity is increased The main consequence is a transfer of purchasing power from drinkers to the Exchequer.

This is one of the limitations on the fiscal approach to the problem of alcohol abuse. As an illustration it is it possible to cite the case of Ireland, where alcohol has been heavily taxed throughout this century, and beer is probably more expensive in relation to income than in any other country, but where none the less excessive drinking causes serious social problems that increased as consumption rose in line with rising incomes during the 1960s and early 1970s. The most obvious consequence of the heavy taxation is the exceptional proportion of personal income (about 10 per cent) that the Irish spend on alcohol.

Another limitation of the fiscal approach to alcohol problems lies in the tendency for high taxes to penalise unduly poorer households where one or more members drink. The risk of 'regressiveness' in this sense is greatest in the case of beer, which is traditionally the workingman's drink in Northern Europe. In addition to this anomalous outcome as between different income groups, heavy taxation of a commodity that may loom large in one household's spending, but not figure at all in others, can generate a sense of arbitrariness and unfairness.

Some consideration should also be given to the question of how to tax alcohol. The traditional British alcohol excise taxes are heavier per litre of alcohol in spirits than in beer. This probably reflects a belief that spirits will bear heavier taxation, but it is also consistent with the view that spirits drinking tends to be more closely associated with problem drinking. A difficulty with excise taxes is the need to adjust them in the annual Budget to keep pace with inflation. In the United States, failure to adjust federal alcohol taxes during the current inflation has resulted in a steady fall in the real level of the tax. In Britain and Ireland the annual Budget increases generate political opprobium for the ruling party.

It would be a foolhardy economist who would venture a judgement that a country's alcohol taxes are too high or too low. Ultimately this verdict must be based on moral and political considerations and not made on narrow economic grounds. The economic ramifications of altering the level of taxation must however be borne in mind when a new policy towards alcohol is advanced.

Brendan Walsh

Clearly, issues to do with alcohol taxation are complex, both from an ethical (e.g. freedom versus paternalism) point of view and from a technical (e.g. ad valorem versus excise taxes) point of view. That alcohol should be subject to taxation seems to be a reasonable presumption, unanimously accepted by those involved in its production, distribution and consumption as well as by those governmental forces most likely to benefit from the revenue thus raised. The questions of an ethical and technical nature, of which the parenthetical examples given above are but the first round, centre upon how it is to be taxed and how much it is to be taxed. For a fuller examination of the specific stands in this debate, readers are referred to 'Economics and Alcohol' another recently published book from Croom Helm (edited by Marcus Grant, Martin Plant and Alan Williams) and in particular to Chapters 9-13, which include a longer contribution from Brendan Walsh himself.

There are, however, other legislative strategies relevant to the prevention of alcohol problems which do not have to do with the determination of appropriate fiscal levels. Broadly speaking it is possible to divide the law's response to the problems caused by excessive drinking into two distinct areas. Firstly, and taxation is part of this area, controls over availability of alcohol can be introduced, laws, that is to say, designed to control the drink. Secondly, given that it is the excesses that the law is seeking to remedy (and setting aside for the time being the state's desire to raise revenue by tidy, predictable, inelastic means) laws can be introduced which are designed to control the drunk. Such laws, seeking to limit the impact of intoxicated individuals upon the rest of society, tend to focus upon the more visible manifestations of drunkenness, such as public inebriety or the phenomenon of the drunk driver. We asked Robin Room, Director of the Alcohol Research Group, Institute of Epidemiology and Behavioural Medicine, Medical Research Institute of San Francisco at Pacific Medical Center, Berkeley, California, to look first at the legislative strategies which relate to drunkenness and then, linking the debate back to Brendan Walsh's contribution, to take up the wider issues of alcohol control laws in general.

Legislative Strategies and the Prevention of Alcohol Problems

For some years now, I have been working alongside a legal scholar, Jim Mosher, as he explores the interaction of alcohol issues with legal questions, and in particular the potential of legislative and regulatory strategies for the prevention of alcohol-related problems. As Jim's tasks and work have gradually unfolded, what has struck me most forcibly is the astonishing diversity of ways in which laws, regulations, and their administration can end up impinging on alcohol consumption and consequent problems. Obscure 'tax-shelter' provisions in an income-tax code can fuel the transformation of a large grape industry from raisin and table grape to wine grape production. Fear of legal liability can shut down a college student representative body's effort to prevent drunk driving by providing bus-service to the border of an adjacent state with a lower minimum drinking age. Changes in mental hospital involuntary-commitment procedures, combined with alterations in state fiscal incentives for local government, can result in the disappearance of 'alcoholic psychosis' as a medical category. These examples, all from the United States, can be multiplied in every country. In a real sense, nearly every prevention strategy considered in the debates in this book is a legislative strategy: alcohol education in the schools, alcohol tax levels, and environmental controls are all shaped by legislation and regulation.

We shall concentrate here, though, on a relatively small range of potential legislative strategies to reduce alcohol-related problems: those which seek to limit or shape the individual's drinking and/or behaviors associated with the drinking, either directly by influencing the individual drinker or indirectly by influencing those around the drinker. The prototypical examples of laws attempting a direct influence are public drunkenness and drunk driving laws; and of those attempting an indirect influence, alcohol control and 'dramshop' (seller's liability) laws. While these by no means exhaust the legislative strategies aimed at influencing drinking and associated behaviors, we shall focus our attention on these three areas.

We are primarily considering here the public health and public order functions of such laws. But disentangling these purposes or functions from others is not always easy. Susanna Barrows has uncovered conclusive evidence of the use of alcohol control laws in the 1850s and 1870s in France as an instrument of political repression, under the cover of preserving public order. The class biases in the enforcement of public drunkenness laws have long been recognized. 'Public health' and 'social sanitation', not to mention 'maintaining peace and order', are often convenient rubrics for other purposes of the powerful. The fact of these other purposes, however, should not divert us from examining the potential role and power of legislative strategies in the prevention of alcohol-related problems.

Public Drunkenness Laws

In the Anglo-American legal tradition, criminal laws penalizing the drunkard and enforced by secular – rather than ecclesiastical –courts date back only to the opening of the seventeenth century. However, the English law of 1606 was preceded by penalties against drunkenness in ecclesiastical law, criminal laws concerning vagrants and 'sturdy beggars' designed to control the labor supply, and legislation designed to discourage tavern-haunting, often by penalizing the tavern-owner. While the 1606 law may have owed something to the growth of Puritan influence in Parliament, it also reflected the atrophy of the authority of ecclesiastical courts. Its preamble spelled out the aims of the act, which were the prevention of sins as well as crimes, not to mention the improvement of industrial efficiency:

Whereas the loathsom and odious Sin of Drunkenness is of late grown into common Use within this Realm, being the Root and Foundation of many other enormous Sins, as Bloodshed, Stabbing, Murder, Swearing, Fornication, Adultery, and such like, to the great Dishonour of God, and of our Nation, the Overthrow of many good Arts and manual Trades, the Disabling of Divers Workmen, and the general Impoverishing of many good Subjects, abusively wasting the good Creatures of God . . .

The Act, which remained the law of England for 266 years, and profoundly affected later legislation in the United States, made no distinction between public and private drunkenness; in fact, concern at the time was more directed at 'inordinate Haunting and Tipling in Inns' than at demeanor on the streets. It was not until 1872 that English law assumed the form in which such legislation is discussed today, of prohibiting only public drunkenness.

A comparative history of criminal laws concerning drunkenness remains to be written. It is clear, however, that national experiences in this respect are very different. Public drunkenness only became a crime in France in 1873, as part of a repressive crackdown that tended to equate immorality with sedition. Public drunkenness is not a crime in Switzerland. Many nations that formally proscribe public drunkenness do not energetically enforce their laws. Judging by the available literature, it is particularly the Nordic and Eastern European societies, along with what have been called the 'Anglomorph' nations, that evince a longstanding and substantial public concern with the control of drunken demeanor, particularly in public places. It is no accident that many of these societies have a strong and traditional cultural association of drunkenness with violence and unpredictable behavior, and that many were strongholds of the temperance movement in the late nineteenth and early twentieth centuries. However, the task of disentangling the historical patterns of interplay between a strong popular movement against drinking, an especial cultural association of drinking with violence and social disruption, and a concern about public drunkenness as a crime *per se*, remains an agenda for future work.

The English Act of 1606 prescribed a fine for tippling, and a stiffer fine for being found drunk; then as now, those unable to pay the fine were likely to be confined instead. As urban police forces became more effective in the early nineteenth century, the result was a steady stream of public inebriates through local gaols and workhouses. By the end of the nineteenth century, one can find evidence all over the English-speaking world that those in charge of the processing of public drunkenness in large cities — the magistrates and the gaol-wardens — were fed up with what later became called the 'revolving door' of the police court and lockup. The 'inebriates' asylums' of the late nineteenth century were in part a response to these complaints. But a wide-ranging and sustained response to these pleas had to await the post-1945 era of the 'welfare state'. At first in Eastern Europe, and then in North America and the Nordic countries, there were moves towards the 'decriminalization' of public drunkenness, and the substitution of medical or social 'sobering-up stations' or 'detox facilities'. In the US these moves came in the wake of a crescendo of public drunkenness arrests, reflecting another outgrowth of the welfare state: 'urban renewal' programs commonly used these arrests as a tool in a war of attrition over possession of the potentially valuable territory occupied by Skid Rows.

There is in fact very little English-language literature directly concerned with the preventive effect of public drunkenness laws with respect to public order. The large numbers of arrests, and the fact that many offenders were arrested repeatedly, were regarded as *prima facie* evidence of the ineffectiveness of public drunkenness laws as either general or specific deterrents. Although even before the last 15 years there were occasional 'natural experiments', when exasperated judges brought the process to a halt by such direct expedients as ordering the destruction of the forms on which public drunkenness arrests were recorded, I know of no US studies of changes in the prevalence of drunken behavior in the absence of criminal sanctions. In line with the concerns of the postwar era, when alternatives to arrests for public drunkenness have been evaluated, the formal criteria of success have not been the effect on public order, but rather whether the alternative saves police effort, or whether the clients are more likely to attain permanent sobriety. In contrast, prior to decriminalization in Finland, there was an experimental study of the 'preventive effect of fines for drunkenness' — i.e. of keeping drunks in gaol for a short sentence in lieu of a fine, as opposed to releasing them the next morning. The study showed that the men did not even recognize that they had been treated differently; those released early assumed that they had not been as drunk as they thought. But while this study played a part in the discussions over decriminalization in Finland, Finnish researchers agree that it did not determine events: decriminalization would have occurred in any case, and in fact the study's results were overinterpreted in the political debate.

Thus, while there is by now an extensive – if often fugitive – North American literature evaluating the great social experiment in the decriminalization of public drunkenness, very little of it is directly concerned with the question of whether and how in fact the behaviors against which public drunkenness laws are directed may be affected by the existence and enforcement of those laws. Nevertheless, the following tentative conclusions may be offered:

(a) Despite a federal policy in favor of decriminalization since the early 1970s, arrests for public drunkenness remain an important police function in many parts of US, and still account for a substantial proportion of all arrests. Even in states which are considered to have complied with the model 'Uniform Act', provisions on compulsory treatment etc. often diverge greatly from the model Act. Though much of the motivation for decriminalization was a concern for the civil liberties of public inebriates (and hence included opposition to long-term compulsory treatment), this agenda has been only partially carried out.

(b) The preferred alternative to public drunkenness arrests, short-term detoxification followed by voluntary treatment, has not worked out as social scientists in the 1960s thought it would: typically only 10-30 per cent of detox clients agree to and go to further treatment. In many places, evaluators have found that those involved in the processing of public drunkenness talk of the 'revolving door' having been replaced by the 'spinning door'. Anecdotally, at least, chronic public inebriates are often reported to spend more total time on the street (and thus drinking) than in the old criminal system, to the annoyance of local merchants and police, and to the detriment of the inebriates' physical condition. Very little is known about the effects of decriminalization on the behavior of a group which is much larger than the Skid Row group, but bulks less heavily in the arrest or detox systems – those who are only sporadically publicly drunk, and who are presumably better candidates for deterrence or treatment.

(c) The new non-police pick-up services for drunks inadvertently discovered a substantial number of chronic drunkenness cases in medical need of detox services, but falling outside the traditional police concern only with public drunkenness. This suggests that a concern only with the latter, whether from a criminal or a non-criminal perspective, is an inefficient way of deterring or dealing with the acute medical complications of heavy drinking.

(d) The experience of the last 15 years suggests that American culture as a whole remains unwilling to tolerate public drunkenness – i.e. to decriminalize it and simply accept it as part of the urban street scene. Moral concerns about the government furthering a drinking habit cut short most experiments with municipal 'wet hotels', which attempt a pragmatic solution to the problem of public drinking by moving it inside. The concern over public drunkenness is not acute in the general population (surveys in urban areas suggest that householders in general are more concerned about beercans and wine bottles in their front yard than about public drunkenness), but it is acute among small merchants, who rightly fear that their customers will dislike stepping over sleeping drunks on their doorsteps, and among the new middle-class 'gentrifiers' moving back into the core cities. Both of these groups are politically potent in local government. Disturbance of the peace by public drunkenness is very much a 'grassroots' issue, and local communities (which tend to perceive public drunks as 'outsiders') are always trying, as they have been since colonial times, to figure out constitutional ways to get them to 'move on down the line'.

(e) In California, at least, public drunkenness arrest figures began to fall in the 1960s, before decriminalization became a national policy. Several factors could account for this: a decline in urban renewal 'Skid Row removal' projects; a decline in Skid Row populations, a decline in civic and police concern with public drunkenness as a crime; a decline in public drunkenness as a behavior. There is scattered evidence supporting each of the first three factors, and no evidence at all concerning the fourth. But, as noted above, there remains a substantial level of public concern with public drinking and drunkenness, and the forms in which decriminalization has been tried have not satisfied that concern. The recent report of the International Study of Alcohol Control Experiences predicted that the current combination of increasing concerns about alcohol problems, the increased acceptance of alcohol in everyday life, and the fiscal crisis of the welfare state may bring renewed tendencies 'towards punitive and disciplinary control of individual deviant drinkers'. This prediction has already been borne out for public drunkenness in California, with the passage of a 1981 law potentially increasing the criminal penalties for public drunkenness.

(f) On the face of it, public drunkenness laws do not seem likely to be highly effective in terms of general deterrence. Unlike drunk driving laws, they include no clear standard of behavior concerning what constitutes an infraction. One of the curiosities of Anglo-American law is the refusal of judges or legislatures to spell out what is meant by being 'drunk'. For public drunkenness laws to be an effective deterrent, this unclear standard presumably has to be kept clearly in mind by the potential lawbreaker through an evening of drinking and deciding where to go next. Though it is possible that this partly reflects a greater effectiveness as a deterrent in other subpopulations, the population segments to which public drunkenness laws are most commonly applied have the least stake in society and thus the least motivation to be deterred by threat of arrest. The high rate of recidivism does not give us confidence in the specific deterrent effect of such laws and lends support to sociological arguments that they are an instrument of 'secondary deviance' which helps to define and create a subculture of repeat offenders.

On the other hand, it is clear from the US evaluations that the alternative of detoxification and voluntary treatment, while often more humane than the drunk tank, is no more effective – and perhaps less effective – in preventing offenses to public order due to drunkenness. For that matter, it is not clear whether offering competing alternatives to public drinking, such as 'wet hotels', will in fact reduce public drunkenness.

For a society which really seriously wants to reduce public drunkenness, however, there does seem to be an effective answer, at least in the short term. Studies of alcohol distribution strikes in Nordic countries suggest that public drunkenness, as a behavior, not just as a criminal statistic – can be dramatically affected in the short term by changes in the availability of alcohol. Even though the overall level of alcohol consumption in such circumstances is often only slightly affected, several studies show public drunkenness and alcohol-related|violence dropping dramatically when normal distribution channels were disrupted or shut off. Such studies strongly challenge the comfortable assumption in the American literature that consumption by late-stage alcoholics will be little affected by control of availability, and lend retrospective credence to earlier studies such as Carter's and Shadwell's accounts of the effect of control measures on public drunkenness in Britain in the First World War. The historical record suggests that such effects can only be extended over the longer term in times of national crisis or in conjunction with a substantial mass anti-alcohol movement.

Drunk Driving Laws

In contrast to public drunkenness legislation, the history of drunk driving legislation is both short and relatively well documented cross-nationally. H. Laurence Ross' recent review, *Deterrence of the Drinking Driver: An International Survey*, provides a handy compendium of the available knowledge. Some concern over drunk driving was shown in many countries quite early in the century, and was expressed in what

Ross terms 'classical' legislation against driving 'under the influence' or 'while intoxicated'. The problem with such legislation, as with laws on public drunkenness, was that it did not offer either the motorist or enforcement agencies a predictable standard of behavior which violated the law. Increased concern as traffic grew in the interwar period, combined with the technological innovation of blood-alcohol measurement, made possible a new kind of law, first adopted in Norway in 1936, in which the presence of a given level of alcohol in the blood became a crime *per se*. In most places within the last 20 years, such laws were gradually adopted not only in other Scandinavian and in 'Anglomorph' nations, but also in French- and German-speaking parts of Europe. (The most stringent European laws are in Eastern Europe, but little is known of their effectiveness in the rather different traffic situation there.)

Cumulatively, this and other changes in the law tended to increase the certainty and the severity of punishent for drunk driving, and sometimes also the celerity. In Ross' view, the changes thus represent a crucial test of the general deterrence model of the effect of criminal laws. It might be added that the population involved in drinking-driving should be more susceptible than the population committing most crimes to deterrent effects, since drunk driving is almost unique among reported crimes in involving large numbers of 'respectable' offenders with much to lose from a conviction. Certainly, we would expect the deterrent effects to be greater in this population than in, say, a Skid Row population.

Ross concludes that there is evidence in each of the countries from which data are available that the introduction of 'Scandinavian-type' laws did have a deterrent effect on drinking-driving behavior. 'In many cases experience has shown that a convincing increase in threatened punishment from drinking and driving has been followed by notable and measurable declines in associated crashes. However, an equally important lesson for the policymaker is that in no case does the accomplishment of deterrence seem to have been permanent . . . Subsequent events have revealed a gradual return of the drinking-driving problems to the level of a pre-existing trend.' Typically, the *perceived* threat of being apprehended initially increased much more than the *actual* threat did, and drivers eventually realized this. A greatly increased actual level of deterrence would not only impinge on protected individual rights in many nations but would require very considerable increases in social resources devoted to traffic control.

In agreement with other writers in the drunk driving literature, then, Ross concludes that, while further developments in legal deterrence are 'feasible and promising' as a strategy of prevention, greater reductions in drunk driving casualties may be attained by working 'for a safer environment for drunks to drive in (sturdier cars, safe highways)'. Ross comments that 'one of the general lessons from the social scientific study of law is that effects are much easier to obtain from laws directed at a small, controllable number of organizational entities than from laws directed to masses of individuals. Desegregation in housing is obtained by edicts directed to housing developers and authorities; taxes are most easily collected through withholding by bureaucratic employers; schools enforce the innoculation of children; and seat belts are installed in vehicles because of rules directed at manufacturers (but lose their efficacy in part becase individual-centered rules are needed to guarantee their use). Safety efforts achievable through manipulation of the vehicle or the road form the object of this most efficacious type of law.'

Alcohol Control Laws

The comments by Ross just quoted provide a good introduction to a discussion of alcohol control laws, since most alcohol control laws are directed at those in the business of making alcohol available, and not at the ultimate consumer. While they are backed by the criminal law as a last resort, they thus operate primarily at the level of economic threats and incentives. Where the state does not itself manage the distribution of alcohol, it licenses others to do so, on condition that they comply with a set of legislative and regulatory conditions. The threat of loss of livelihood involved is often a stronger threat and a cheaper one to enforce than serious criminal penalties, and thus is a potentially very powerful instrument of the state. But by the same token, those affected by such controls are often better organized and positioned than are the mass of individual voters or consumers to defend themselves from state action in a pluralistic political order. In the absence of strong public sentiment, state regulatory powers tend thus to be a ratchet mechanism, wound in only one direction − in the direction of gradually looser controls − by the vested interests the state has licensed.

As implied above, state control over the drink-seller generally predates state control over the drinker. In medieval England, state control over the sale of alcohol began primarily in the form of price fixing statutes, enforced after 1330 by the provision that violators should not be permitted to reopen until they had 'the King's Licence'. Acts of 1552 and 1553 gave local justices of the peace power to select and require bonds of those keeping alehouses and wine shops. By these Acts, the retailers were made responsible for the behavior that they permitted among their customers. In America as in Britain, the subsequent history of alcohol control measures, to the extent they were maintained, remained until well into the nineteenth century a matter for local consideration, oriented primarily around controlling disruptive behavior or idleness associated with taverns. The British history included two periods when licensing was effectively abolished for at least part of the retail trade (1690-1743 and 1830-69); both experiments seem to have produced a disastrous increase in heavy drinking, curtailed only with great difficulty.

In the functional sense of state regulation of alcohol trades, alcohol control thus has a lengthy history, extending in fact back to some of the first laws of which there are written records. But in the last century 'alcohol control' took on an added level of meaning, in terms of a general strategy for managing and reducing the public health and order problems associated with drinking. As a self-conscious strategy, alcohol control emerged in reaction to and as an alternative to the strategy of prohibition, both at the local level (local control vs. local option) and at national levels (state or national prohibition vs. state and national control systems). To a large extent, this self-conscious strategy of alcohol control initially took the form of a strategy of local or state monopoly over at least part of the alcohol trade. But even the most thoroughgoing monopoly systems did not monopolize all parts and levels of the trade, and the concept of alcohol control came to include the older and alternative strategy of state licensing of private and co-operative enterprises.

The concept of a state monopoly over psychoactive drugs was by no means new in the nineteenth century. The old regimes all over Europe had copied the Venetian state monopoly on tobacco as the most lucrative way of organizing tobacco revenues (these monopolies have survived all subsequent revolutions and changes in government in such countries as France and Austria). But these older monopolies had been primarily motivated by the state's need for revenue. When the town of Gothenburg in Sweden installed a municipal monopoly of alcohol sales in 1865 (following an earlier initiative in 1850), the primary motivation was the prevention of alcohol-related problems.

The idea of a municipal or county alcohol monopoly spread all over the Nordic and English-speaking world in the succeeding decades, surfacing in such far-flung forms as municipal beer-halls in southern Africa and the 'community hotel' in Renmark, South Australia. A number of communities in US Southern states adopted a municipal 'dispensary system', beginning in 1891. By that time, the alternative of a monopoly organized at the state or national level had emerged: Switzerland set up a Federal Alcohol Monopoly on spirits in 1885; the first US state monopoly system was set up in South Carolina by Ben Tillman in 1893. The British cabinet came within one vote of nationalizing the beer industry during the First World War, but in the event a state monopoly was installed only in two shipyard areas in Britain.

Like many such schemes, Tillman's dispensary system had been explicitly adopted as an alternative to statewide Prohibition. The idea of at least a partial state monopoly thus re-emerged as a potential alternative as dissatisfaction grew with the national and provincial prohibitions installed in Nordic and North American countries in the 1910s and 1920s. An influential study commissioned by John D. Rockefeller recommended the system for the US State alcohol monopoly systems were set up in all Canadian provinces, in Finland, Sweden and Norway, and in 19 US states. Other American states adopted the alternative of a highly-regulated and relatively coherent license system, governed by an Alcoholic Beverage Control (ABC) code.

In their broad outlines, these systems installed at the repeal of the various national prohibitions remain intact today. However, the International Study of Alcohol Control Experiences, which included three study sites (Finland, Ontario and California) which had experienced prohibition and four (Switzerland, the Netherlands, Poland and Ireland) which had not; found that in all of the study sites there had been a gradual erosion of alcohol controls in the 30 years after 1945. The most far-reaching changes occurred in the two sites (Finland and Ontario) which had had the most stringent alcohol control systems. In places like California, while the form of an alcohol control system remains, encrusted by now with a baroque superstructure of special exceptions, in its functioning the system is primarily concerned with adjudicating between competing interests in the alcohol trades. There are some signs in many countries of a halt in the late 1970s to the 'ratchet-mechanism' of further liberalizations. There are even some minor increases in control, including raising of minimum drinking ages in the US and Canada, shortened opening hours in Finland, Norway and Alaska, and requirements that alcohol be physically separated from other commodities in stores in Ireland and Switzerland. But in terms of net effect, the availability of alcohol has been considerably increased in most industrialized nations in the last 30 years.

In US discussions of alcoholic beverage control, it has often been fashionable to decry the incredible complexity of the ABC system in its current form, to point to the inconsistencies from one place to another in legal provisions, and simply to assert the ineffectiveness of alcohol control laws as a strategy of prevention. There is always a strong temptation to conclude that a longstanding law is ineffective, since its failures will tend to be apparent while its successes remain hidden. But the only true test of the effectiveness of laws is to watch what happens when they change.

In recent years, evidence has been building up from a variety of sources that, given the right circumstances, controls on alcohol availability can be surprisingly effective, both in altering the level and patterning of alcohol consumption and in affecting the incidence of alcohol-related problems. The relaxations of control in Finland were followed by a considerable increase in alcohol consumption and in alcohol-related problems; lowering the drinking age in US states in most cases produced an increase in teenage drunk-driving casualties; interrupted time-series analyses with Nordic data show a temporal association between increases in alcohol consumption and increases in the rate of violent crimes. In the other direction, a series of 'strike studies' in Finland, Norway, Sweden, Poland, Australia and Canada have shown that temporary reductions in the supply of alcohol have often produced surprisingly strong reductions in alcohol-related problems.

Cumulatively, these studies make clear that in some circumstances alcohol control measures have an effect on consumption and alcohol-related problems separate from any effects of cultural or other factors. But any practical application of this general finding must take into account the particularities of cultural patterns and change. Short-term changes as in a strike period are not necessarily the same as long-term changes. General principles of social justice or equity were often involved in the liberalizations of control that occurred in the postwar period, and there is little sign in any industrialized country of a really substantial shift towards a restrictive control system. In technical terms, alcohol controls may be a potentially powerful preventive tool, but decisions on whether and how the tool is to be employed are properly decisions for the political process.

Two conclusions which could be drawn from the alcohol control studies also apply more generally to studies of legislative approaches to prevention. Classic legal-impact study designs are designed to measure the effect of a discrete legal change, irrespective of its environment. But the effectiveness of a particular legal change is often dependent on the environment in which it occurs: an isolated change may be much less effective than the same change occurring in a supportive environment of related changes. Both in research and in designing prevention strategies, attention must be paid to the whole system of law and custom in which the changes occur.

Secondly, in gauging the effect of alcohol controls and other legal measures, it is important to pay attention not only to the face value of the laws involved, but also to different cultural traditions of the meaning of legislative action. It is my impression that Nordic and perhaps British researchers have often been puzzled by the attention that Gusfield and other American social scientists have directed to the symbolic dimensions of law. There is a symbolic aspect to lawmaking in all societies, but it seems that American legislators are more likely than Nordic legislators to give primacy to the symbolic dimension. Unlike some American laws, a Scandinavian law means what it says, even if it also has other meanings. In the field of alcohol controls, the US is by no means at an extreme in terms of symbolic and unenforced legislation. A recent study for the Pan American Health Organization has uncovered a rich archaeology of forgotten alcohol control laws in Central American republics.

As I have implied in the course of this discussion, the recent history of legislative approaches to the prevention of alcohol problems in industrialized countries is marked by inconsistency: there has been a heavy reliance on criminal law approaches to drunk driving, while legal and regulatory approaches tend to have been de-emphasized in the fields of public drunkenness and alcohol controls. In terms of the most effective possible strategies for reducing the level of alcohol-related problems, what is needed is a convergent approach involving a variety of mutually reinforcing strategies. There are limits to what can be accomplished with legislative strategies; on the other hand, legislative and regulatory approaches will be an important component of any effective integrated policy. Laws and regulations that are directed not at persuading or threatening the alcohol consumer, but rather at influencing the fact and environment of consumption and preventing untoward consequences, will play a crucial part in such a policy.

Robin Room

In a way, therefore, what emerges from this chapter is that the debate is not just whether the law can contribute to the prevention of alcohol problems nor how best to develop existing imperfect strategies. Rather, it has to do with two separate and distinct legislative thrusts, one directed towards the problematic individual and the other towards society as a whole, which have not in the past been seen as having too much to do with each other. Indeed, from an historical perspective, it would be possible, as Robin Room does to an extent, to see the changing legislative response to alcohol problems as the story of the relative emphasis given at different times to 'drink laws' and 'drunk laws'. The question posed by this debate is whether it might not be more rational and to the greater good of society to attempt to achieve a reconciliation between these two approaches and to adopt a more integrated style of law-making designed to confront the whole range of alcohol problems and not just those which are most visible.

16 THE ETHICAL DEBATE

Population surveys in Britain and the USA commonly find that most people support the view that a man's drinking is his own affair and not the concern of anyone else. Advocates of alcohol control policies commonly earn epithets such as killjoys or busybodies. Those who criticise them are perhaps concerned that the state is interfering with their own freedom to drink. The issues underlying this common argument raise important questions concerning individual rights and responsibilities. We felt that the ethical debate surrounding state interventionism required careful analysis and asked two philosophers, both of whom have been involved with alcohol policy, to look closely at the relationship between the individual, the state and alcohol.

Professor Dan Beauchamp of the Department of Health Policy and Administration at the University of North Carolina opens the debate and this is followed by a commentary on his views by Dr. Ian Thompson of the Scottish Health Education Group.

The Individual, the State and Alcohol

The renewal of interest in alcohol policy in recent years raises basic questions about the relation of the individual and the state. In seeking to minimise the damaging consequences from alcohol, the state in Western democratic societies must consider the rights of individuals. Basic rights include the rights of free speech, free assembly, religion, and so forth. Many also would include the right to make one's own choices and to determine one's own good. This may be called the right of autonomy. To override an individual's right of autonomy in order to protect the interest of that same individual is considered paternalistic. In this view the state has little legitimate interest in protecting the individual from himself. As John Stuart Mill argued over a century ago in his famous essay *On Liberty*, the only legitimate interest the state has in limiting the liberty of an individual is to prevent harm to others (Mill 1974).

Mill's essay contains many references to questions raised in dealing with alcohol policy. Mill was even opposed to the use of taxes to promote the good or the welfare of the drinker. Despite Mill's argument, most democratic societies have maintained strong powers to regulate drinking. Still, there is something of a guilty conscience about their use. This is because we have increasingly become 'liberal' societies, all professing the freedom of the individual to pursue his own good as long as this freedom does not work to harm the interests of another. The main idea behind objections to paternalistic legislation is that the state should only enforce valid duties. Individuals cannot have dutites to themselves. Individuals can only have duties to others. When we say that individuals 'ought' to safeguard their health, we use 'ought' in the prudential and not in the moral sense. Prudence pertains to calculations of self-interest, not regard for others. Thus, when we say that someone 'ought' not to drink so much, we are not speaking of a moral motive but rather a prudential motive. Mill has this to say about these so-called 'self-regarding faults'. (Mill 1974)

> Self-regarding faults . . . are not properly immoralities . . . They may be proofs of any amount of folly or want of personal dignity and self-respect, but they are only a subject of more reprobation when they involve a breach of duty to others, for whose sake the individal is bound to have care for himself. What are called duties to ourselves are not socially obligatory unless circumstances render them at the same time duties to others . . .

This difference between prudence and morality is why we find so many efforts to connect what the drinker does to the interests of the larger community. The drinker, especially the heavy drinker, imposes 'costs' on the larger community in the form of higher insurance rates, increased health care costs, and increased risks for others through careless driving, violence, and so forth.

While it is certainly true that the heavy drinker and often the so-called 'social drinker' impose serious costs on the larger community, I believe that limiting our thinking about controlling drinking and alcohol consumption in terms of the categories of self and other is misleading. The basic principle underlying the restriction of the consumption of alcohol is not to prevent harm to others or to the self. Alcohol policy, and health and safety policy more generally, rest on a common interest of all, or what is sometimes called the common good.

Common interests can be individual interests but they are not private interests. Common interests are called common because they are basic and shared by every individual alike. Common interests are common because they can only adequately be secured through collec-

tive action and organisation. As John Dewey argued, the government is needed to develop rules for the protection of those common
interests for which the private market and prudential motives would
be inadequate (Dewey 1927). We touch here on the fundamental
motive of government. Governments are formed not simply to adjudi-
cate disputes and prevent injuries to others: the more basic reason for
their existence is to secure a level of welfare and security which
individuals acting alone or on the basis of self-interest can never
achieve. The fundamental motive for government is not autonomy.
The fundamental motive is welfare and security. This does not mean
that we are willing to sacrifice autonomy willy-nilly for ever-
increasing levels of welfare. We clearly are not willing to do so and
for fundamental reasons of privacy and respect for individuals. But
where we see that individual calculations to prudence and self-interest
are inadequate for achieving higher levels of safety and the health of
the public in the market place, in the long run we usually opt for higher
levels of security if rather minor sacrifices of liberty are at stake.

There is an excellent sample found in the field of alcohol policy
itself that makes the limitations of self-interest and prudence very clear.
A widely discussed norm for so-called safe drinking has been Anstie's
Limit. This limit was devised by Francis Anstie, a nineteenth century
English actuary who observed that individuals who drank no more
than one and a half ounces of absolute alcohol daily (roughly three
ounces of whisky) were under no risk of developing health complications (Beauchamp 1980). For the sake of discussion, let us assume that
this assumption of Anstie was correct. Let us further assume that this
limit is a limit dictated by prudence. This seems a reasonable assumption because the limit was explicitly drawn up as a rule of thumb of
safety for the individual drinker. Thus, if prudential rules were the
basis for most drinking, the norm for drinking in society should approx-
imate to Anstie's Limit.

Now the surprising thing is that for most Western societies the
typical (model) drinker drinks far less than one and one half ounces of
absolute alcohol per day. In both the United States and England, for
example, the average individual drinks far less than would be indicated
if he followed simple precautionary measures dictated by prudence. In
the United States roughly eight or nine out of ten drinkers drink less
than an average of one ounce of absolute alcohol every day.

I submit the reason we find this apparent anomaly is because the
broad rules governing drinking —rules rooted in customs and societal

values — are not based on individual or prudential motives at all, but rather on rules that seek to protect the interests of the entire community, including all drinkers generally. Some of the norms are historical relics, such as the norm that women should drink less than men. Nevertheless, the fact remains that these very conservative limits for drinking are based on taking into consideration what might happen if social or community-wide rules were abandoned altogether and instead individuals were left to determine what level of drinking would be advisable taking into account their specific and private interests.

This line of thinking, a perspective I suggest is the fundamental line of thinking behind ever increasing demands for safety and health protection in democratic societies, is not paternalistic. This is because the motive is not one arising from the desire to look over the shoulder of the drinker, forcing him to employ greater prudence. The state is not seeking to assure that the drinker work harder to protect his own interests. Self-interest and prudence are the source of the failure of private markets to safeguard the health of the public. The individual drinker (and more importantly the entire alcohol industry) is asked to accept restrictions on alcohol commerce and on drinking because self-interest and the rules of the market place provide levels of safety and health in the aggregate that are simply unacceptable. The goal is to avoid consequences that are deemed highly undesirable from the standpoint of the entire community and from the perspective of the entire group of drinkers.

How do we seek to balance the fundamental interest in health and safety with the interest of autonomy and individual choice? In general and in the long run we seem to adhere to the principle that the liberty and autonomy of the individual will not ordinarily be barriers to significant improvements in the welfare of the community. Nevertheless, we reject or refuse to adopt legislated measures that violate the fundamental autonomy of the individual. A crucial point seems to be the degree of invasiveness of the governmental restriction. Putting fluoride in the water supply to protect the dental health of the public seems acceptable while posting an inspector in every home to determine whether individuals observe the rules of good dental hygiene is plainly unthinkable.

Notice that when we advocate tighter alcohol control policies we rarely go beyond those meaures that operate generally and at a distance from the individuals affected, although Prohibition is an obvious exception. I have in mind closing hours, price, age limits, or restrictions on advertising. Each of these measures seeks to control the general effect of having alcohol available in society, attempting to mitigate these effects with broad policies of restriction. No individual is told in any detail how much he should drink, nor are individuals prevented from drinking heavily. Of course, this is not to say that these policies do not restrict the liberties of drinkers. Clearly they do. But they do not do so for the purpose of replacing the prudence of the drinker with the prudence of the state.

Paternalism, properly defined, should only be applied as a label to those policies that seek to replace the individual's judgement of his own interest with the judgement of the state. The root legal doctrine for paternalism is *'parens patriae'*, or the doctrine permitting the state to supervise the conduct of individuals who are incapable of judgement such as minors, mental defectives and so forth. Nothing even close to this doctrine is involved in measures seeking to limit the availability of alcohol to protect the health and safety of drinkers generally.

The employment of instruments of legislation in order to protect the health and safety of drinkers and the larger community stems from a very basic question. This is the question of what might happen if everyone, including the alcohol industry, were free to determine for himself what would be in his own interests regarding the use of alcohol. Such a *'laissez-faire'* approach to alcohol has few friends. Paternalism as an objection to alcohol control policy is, I would submit, a false issue. Those who support stricter controls over alcohol ought not to feel guilty about their underlying motives. The goal of alcohol policy is not to seek to shape private conduct in any close, intimate way. No responsible authority is today calling for Prohibition. The reason is obvious. Totally abolishing alcohol, or anything close to this policy, actually defeats the goal of protecting the common good. Prohibition can lead to conseqences which simply outweigh any gains to the health and safety of the public. (This is why an individual can with consistency be for the prohibition of handguns or even heroin, but still oppose the prohibition of alcohol.)

At the risk of repetition, I am not denying that alcohol policies restrict the freedom of the drinkers. I am only denying that they do so to make the drinker do for himself what he ought to do voluntarily and without coercion. As I have argued, alcohol policy and health and safety policy generally place burdens and restrictions on individuals and groups for the common good, which no individual should be expected to undertake except in the expectation that everyone in similar circumstances is similarly burdened.

Dan E. Beauchamp

Dr. Ian Thompson of the Edinburgh Medical Group and the Scottish Health Education Group was invited to respond to this position and takes a rather different view of some of the terms used by Dr. Beauchamp. He also extends the ethical debate into the arena of health education.

In developing his argument that it is justifiable for governments to adopt alcohol policies that restrict the freedom of drinkers for the common good, Dan Beauchamp tries to maintain a position which is consistent with defending the autonomy of individuals. What he means by 'the common good' is not altogether clear and as a result no coherent picture emerges of what moral or practical criteria would justify interventionist alcohol policies on the part of any government.

While not disagreeing with his general thesis that restrictive alcohol policies may be justified for the common good, I find myself asking for clarification of two kinds of questions: the first concerns the philosophical basis of the moral judgements being made, the second, the conception of health education underlying the whole discussion.

Traditionally philosophers have argued that individual rights follow from the principles of respect for persons. *Respect for persons*, that is respect for their dignity and moral autonomy, is a logically primitive notion in ethics. It is the basis for the attribution of rights and responsibilities to individuals. In this respect it does not make sense to speak of a 'right to autonomy' along with the right to freedom of speech, etc. Moral autonomy is the normative presupposition of all other rights. Individual rights are the means to the attainment of moral autonomy and the expression of it. In that sense autonomy is a *principle* in terms of which we make judgements about what rights to attribute to individuals and serves as a criterion by which we judge the means necessary to enable people to achieve full autonomy or whether actions taken restrict their autonomy. It was for this reason that Kant (1949) referred to respect for persons as a 'categorical imperative' of ethics.

However, Kant and other philosophers have recognised that you cannot build a coherent ethics on the basis of the principle of respect for individual persons alone. We need in addition what Kant called the 'principle of universalisability', namely the principle that any moral rule on which we act should be capable of being universalised to apply to everyone or it fails to qualify as a moral rule, by the criterion of *justice*. Justice demands that moral rules should be capable of being applied universally, without unfair discrimination (eg on the grounds of sex, religion, social class or race, etc.). The demands of this second principle or criterion of ethics may well conflict in particular cases with the unrestricted expression of individual autonomy, and a great deal of moral debate centres around questions of which principle is to be given priority in particular cases. This necessitates on the one hand the clearer definition of individual rights — to spell out what is implied in facilitating the moral autonomy of individuals. On the other hand it means distinguishing between the positive and negative meanings of 'justice': what have been called distributive justice and retributive justice.

In the attempt to universalise the requirements of the principle of respect for the dignity and autonomy of individuals, we come to the notion of the common good. Distributive justice attempts to ensure fairness in the distribution of benefits, goods and services to all in the exercise of their rights, to ensure equality of opportunity in the stuggle to attain full personal autonomy and to facilitate equality of outcome in terms of access to the social, material, financial and health resources necessary to achieve this goal. Retributive justice attempts to ensure fairness in the application of sanctions to those who infringe or violate the rights of others by whatever means — injury, exploitation, robbery, etc. Both distributive and retributive justice are concerned with protecting the rights of individuals, but in such a way that the interests of all are safeguarded as is best possible.

This safeguarding or protective function has to be exercised by individuals (or by the community) on behalf of one another and particularly on behalf of children, incompetents and vulnerable people. This points to the necessary requirement for a third kind of moral principle fundamental to ethics — what has been called the principle of reciprocity or the principle of *beneficence*. In its most familiar form 'do unto others as you would have them do unto you', it simply expresses the requirement that we act to promote or protect the rights of others as we would hope they would respect our own, in recognition of the demands of justice. The principle that the state (or its representative) in certain circumstances should act *'parens patriae'* or that the doctor 'should do no harm' spells out the implications of moral life as involving not only responsibility for our own actions but responsibility for others. This responsibility for others may be formalised in lawyer/ client, doctor/patient relationships, as the individual entrusts himself into the care of another and the professional acquires 'fiduciary responsibility', but it has a more general form, namely, the responsibility of the individual and community to promote and protect the rights of others for the common good.

These three principles of respect for persons, justice and beneficence have been traditionally regarded by philosophers as mutually implying one another, but more recently the Ethics Advisory Board of the US Department of Health Education and Welfare (1978) has coherently argued that social policy on matters ranging from research involving human subjects to health education cannot be satisfactorily discussed without recognising the inter-relationships of these three principles. In dealing with alcohol policy it may be argued that the same is true. Emphasis on autonomy alone cannot lead to a coherent policy and leads in practice to anarchy. Emphasis on justice uninformed by concern for individual rights becomes legalistic and formal and potentially totalitarian, and the principle of justice without the beneficent motivation and will to do something about it is useless. Beneficence which is not qualified by respect for individual rights becomes paternalistic and authoritarian, and uninformed by the practical demands of justice is at risk of becoming sentimental and ineffective. Each principle is necessarily involved, but to different degrees in each situation.

Dan Beauchamp seeks to demonstrate (against Mill) that the state is not only justified in limiting the liberty of individuals to prevent harm to others, but also may be justified to 'place burdens and restrictions on individuals *for the common good*' provided only that 'no individual should be expected to undertake (these) except in the expectation that everyone in similar circumstances is similarly burdened'.

Part of his purpose is to dispose of the objection that advocating more stringent control over alcohol smacks of paternalism and violates individual autonomy. He contends that 'those who support stricter controls over alcohol ought not to feel guilty about their underlying motives', because the charge of paternalism would only stand if the state arrogated to itself the right to decide what is in the best interests of individuals ('to replace the individual's judgement of his own interest with the judgement of the state') whereas the state is simply the means of achieving a greater 'level of welfare and security (than) individuals acting alone or on the basis of self-interest can achieve'.

However, there are several kinds of ambiguities and difficulties in this argument. While he implicitly recognises the complementary relationship between the principles of respect for persons and justice (in emphasising that restrictions of individual liberty could only be justified for the common good and provided they were applied universally without discrimination), he does not distinguish between the concepts of distributive and retributive justice which are both implied in promoting and protecting the common good. The phrase 'alcohol policy and health and safety policy' covers both these functions in theory and in practice. Whilst it is true that legal and fiscal measures to control closing hours, price, age limits and restrictions on advertising 'operate generally and at a distance from the individuals affected', the sanctions of the criminal law related to drunken driving, drunken and disorderly behaviour, health and safety at work, do apply directly to individuals and may in fact specify in detail how much individuals may drink, and act as a deterrent to heavy drinking. Alcohol policy cannot be discussed realistically apart from the protective functions of retributive justice.

It is naive to suggest that the state can be used non-paternalistically as a means to achieve greater security and welfare for all. There is danger in this argument of viewing the state as a being with a life of its own, separate from the individulas who comprise it or the ministers who control the levers of power. Policies are the policies of groups or individuals (even individual ministers) and the authority with which they are implemented for the common good is that of individuals acting (whether wisely or misguidedly) 'in the best interests of others'. If we are not to hypostatise the concept of the state and attribute to it superhuman powers, then we have to recognise that the basis of corporate action for the common good must be the principle of beneficence (even beneficent paternalism). Acting to promote or protect the well-being of others is to exercise fiduciary responsibility on their behalf. Politicians, bureaucrats and their professional advisers may act arbitrarily, tyrannically and viciously or they may act rationally, justly and magnanimously in the common interest. In either case the moral authority for acting as they do derives from the principles of beneficence or reciprocity. In the one case that authority is abused in a destructive authoritarian way. In the other case the authority is used to augment the well-being of the community they serve (and to whom they are accountable).

Dan Beauchamp's argument is not helped by taking the line he does. Paternalism is not inconsistent with moral autonomy. On the contrary, paternalism exercised with beneficence by a father may facilitate and promote the moral autonomy of his son. The principles of beneficence relate to the responsibility of individuals/the state both to *promote* and *protect* the rights and well being of others. That responsibility may be exercised in an authoritarian manner or in a manner which is paternalistic in the best sense of facilitating fatherhood.

Further, an alcohol policy must meet the demands of both kinds of justice – distributive and retributive – if it is to promote and protect the rights of others. The case for the stricter control of alcohol has to be made in terms of two kinds of criteria (in so far as it is a health matter) – relevant evidence of how this can *promote* the better health of the community ('complete physical, mental and social well-being and not just the absence of disease'), and relevant evidence of how alcohol controls can *prevent* morbidity, accidents, violent crime, etc. If the ministers of the state are to enact controls over the price, sale, advertising, distribution and availability of alcohol, they need the authority to do so. As elected representatives in a democracy their moral authority to exercise power over us is based on the three principles of respect for persons, justice and beneficence. The exercise of this power or fiduciary responsibility will only satisfy these three principles if it is based on truth and public accountability.

The difficulty with Dan Beauchamp's argument is that he pays too much deference to individual autonomy without recognising the practical demands of justice and the necessity for individuals as agents of the state (and representatives of the people) to exercise beneficence on behalf of others for the common good. The danger of this line of argument is that moral notions become privatised and subjective. The public and objective meaning of justice is lost in talk about aspirations for the achievement of individual moral autonomy.

The sanctions of the criminal law against drunkenness and its consequences are a reminder of the objective realities of public life to which ethics properly relate. The protection of individuals from injury caused by others who abuse alcohol, is not the only concern of justice. In promoting the well-being of the whole community, in the interests of distributive justice, an alcohol policy which resulted in restriction of individual liberty for the common good would be justified not only if it was applied in a non-discriminatory way but also *if it could be demonstrated* that it did improve the health, safety and well-being of the community.

One need not be apologetic about introducing stricter control of alcohol if one can demonstrate (a) that excessive alcohol consumption causes harm to the drinker and to others, and (b) that the application of the proposed controls does contribute to the common good. These are not matters of opinion but attestable fact or matters which may be verified by trial and error. Excluding the more questionable motives or vested interests which may influence politicians in advocating relaxation of controls on alcohol or the reintroduction of stricter controls, the argument must rest on evidence, some of it medical evidence and criminological evidence, and health educators do not need to be apologetic about facts, nor hesitant in advocating changes in public policy on the basis of facts. That is their responsibiliuty as health professionals.

A more subtle reason for current inhibitions about the use of legal and fiscal measures, when our Victorian ancestors did not shrink from using the law to protect and promote public health, relates to a shift in public attitudes to the relationship between law and morality. In particular this change has come about in the campaign to liberalise the law in relation to the control of sexual behaviour and its consequences (eg in relation to homosexual acts between consenting adults, prostitution, adultery, abortion, etc.). While the decriminalisation of unconventional forms of sexual behaviour is to be welcomed, it has lent credence to the view that the law has no part in regulating moral behaviour, that personal conduct is a private matter and that in that sense the choice of moral values is a private concern of individuals in which the state has no right to interfere. The law in this view exists solely to prevent individuals from doing harm to others or to ensure redress when individuals in the exercise of their personal autonomy do injury to others. The law has to do with the public sphere, morality with private interests.

If this was a tenable view, then no public system of education which attempts to mould attitudes or to change attitudes and values would be justified, least of all health education in matters related to smoking, diet or alcohol and drug abuse, and *a fortiori* not to sex education and contraception! The fact is that in theory as well as practice we cannot separate the functions of law and morality. A.D. Woozley (1981) in a paper on *Law and the Legislation of Morality* has argued powerfully against the common trend to separate law and morality. As he says: 'In a representative democracy of any degree of civilisation, law and morality cannot be unrelated; at the very least if we accept the authority of law and are not merely subservient to it, the idea of morality is involved.' Further, if the argument developed earlier in this paper is coherent then a private morality that is exempt from the criterion of universalisability is incoherent both in theory and in practice. The principles of beneficence, by which we recognise a public responsibility to promote the common good, including the personal rights of individuals, through appropriate political and legal institutions, is a moral concept of fundamental importance which is not and cannot be restricted to the private sphere.The public responsibilities of the state in relation to security, health, education and welfare are without authority unless they are seen to arise from and rest on fundamental moral principles such as respect for persons, justice and beneficence. The exercise of political power on other than these grounds would be amoral, arbitrary or capricious (and probably immoral and tyrannical).

Woozley discusses the moral aim of the law in terms of the creation of the conditions favourable to the realisation of full personal autonomy and the security and welfare of all. In this respect the law at any given time has a two-fold character — to embody the existing moral attitudes and consensus of the society, and to create a context where these attitudes and values may be perpetuated and protected. In this respect the law may be directly used to educate and influence attitudes (eg laws relating to race or sex discrimination) but even implicitly and indirectly the law creates the context and safeguards which ensure the flourishing of a certain kind of society and certain kinds of values. Whether or not the law is deliberately used as an instrument of social engineering, the fact is that it is characteristic of law that 'it does inculcate moral attitudes'. As Woozley concludes: 'Morality is legisated, not by the mere enactment and implementation of a law, but by the way we live under it and absorb it into our moral bloodstream.' (Caplain & Callahan 1981).

In a sense the morally prescriptive functions of law have to be faced. It is rather timorous and disingenuous to deny these. What is required is that health educators should be more positive about the value of health, more positive about the need to change institutions and laws for the sake of public health. In the absence of alternative values and laws which promote and protect the security and well-being of the people, the laws and institutions of the *status quo* simply perpetuate the conditions of ill health in the community, simply consecrate *in aeternam* the attitudes and values which created the *status quo*. Conservatism is not a morally neutral position, but is a positive endorsement (for whatever reasons or motives) of the values, embodied in existing laws and institutions. The challenge of achieving social change, of positive improvements in public health, is the real challenge facing health education.

Health education can be conducted in an officious, interfering, even totalitarian manner, or it can be with the consent and co-operation of the people. This raises the whole question of what we mean by 'health education'. Briefly we may distinguish four approaches, each with a different rationale and with different advantages and limitations. It is arguable that in attempting and achieving social change which contributes to the better health, welfare and security of the whole community, all four approaches are necessary. These approaches may be described as the medical, educational, political and community development models.

The traditional medical model, based on the scientific diagnosis of disease and understanding of its aetiology and epidemiology seeks to achieve prevention by giving the public information, screening, immunisation and other preventive measures. This approach of giving people the facts and letting them choose, respects individual autonomy but tends to be inherently conservative insofar as it addresses individuals, assuming that facts alone will be sufficient to change attitudes and behaviour and insofar as it fails to address the root causes of motivation, the structural socio-economic conditions in which people live, and the need to change laws and institutions by political means.

This points to the need for the other approaches. The dissemination of information about health hazards and disease prevention provides the necessary background to justify educators intervening more directly to influence people's attitudes and mould their values in order to change their behaviour. It also informs and influences public opinion both to support and sanction political measures to improve public health, including the use of legislative and fiscal controls (eg in relation to the price, availability, advertising of tobacco, alcohol and drugs, or in relation to seatbelt legislation or fluoridation, etc.). Further, together with the impetus of education and the incentives or disincentives created by laws and taxes, the need may be recognised to address the health problems in areas of chronic poverty and multiple deprivation.

The painstaking, psychological and moral persuasion of teachers and the political controls of the state may have little impact in changing the conditions of those for whom smoking and alcohol abuse are a way of life and the only diversions from depressing socio-economic conditions. However, information, education and legislation can create the conditions favourable to change, but it may take the further initiatives of community development, encouraging self-help and practical measures to change the environment before real change can occur.

Alcohol policy requires, in order to be effective, all four kinds of approaches by the state (or representative individuals and responsible health professionals). Legislation alone will not control or eradicate alcohol abuse in areas where the motivation is lacking and the socio-economic conditions militate against it. Alcohol policy must concern itself not only with the issues of control, but also the means to facilitate community development and to create the conditions favourable to better public health.

I.E. Thompson

The issues raised here find echoes in all our other debates. We have seen that some measures are more intrusive than others and it is important that controls are seen to be fairly imposed. In the end it is likely that the ethical choices made by a community and the balance of state control which is accepted will be influenced by the political flavour of that community. It is clear from this chapter that we need to establish criteria for intervention along with a forum in which the moral choices can be debated. Sadly such a forum rarely exists.

17 THE WAY AHEAD

In the preceding chapters we have identified what we think are the key debates which sooner or later impinge on decisions about the prevention of alcohol related problems. Each remains largely unresolved, waiting amongst other considerations for the reader to cast his or her own vote. We believe it would be hard to pursue a coherent preventive policy without addressing the issues our correspondents have debated but we would not pretend that they represent an exhaustive list of the issues which need to be considered.

In our debates we have, for instance, largely ignored the biomedical aspects of alcholism. They have been the subject of much research — the vast majority of research funds are devoted to biomedical rather than social research in this field — but disappointingly few practical consequences have so far come from this investment. We have chosen not to consider ways in which drugs, by protecting the liver or alleviating hangovers, might be developed to prevent some of the harmful consequences of drinking, but we could not ignore recent research into the inheritance of alcoholism which must be a significant consideration in planning priorities in prevention. We therefore asked Dr. Robin Murray of the Institute of Psychiatry in London to contribute to the concluding section of this book by summarising contemporary views about the genetics of alcoholism and considering their implications for prevention.

A Genetic Contribution to Alcoholism?

The resurgence of interest in the genetics of alcoholism has its origins in the indisputable evidence that alcoholism is a family disorder. Without exception every study, irrespective of country, has shown higher rates among relatives of alcoholics than in the general population. But until recently it has been assumed that this was due to imitation rather than inheritance. One reason for favouring this environmental explanation is that although the risk for first-degree relatives (e.g. parents and siblings) is over 20 per cent, the risk for grandsons and half-brothers is almost equally high. Genetic theories predict that these second-degree relatives should have a lower risk than parents and siblings. Such high rates are only compatible with genetic laws if alcoholics tend to marry individuals who have a drinking problem; of course there is some evidence that this assortive mating does occur.

One way to tease apart the effects of heredity and environment is to hold the family environment constant by comparing the drinking habits of genetically identical twins with those of non-identical twins who share only 50 per cent of their genes. Kaij (1960) located 174 Swedish twin pairs where one member had appeared on a national register of alcohol abusers. Significantly more identical than non-identical twins had similar drinking habits; indeed, where one twin was a heavy abuser so was the other in 70 per cent of identical, but in only 32 per cent of non-identical twins. Since the twin pairs shared the same upbringing, the greater similarity in drinking history of the former may have been due to their closer genetic identity. In a subsequent Finnish study the evidence found by Partanen and Bruun (1966) was more equivocal. There was no difference between identical and non-identical twins in regard to addictive symptoms or consequences of drinking, but the frequency of drinking and the amount drunk at a session showed a moderate degree of heritability.

The most impressive evidence in favour of a genetic component to alcoholism has come from a series of studies using the Danish adoption and psychiatric registers. In 1973 Goodwin and his colleagues reported that the sons of alcoholics separated from their alcoholic parents early in life and raised by foster parents were nearly four times more likely to become alcoholics than were adoptees without alcoholic biological parents. Since both groups were brought up by similar non-alcoholic foster families, the difference in the frequency of alcoholism must have been due to the genetic transmission of a factor predisposing to alcoholism from the alcoholic biological parents. Another study comparing adopted-away sons of alcoholics with their brothers raised by the alcoholic parent revealed rates of alcoholism of 25 and 17 per cent respectively. The more severe the father's alcoholism, the more likely was the son to be alcoholic. Goodwin concluded that 'environmental factors contributed little, if anything, to the development of alcoholism in sons of severe alcoholics in this sample'. Such a statement is to say the least an exaggeration, given that the availability of alcohol is itself an environmental factor!

Two further papers by the same workers, examined the daughters of alcoholics. Daughters, both adopted and non-adopted, had a greater risk of alcoholism than the general population, but so did adoptees without alcoholic biological parents. Thus, a clear genetic contribution to alcoholism in women could not be inferred. Neither group of adoptees showed more depression than expected, but daughters brought up by their alcoholic parents were significantly more prone to depression, suggesting that depression in the daughters of alcoholics may often be a consequence of the unfortunate circumstances of their upbringing.

Goodwin's findings remain controversial and have been much criticised but they have been supported by two other adoptive studies. Cadoret and Gath (1978) investigated 84 American adoptees separated from their parents at birth, and found alcoholism more frequently in those who had a heavy drinking or alcoholic biological relative. Bohman (1980) used the Swedish criminal records and register of alcoholics in an examination of the biological and adoptive parents of 2000 adoptees. There was no relationship between crime in biological parents and their adopted-away offspring, but, once again, there was a significant correlation between alcoholism in biological parents and in their adopted-out sons.

Despite deficiencies in both the twin and adoptive studies, it seems likely that genetic factors do contribute to alcoholism in men, although not necessarily in women. Is what is inherited a biochemical predisposition to alcohol dependence, or is it some personality inadequacy which may lead to secondary alcoholism? Neither the twin nor the adoptive studies produced any evidence in favour of a personality predisposition and there has been increasing interest in a possible pharmacogenetic mechanism. It is known, for instance, that inbred strains of rats and mice differ in their preference for, or avoidance of, alcohol, and that the drinker strains tend to have higher alcohol dehydrogenase activity The existence of an atypically active form of alcohol dehydrogenase has also attracted a great deal of notice. Only a small proportion of Europeans have this enzyme variant but it is found in 85 per cent of the Japanese population. The unpleasant flushing reaction which many Orientals have to alcohol could be due to their more active alcohol dehydrogenase producing higher acetaldehyde levels than in Europeans; as a consequence heavy drinking could be less attractive to Asian people. Such a theory does, however, appear incompatible with the recent dramatic increase in the consumption of whisky in Japan, unless one assumes that the Japanese are very determined to overcome their enzymatic disadvantage!

The Public Health Implications of the Genetic Findings

In stating that genetic factors do contribute to the occurrence of alcoholism, I am not denying the undoubted effects of the social environment on drinking patterns. Genetic factors do not explain why barmen are more prone to alcoholism than Methodist ministers. But, by no means all barmen become alcoholics, and different genetic loading may help us to understand why some individuals develop a drinking problem while others exposed to the same social pressures continue to drink normally.

Contrary to popular belief, there is no need to adopt a fatalistic attitude towards the occurrence of a disorder just because it is known to be subject to hereditary influence. Indeed, recent experience has shown that it may be easier to prevent some such disorders manifesting themselves than to alter the behaviour patterns which cause social diseases like obesity and lung cancer. One example concerns phenylketonuria, which is a hereditary disorder resulting in mental deficiency. While we can do nothing to prevent the transmission of the causative metabolic error, we can detect children with the abnormality, and, if they take a low phenylalanine diet thereafter, they develop normally. The genetic factors predisposing towards alcoholism certainly do not obey the simple Mendelian Laws of recessive inheritance which operate in phenylketonuria, so it would be foolish to hope for such an easy solution. Nevertheless, one should not despair of counteracting any hereditary influence on alcoholism. Indeed, the fact that alcoholism runs in families provides us with a high risk group towards which we can direct our preventive efforts. One need not even assume a genetic hypothesis to realise that identifying and following-up the relatives of alcoholics would be a much more cost-effective strategy than screening whole populations for alcoholism.

Robin Murray

Murray et al have themselves studied 78 twin pairs when the concordance rates for alcoholics were 25 per cent for non-identical twins as against 21 per cent for identical twins. When asked about this and some of the criticisms of the studies reported above, Murray replied.
There is no doubt that there are methodological deficiencies in the Kaij twins study and in the Goodwin adoption study. However, I doubt whether the methodological deficiencies are sufficient to explain away either of these findings. My view on this is fortified by the fact

that 1981 saw the publication of a large twin study from the States, Hrubec and Ommen (1981) which largely agrees with Kaij's findings. In addition to the other two adoption studies which I mentioned earlier, there has been a further and very sophisticated analysis by Cloninger (1981) of Bohman's adoptees, which again supports some genetic influence on alcoholism.

Murray felt that, despite the contradictory evidence suggested by his own work with Clifford and Gurling (1983) he can still conclude:

My present position is that it seems likely that heredity makes a modest but nevertheless significant contribution to liability to alcoholism . . . I think time has long passed the simplistic argument over nature versus nurture. The trouble is that such arguments tend to become ideological, based on prejudice rather than real evidence. The issue is complicated one, and a sober review of all the evidence would have to be very much longer.

Such a review is provided in Murray et al (1983). The debate rests with, we believe, clear evidence that the genetic argument must be taken into account but it does not contradict or outweigh the importance of environmental factors. It is important in part of the evidence which must be taken into account when piecing together a preventive plan.

It is also clear that for many countries the question of the need for a national alcohol policy has never been seriously acknowledged, or it has been recognised but rejected. The prevailing value systems and political structures of a country will obviously determine the pattern of responses which proves culturally acceptable, but there is evidence of policies existing in very diverse socio-political settings. In this section we asked Mrs. Joy Moser (until recently with the World Health Organisation) to review trends in the development of preventive strategies throughout the world. Her review provides good evidence that the debate is not confined to the rich man's club of industrialised societies but is relevant to all parts of the world.

Public Health Approaches

Drunkenness and alcoholism are seen as important individual problems, but increasing recognition is now being given to the repercussions of drinking behaviour on the family, the community and the population at large. At the same time, there has been a development of understanding that broad social forces help to shape individual drinking patterns.

Despite a lack of consensus about the relative importance of the causative factors, it is now widely agreed that alcohol problems cannot be attributed to a defect in the individual alone, nor solely to the 'demon alcohol', but that social changes too can affect the occurrence of these problems. A growing appreciation of the burden on society, and the disappointing results of individual treatment, have led to a search for more effective means of prevention that will lower the extent, gravity and duration of alcohol problems in total populations. The World Health Assembly, in 1975, asked the World Health Organisation (WHO) to direct special attention to the 'extent and seriousness of the individual, psychological and social problems associated with the current use of alcohol in many countries in the world and the trend towards higher levels of consumption; and to study what measures could be taken to control the increase in alcohol consumption involving danger to public health'. A further resolution, in 1979, recognised that alcohol problems 'rank among the world's major public health problems'.

The public health approach implies knowledge of the nature and extent of the problems to be prevented and the changing trends in their incidence and prevalence; the types of measures that are or could be taken; and the factors within the population that could affect the application of various measures. WHO has stimulated many countries to compile and record relevant data as a base for planning and monitoring preventive endeavours (Moser 1980; Moser, in preparation). In some countries detailed reviews of the situation have been prepared (e.g. Single, Morgan and De Lint 1982).

A clearer picture of the patterns and prevalence of alcohol problems is beginning to emerge from such documentation. There is general agreement that in addition to the disabling consequences of alcoholism, a heavy burden is laid on society by widespread short-term or prolonged excessive alcohol consumption which may never reach the stage of dependence (Edwards, Gross, Keller, Moser and Room 1977). The effects are seen on the physical and mental health of the drinker as well as on working efficiency, traffic and industrial safety, and family welfare. In many areas studies have revealed the rising prevalence of such problems and a changing composition of the high risk groups, which are extending to include women and younger age groups.

Multiple Preventive Approaches

Increasing emphasis on the careful investigation of the nature and extent of alcohol problems in defined populations, and of the resources for confronting these problems, has led to two conclusions that are now fairly widely accepted. One is that the heavy toll of alcohol problems in the world cannot be reduced to any appreciable extent through currently available treatment and management measures. A second realisation is that no single approach to the prevention of alcohol problems is likely to be effective on a population basis (WHO 1980).

According to the public health model, preventive action aims at cutting the links between agent, host and environment. The approaches may be subsumed under three main headings: controls on the availability of the agent – alcohol; education encouraging the host – the drinker, or potential drinker – to accept such limitations and to exercise his own controls; and social measures designed to modify environmental factors that are known to promote harmful drinking.

A bewildering variety of laws and regulations for the control of production, distribution and sale of alcoholic beverages have been promulgated, but their impact has rarely been evaluated. The main purpose of some has been to increase state revenues. However, there are now fairly clear indications that raising prices in pace with rising average incomes, and controlling the distribution of outlets as well as opening times and minimum legal age for purchase and consumption, are likely to be effective measures for stabilising, or even reducing consumption. There is also a growing appreciation of the need for national and international controls on the production and promotion of alcoholic beverages to halt rising consumption.

If such measures are to be widely accepted and enforced, much additional effort is required to overcome the resistance of those who view alcohol as solely a source of pleasure or profit, without being conscious of the potential degrees of alcohol harm in specific situations and risk groups. Much debate and planning may be involved in seeking acceptable alternatives to excessive alcohol production and consumption. Progress has been made in determining educational methods likely to be most successful in enabling individuals to come to responsible decisions concerning their own drinking behaviour, rather than merely increasing knowledge about alcohol and its effects, or changing attitudes to drinking and drunkenness. In a number of countries, important education programmes on alcohol problems have been mounted for the general public, for school populations and in some cases for specific groups likely to be at high risk of suffering from, or causing, alcohol problems – such as drivers. Both UNESCO and WHO have helped to promote the exchange of information and experience on such educational programmes.

A further area for focusing preventive effort is the socio-cultural environment. Alcohol problems are giving rise to a particularly serious situation in some parts of the world undergoing rapid socio-economic change: yet it is hardly feasible to reverse such profound alterations in society. The response in some areas — such as Greenland and parts of North America — has been to make a very careful study of the local situation, to engage the local population in debate on suitable preventive measures and to ensure community involvement in their application. In addition to controls and education, measures such as increase in employment and leisure time opportunities have been suggested as supplying alternatives to drinking.

In general, preventive action directed at the environmental aspect of the three-pronged public health approach will have implications going far beyond alcohol problems. However, more restricted proposals have been made to alleviate some of the social repercussions of drinking. These include provision of support for the spouse and children of excessive drinkers; enforcement of measures to reduce alcohol-related traffic accidents; and specific programmes for early intervention in employment.

Constraints on Implementing Approaches

No blueprint can be produced for a cut-and-dried preventive programme easily implemented all over the world. No vaccine is available to prevent inappropriate drinking and its consequences. The physical, psychological and social reasons for the kinds of drinking that lead to problems are also complex and only partly understood. Despite the important volume of costly biomedical research on alcoholism in recent years, little new knowledge is as yet to hand that is relevant for preventive programmes.

Some other constraints include an unwillingness to relinquish the pleasure of alcohol, even in dangerous circumstances, such as driving. In addition, the moderate drinker may consider that preventive action should focus only on the minority who drink unwisely. Also, in many areas it would be difficult for the producer, salesman and tax authorities to find sources of profit as remunerative as alcohol, or alternative employment for those involved in production and trade.

A further impediment to embarking on a programme to prevent alcohol problems is the fear that alcohol might be replaced by another, perhaps more harmful, substance. Moreover the authorities in any coun-country have to face the competing demands on resources for dealing with a wide variety of health and social problems and those related to alcohol may be seen as of minor importance, or as intractable in the prevailing situation.

Main Themes of Prevention Approaches

The 1982 WHO Technical Discussions on Alcohol Consumption and Alcohol Related Problems showed that many nations are now aware of the threat to public health and welfare from the rising levels of alcohol consumption. While recognising the obstacles to developing preventive programmes, the delegates participating in the discussions — coming from more than 100 countries — gave examples of how these difficulties are being overcome. Other examples came from responses to a pre-circulated WHO inquiry (Moser, in preparation).

Some of the main themes of preventive approaches are reviewed below.

(1) Co-ordinated approach to alcohol problems within general health and development programme

There was a general agreement that programmes concerning alcohol problems should be established as part of general programmes aimed at promoting health and socio-economic development. However, to ensure that alcohol problems are given adequate attention, many countries have set up special bodies or commissions at national level comprising participants from a variety of governmental and voluntary bodies, as well as religious, educational and research intitutions. Such multi-disciplinary groups have proved valuable in reviewing the complexities of alcohol use and problems within the specific situation of their own country, and in making recommendations for preventive action. In some countries, a co-ordinating body of this type has responsibility for continued monitoring of the situation and assessment of the effectiveness of the preventive approaches selected. Another role of such a body may be the promotion and review of relevant research and the use of the findings for preventive action.

(2) Prohibition and temperance: east and west

In contrast to this broad approach to what is considered a complex range of problems, some countries are applying what might appear to be a more direct approach of prohibition. A closer study of the history of prohibition reveals, though, that it can also be a complex approach to prevention.

According to Baasher (1981), the Koranic injunctions that led to complete prohibition were the result of a step-by-step approach adopted by Islam in 'transforming animistic beliefs and pagan traditional practices into a new religious system and a completely different way of life'.

The prohibition doctrine is still adhered to in Saudi Arabia and several other Arab states, whereas in Bahrain, for example, production and consumption by Moslems is prohibited but the use of alcohol by foreigners is permitted. In some neighbouring countries, such as Iraq, Egypt, Lebanon and Sudan, which have a considerable non-Moslem population, abstinence is the rule among some groups but prohibition is not in force. In certain African countries, such as Senegal, where the Islamic influence is powerful, abstinence is not observed by all the Moslem groups.

The objective of achieving prohibition became a directive principle set out in the Constitution of India after independence, and in 1955 the Central Prohibition Committee drew up detailed guidelines for the gradual restriction of alcoholic beverages, to be implemented by State governments. The expectation of complete prohibition within a few years, however, has not been fulfilled.

Profound socio-cultural and economic changes and adjustment to the impact of other cultures through increased communication have affected areas where prohibition has been widespread for centuries. In some cases the effect has been a general relaxation of laws and customs, accompanied by an increase in smuggling, illegal production, and consumption of non-beverage alcohol. Elsewhere the response to the situation has been a tightening up of alcohol regulations and enforcement of heavy penalties for infringement.

The development of prohibition in North America and several European countries was linked with the spread of the Protestant ethic and the rise of the temperance movement. The stress on self-discipline led to concern with working class conditions and emphasis on alcohol control systems (Mäkelä, Room, Single, Sulkunen, Walsh *et al* 1982). With the decline in religious and moral influences, and in tune with general social, economic and political changes, prohibition broke down and controls became less strict. Increasing production and marketing of alcoholic beverges added to the pressure towards liberalisation.

A review of the most recent policies in such countries has shown a tendency to reinforce controls in order to counteract rising levels of alcohol-related damage. This is clearly seen in the Nordic countries. In Norway,for example, a 1980 white paper defined the major objective of alcohol policy as the reduction of the total consumpton of alcoholic beverages in the interest of health.

Strong opposition to such proposals has been voiced particularly by the big alcohol-producing countries where governments, even when recognising the potential dangers of increased production, may prefer to stress the importance of individual choice and responsibility. Producers themselves − which in some countries means the State − may acclaim the value of educational measures advocating 'sensible' drinking. So far there has been little or no evidence that such a policy leads to a reduction in levels of consumption and damage.

(3) Controls and Education in Latin Cultures

In most Latin cultures of Europe and the Americas, where *per capita* alcohol consumption levels tend to be the highest in the world, attention has only recently turned to the concomitant risks. Alcoholic beverages have been looked upon as a necessary part of meals and normal everyday life, even as essential to health, or at least as an important attribute of manhood. Such deeply rooted attitudes are difficult to change, especially in countries where a notable percentage of the population is engaged in alcohol production and trade. Moreover, prohibition is unlikely to be acceptable in cultures strongly influenced by Roman Catholicism. Yet several governments in these countries are now seeking appropriate ways of reducing the heavy burden of alcohol problems. France, for example, has prepared detailed proposals for a co-ordinated national policy, based on a review of the existing situation. A proposal to improve the quality and lower the production of wines is coming into effect and a new decree raising taxes on spirits of over 25° will come into force in 1983. Regulations on advertising of alcoholic beverages are being enforced.

In Latin America, alcohol problems have been considered until quite recently mainly in terms of alcoholism requiring treatment, for which resources and knowledge are inadequate. However, several important meetings in the region in the last few years, and the high proportion of responses to the WHO inquiry for the technical discussions, indicate governmental concern about the need for prevention programmes. So

far, though, there has been little evidence of strong action to counteract rising production and, in some areas, importation. On the other
hand, several countries, such as Chile and Costa Rica, have developed
detailed school education programmes on alcohol and related problems.

(4) Counteracting Expansion of Alcohol Trade

At several World Health Assemblies, and during regional meetings,
numerous African delegates referred to rising levels of alcohol consumption and harmful consequences. Among proposals for preventive
action were limitation of importation of alcohol, and this step has been
taken in several countries. However, the main reason may have been to
save foreign currency.

In some of the developed countries, alcohol consumption has started
to decline, despite increased production. Producers are, therefore, energetically promoting exportation of their products to new markets. For
instance, on a *per capita* basis, the importation of spirits into South
America increased by 60 per cent between 1970 and 1977 and by 200
per cent in Africa. Beer exports are less remunerative and foreign corporations have preferred to 'assist' the developing world through the
establishment of subsidiary companies, joint ventures and licensing
agreements. Partly as a result of such activities, massive increases in
beer production and consumption have occurred in some areas. Between
1960 and 1980, for example, beer production increased by nearly 200 per
cent in Latin America, more than 400 per cent in Africa and 500 per
cent in Asia. Recognition of the urgent need to deal with this situa-
is reflected in a further World Health Assembly resolution requesting
WHO to review existing trade practices and agreements related to
alcohol.

At a regional level, the European Economic Community (EEC) has
given consideration to regional control of the production of alcoholic
beverages and the relevant trade: but not always with the objective of
preventing alcohol problems.

(5) Community Involvement in Research and Action

Reference has been made to preventive approaches to alcohol problems at the national and international levels. In recent years, stress has
been laid also on the importance of community involvement in health
and development programmes. Thus WHO, through its more than 160
member states, is investigating means of improving primary health care.
In this perspective, a WHO project on Community Response to Alcohol-

Related Problems has been developed, initially in rural and urban communities in Mexico, Scotland and Zambia (Rootman & Moser 1982). This action-oriented research project has clearly shown the need to study alcohol problems within defined populations. A vigorous attempt has been made to involve the communities not only in the research but also in determining appropriate ways of dealing with the problems in the specific setting. In the three countries, the results of the first phase of the project and plans for action have been discussed with national authorities, since national involvement is essential for changes such as restrictions on the availablity of alcohol. Recognition has been given also to the importance of collaboration with voluntary bodies already carrying out preventive work.

Joy Moser

It appears that preventive approaches to a wide range of alcohol problems need to be based on studies of drink, the drinker, the context and the consequences. There is evidence of widespread agreement on the need for multiple preventive approaches, whereby co-ordinated programmes for alcohol controls, education and motivation can be planned, to respond to the socio-cultural and economic conditions prevailing in defined populations. Finding and implementing appropriate prevention approaches involves collaboration at community, national and international levels.

What, then, after so many points of view on so many issues, remains to be said? There is no consensus, no neat bottom line that can round off this series of debates. Alcohol problems are indeed so manifestly diffuse, so ubiquitously pervasive and so cunningly inconspicuous that single solutions can only deal with fragments of the great debate which lies behind all the other debates in this book.

It is no accident that it has taken us nearly four years to produce this book, nor is it an indication of a lack of commitment either on our part or that of the contributors. Rather, it is an indication of the complexity of the problem, a complexity which became increasingly apparent the further we advanced into the work. Preventing alcohol problems means balancing the interests of hosts of different points of view. It requires the simultaneous acceptance of irreconcilable arguments. It requires patience, diligence and imagination.

But self-congratulatory rhetoric brings home no bacon. Irritated readers, growing hourly more exasperated as they have ploughed through the special pleading of contribution after contribution, may now feel like throwing the book down in disgust, calling 'a plague on all your houses' and reaching for the whisky decanter. All we can hope to do in this conclusion, perhaps, is to wheedle a little more, our wheedling being directed towards the simple objective of establishing that the prevention debate, far from being empty bombast and untested prejudice, represents the core of the community's response to the alcohol problems that it has created and that, in turn, it is called upon to solve.

There are, in this regard, five separate strands to our argument. They are strands which run through the whole of this book, linking the general issues raised in the introduction to the specific and frequently conflicting points of view advanced by the contributors to the debates themselves.

The first and most important strand to our thinking is that alcohol problems are serious enough and pervasive enough to warrant action being taken to alleviate them; that alcoholism treatment of doubtful efficacy but undoubtedly expensive, is not in itself a cost-effective solution; that prevention strategies, whilst requiring much more and much clearer planning, do seem to point the way towards practical benefits. In other words, we are arguing that lack of consensus is no impediment to a commitment to continue. If this book has helped at least to clarify the terms in which the battles have to be fought, then it has been worthwhile. What we are asserting is simply that it is necessary to continue. The debate has begun, but nobody is yet calling the votes.

The second strand to our thinking is that specific problems are likely to require specific solutions. No review of the many courses of action recommended by the contributors to this book could fail to identify that each presumes a priority hit-list of problems to be confronted and that it is not always the same items that appear at the top of everybody's list. Devising preventive strategies involves making decisions about priorities. These decisions are likely to be influenced both by the severity of the problems under attack and by the estimated effectiveness of the proposed plan of campaign. Another part of the purpose of this book is to argue that both these factors need to be considered simultaneously and that modest but attainable impact upon particular problems may be a great deal more imporant than rousing battle cries about universal scourges and endless misery.

The third strand, which has to run beside the previous one, is that, although specific solutions must be sought for specific problems, it is important not to lose sight of the global perspectives. Alcohol problems are not just the affair of one district or one region or even one country. They are the world's problem and have to be confronted with as much of an integrated approach as possible. Differences between countries, between regions, even between districts are important and will exert influence upon the way that strategies are interpreted for that district, region or country. But beyond the particular, there is a general truth and the inability of some treaters, researchers, educators or social planners to look beyond their own backyard is bound in the end to limit the effectiveness of preventive strategies in a serious and unaccountable way. This book is arguing for particularity but against parochialism.

The fourth strand concerns individual responsibility. We commonly feel dwarfed by talk of government committees, international treaties or a concourse of 'experts'. Many individuals, including those active in helping alcholics, feel that prevention is too remote a concern for themselves and turn back hurriedly to attend to the casualties. We think this book shows that each individual must decide where he or she stands on the issues raised. Despite the complexity of effective prevention, the individual is not powerless over his own environment. As the debate in Chapter 14 shows, a group of interested individuals can influence the level of alcohol problems in their neighbourhood and indeed they are likely to be all the more effective because they are close to local customs and attitudes.

Fifthly, this book is intended as a demonstration of what it advocates – debate. There are those, seeking to advance their own arguments, who wish to exclude others from the debate. To exclude doctors, or to exclude non-doctors; to exclude recovered alcoholics or to include only recovered alcoholics; to exclude the beverage trade, or to silence the neo-prohibitionist; to pour millions into education or to shut up health education as tokenistic claptrap; to impose draconian laws or to clear the way for a free market economy; to ban advertising; to ban private clinics; to ban WHO from looking at marketing practices; to ban the government from spending alcohol revenue except on alcohol problems; to ban, finally, alcohol itself.

We are, of course, the moderators of these debates, the liberal proponents of free speech, against banning anything unless it is clear that no other course of action is possible to protect society from devastating harm. Our presumption is that the debates illustrate the pressing need to involve everybody who is willing and able to be involved. The issues are complex. The public health perspective is not necessarily the overriding force in human affairs, just as the expansion of commercial interests is not necessarily hostile to the benefit of the majority of man-

kind. Frequently, conflicts arise as much from a lack of understanding as from genuinely irreconcilable points of view. That is not to say that the prevention debate will not yield clashes. It will. We are not advocating a blurring of distinctions, a blind eye being turned to legitimate and important differences. What we are advocating is a continuation of the debate. Not as an alternative to action, but as an integral part of the action.

In simpler times many villages had the custom of holding a convocation of villagers to discuss issues which threatened the common good – issues such as drought, invasion from neighbouring tribes or the problem of drunkenness. The capacity to debate such issues, giving due recognition to the diversity of viewpoints and interests, has become institutionalised or fragmented or, in some societies, utterly lost. If the debates opened here are to be continued, where are they to be heard and how can conclusions be implemented? In Britain, as in many other countries, no forum for this kind of debate currently exists. There is no single executive body which can effect a co-ordinated alcohol policy, although it is interesting that in Britain the Central Policy Review Staff did recommend that 'an Advisory Council on Alcohol Policies should be established with associated internal co-ordinating arrangements'. (Bruun 1982). This recommendation was not adopted. Without some visible co-ordinating executive, the protagonists in the debate may well become exhausted and retreat to plough their own furrows or cultivate their own vineyards. Our hope is that, in providing the limited forum of this book, we have taken these debates far enough that it will be in everybody's best interests to see them continued. And, if they are to be continued, they will need to find their own larger forum, so that the contributors to the debates will include not only the select few who have squeezed between the covers of this book, but the whole range of people around the country and around the world who feel that they too have something they want to say in the great alcohol debate.

REFERENCES

Aitken, P. (1978) *Attitudes and Behaviour of 10-14 Year Old Children in Relation to Alcohol*, HMSO, London

Aitken, P.P. and Leathar, D.S. (1981) *Adults' Attitudes Towards Drinking and Smoking Among Young People in Scotland*, HMSO, Edinburgh

Ajzen, I. (1971) 'Attitudinal vs. normative messages: an investigation of the differential effects of persuasive communication on behaviour', *Sociometry*, *34*, 263-80

Ajzen, I. and Fishbein, M. (1977) 'Attitude-Behaviour Relations: a theoretical analysis and review of empirical research', *Psychological Bulletin*, *84*, 888-918

Arroba, T. (1977) 'Styles of decision-making and their use: an empirical study', *British Journal of Guidance and Counselling*, *5*, 3

Ashley, R., Granger, C.W.J. and Schmalensee, R. (1980) 'Advertising and Aggregate Consumption: an analysis of causality', *Econometrica*, *48*, 5

Baasher, T. (1981) 'The use of drugs in the Islamic world', *British Journal of Adidiction*, *76*, 233

Barthes, R. (1972) *Mythologies*, Penguin, London

Beauchamp, D.E. (1980) *Beyond Alcoholism: Alcohol and Public Health Policy*, Temple University Press, Philadelphia

Breed, W. (1982) Personal communication

Breed, W. and De Foe (1982) 'Effecting media change: the role of co-operative consultation on alcohol topics', *Journal of Communicaton*, *32*, 100-111

Brewers' Society (1981) *A Strategy for the Prevention of Problem Drinking*, Brewers' Society, London

Bowman, M.S.(1980) 'A prospective, longitudinal study of children registered for adoption', *Acta Psychiatrica Scandinavica*, *61*, 339-55

Bruce, D. (1980) *Changes in Scottish Drinking Habits and Behaviour Following the Extension of Permitted Evening Opening Hours*, Statistical News No. 48, HMSO, London

Bruun, K., Edwards, G., Lumio, M., Mäkelä, K., Osterberg, E., Pan, L., Popham, R.E., Room, R., Schmidt, W., Skog, O.L. and Sulkunen, B. (1975) *Alcohol Control Policies in Public Health Perspective*, Finnish Foundation for Alcohol Studies, Vol. 25, Helsinki

Cadoret, R.J. and Gath, A. (1978) 'Inheritance of Alcoholism in Adoptees', *British Journal of Psychiatry*, *132*, 252-258

Caplan, A.L. and Callahan, D. (1981) *Ethics in Hard Times*, Plenum Press, New York

Caplan, N. and Nelson, (1973) 'On being useful: the nature of consequences of psychological research on social problems.' *American Psychologist* (March), 199-210

Casswell,S. and Mortimer, D. (1982) Evaluation of school based alcohol education programmes', *Proceedings of International Institute on the Prevention & Treatment of Alcoholism*, ICAA, Geneva

Chiplin, B., Sturgess, B. and Dunning, J.H. (1981) *Economics of Advertising*, Holt, Rinehart and Winson

Cook, J. and Lewington, M. (1979) *Images of Alcoholism*, BFI/AEC, London

Clayson, C (1973) *Report of the Departmental Committee on Scottish Licensing Laws*, HMSO, London

Cloninger, C.R., Bohman, M. and Sigvarsson, S. (1981) 'Inheritance of alcohol

Abuse', *Archives of General Psychiatry, 38*, 861-8

Cork, R.M. (1969) *The Forgotten Children*, ARF, Toronto

Cowley, J. (1978) 'Decision-making skills – can they be taught?', *Monitor*, No. 50

Davidson, A.E. and Jaccard, J.J. (1975) 'Population psychology: a new look at an old problem', *Journal of Personality &Social Psychology, 31*, 1073-82

Davies, J. and Stacey, B. (1972) *Teenagers and Alcohol: a Developmental Study in Glasgow*, HMSO, London

Davies, J. and Stacey, B. (1972) 'Alcohol and health education in schools', *Journal of Health Education, 17*, 1-7

De Haes, W. and Schuurman, J. (1975) 'Results of an evaluation study of three drug education methods', *International Journal of Health Education, 18*, 4

Dewey, J. (1927) *The Public and its Problems*, Henry Holt & Co., New York

DHSS (1981) *Prevention and Health: Drinking Sensibly*, HMSO, London

Dight, S. (1976) *Scottish Drinking Habits*, HMSO, London

Docherty, S.C. (1981) 'Sports Sponsorship – a first step in marketing health?', in Leathar, D.S., Hastings, G.B. and Davies, J.K. (eds.), *Health Education and the Media*, Pergamon, Oxford

Dorn, N. (1972) 'Drug Education – is it effective?', *Drugs and Society, 9*, 1

Dorn, N. (1977) *Teaching Decision-Making Skills about Legal and Illegal Drugs*, ISDD/HEC, London

Dorn, N., Swift, B. and Thompson, A. (1974) *Evaluation of drug education*, ISDD, London

Dorn, N. and Thompson, A. (1976) 'Decision-making skills: a possible goal for drug education?', *Health Education Journal, 35*, 4

Drinkhall, J. (1981) 'Tire explosion cases could cost companies hundreds of millions,' *Wall Street Journal*, March 6th, 1

Duffey, J.C. (1977) 'Alcohol consumption, alcoholism and excessive drinking', *International Journal of Epidemiology, 6*, 275-379

Duffey, J. (1982) 'The effects of advertising on the total consumption of alcoholic drinks in the UK: some econometric evidence', *Journal of Advertising, 1*, 105-118

Eades, M. (1978) 'Alcohol education; evaluation of a teaching programme aimed at changing or reinforcing attitudes', unpublished

Edwards, G., Chandler, J. and Hensman, C. (1972) 'Drinking in a London Suburb', *Quarterly Journal of Studies on Alcohol, 6*, 69-73

Edwards, G., Gross, M., Keller, M. and Room, R. (1977) *Alcohol-Related Disabilities*, WHO Offset Publication No. 32, WHO, Geneva

Egger, G. (1979) 'A mass media approach to anti-smoking education', proceedings of General Symposium, 49th ANZAAS Congress. *Smoking: Stubbing out the Habit*, University of Auckland

Evans, R.I., Rozelle, R.M. Lasater, T.M., Dembroske, T.M. and Allan, B.P. (1970) 'Fear arousal, persuasion and actual versus implied behavioural change: new perspectives utilizing a real life dental hygiene program', *Journal of Personality and Social Psychology, 16*, 220-7

Evans, R.I. *et al* (1978) 'Deterring the onset of smoking in children: knowledge of immediate psychological effects and coping with peer pressure, media pressure and parent modelling', *Journal of Applied Social Psychology, 8*, 126-135

Fishbein, M. (1967) 'Attitude and the prediction of behaviour', in Fishbein, M. (ed.), *Attitude Theory and Measurement*, Wiley, New York

Fishbein, M. (1975) *Belief, Attitude, Intention and Behaviour*, Addison-Wesley

Gagne, R.M. (1957) *Essentials of Learning for Instruction* Dryden Press

Goldsen. R. (1980) 'The Great American Consciousness Machine: Engineering the Thought-Environment', *Journal of Social Reconstruction 1*, 87-102

Goodstadt, M. (1978) *The Status of Drug Education in Ontario 1977*, Addiction Research Foundation, Toronto

Goodwin, D.W., Schulsinger, L.F. and Hermansen, L. (1973) 'Alcohol problems in adoptees', *Archives of General Psychiatry, 28*, 238-43

Grabowski, J.G. (1976) 'The effects of advertising on the inter-industry distribution of demand', *Explorations in Economic Research, 1*, 21-75

Grant, M. (1982a) 'Alcohol Advertising and Young People: Ethical, Legal and Regulatory Issues', in Jeanneret, O. (ed.), *Child Health and Development, Volume 2: Alcohol and Youth*, S. Karger AG, Basel

Grant, M. (1982b) 'Young People and Alcohol Problems: educating for individual and social change', *proceedings of 10th International Congress of the International Association for Child and Adolescent Psychiatry & Allied Professions, Dublin*

Grant, M. (1982c) 'The Impact of Alcohol Education: implications for the development of national policies', *proceedings of the 11th International Conference on Health Education, Hobart*

Grant, M., Plant, M.A.and Williams, A. (eds.), (1983) *Economics and Alcohol: Consumption and Control*, Croom Helm, London

Hancock, D.C. (1970) 'We can reduce and prevent alcohol problems by changing attitudes and prejudices' in Brock (ed.), *Selected Papers Presented at the General Sessions, 21st Annual Meeting of the North American Association of Alcoholism Programs, San Antonio, Texas*

Hawker, A. (1978) *Adolescents and Alcohol*, B. Edsall, London

Hawley, A. (1973) 'Ecology and population', *Science, 1979*, 1196-201

Hovland, C.K., Janis, I.L. and Kelley, H.H. (1963) 'A summary of experimental studies of opinion change' in Hovland, C.I. *et al* (eds.), *Communication and Persuasion*, Yale University Press

Hrubec, Z. and Ommen, G.S. (1981) 'Evidence of genetic predisposition to alcoholic cirrhosis and psychosis', *Alcoholism, 5*, 207-15

Jahoda, G. and Crammond, J. (1972) *Children and Alcohol,*, HMSO, London

Jessor, R. and Jessor, S. (1977) *Problem Behaviour and Psychosocial Development: A Longitudinal Study of Youth*, Academic Press, New York

Kaij, L. (1960) *Studies on the Etiology and Sequels of Abuse of Alcohol*, Almquist and Wishell, Stockholm

Kant, I. (1949) 'Groundwork of the Metaphysic of Morals' in Beck, L.W. *Critique of Practical Reason and Other Writings in Moral Philosophy*, University of Chicago Press, Chicago

Kendell, R.E. (1979) 'Alcoholism: a medical or political problem', *British Medical Journal, 5*, 367-71

Kendell, R., de Roumanie, M. and Ritson, E.B. (1983) 'The influence of economic factors on alcohol consumption' (in preparation)

Knight, I. and Wilson, P. (1980) *Scottish Licensing Laws*, HMSO, London

Kricke, L.J. and Clark, P.M.S. (1979) *Biochemistry of Alcohol and Alcoholism*, Ellis Hallwood, Chichester

Kyle, P.W.(1982) 'The impact of advertising on markets', *Journal of Advertising, 1*, 345-59

Labonte, R. and Pengold, S. (1981) 'Canadian perspectives in health promotion: a critique', *Health Education*, (April), 4-9

Lambin, J.J. (1976) *Advertising, Competition and Market Conduct in Oligopoly Over Time*, North-Holland/American Elsevier

La Piere, R.T. (1934) 'Attitudes vs. Action', *Social Forces, 13*, 230-7. Reprinted (1975) in Liska, A.E. (ed.), *The Consistency Controversy*, John Wiley, New York

Lancet (1977) Leader. 488-90, September 3

Levine, H. (1978) 'Demon of the middle class: self-control, liquor and the ideology of temperance in 19th Century America', Ph.d. Dissertation, Sociology, University of California, Berkeley

Lowry, D.T. (1981) 'Alcohol Consumption Patterns and Consequences on Prime Time Network Television', *Journalism Quarterly* (Spring)

McGuinness, T. (1979) *An econometric analysis of total demand for alcoholic beverages in the UK*, SHEG, Edinburgh

McGuinness, T. (1983) 'The demand for beer, wine and spirits in the UK 1956-1979', in Grant, M., Plant, M.A. and Williams, A. (eds.), *Economics and Alcohol: Consumption and Controls*, Croom Helm, London

McQuail, D. (1977) 'Influence and effects of mass media', in Curran, J., Gurevitch, M. and Woollacott, J. (eds.), *Mass Communication and Society*, Edward Arnold/Open University Press, London

Mäkelä, K., Room, R., Single, E., Sulkunen, P., Walsh, B. *et al* (1981) *Alcohol, Society and The State. Volume 1: A Comparative Study of Alcohol Control*, Addiction Research Foundation, Toronto

MORI (1981) *The Effects of Advertising on Alcohol Consumption*, research study conducted for the National Consumer Council by Market Opinion Research International

Milgram, G.G. (1975) *Alcohol Education Materials: An Annotated Bibliography*, Rutgers Center of Alcohol Studies, Brunswick

Milgram, G.G. and Page, P.V. (1979) 'Alcohol Education Materials, 1978-79: an annotated bibliography', *Journal of Alcohol and Drug Education, 24*, 4

Milgram, G.G. and Page, P.B. (1980) 'Alcohol Education Materials,1979-80: an annotated bibliography', *Journal of Alcohol and Drug Education, 25*, 4

Mill, J.S. (1974) *On Liberty*, Penguin, London

Moser, J. (1980) *Prevention of alcohol-related problems: an international review of preventive measures, policies and programmes*, Addiction Research Foundation, Toronto

Moser, J. (in preparation) Alcohol problems and national policies: a review based on the Technical Discussions held during the 35th World Health Assembly, 1982, WHO Geneva

Murray, R.M., Clifford, C. and Gurling, H.M. (1983) 'Twin and Adoption Studies', in Gallanter, M. (ed). *Recent Developments in Alcoholism, Volume I*. Gardner Press, New York

Neubauer, D. and Pratt, R. (1981) 'The second public health revolution: a critical appraisal', *Journal of Health Politics, Policy and Law, 6*, 205-228

O'Connor, J. (1978) *The Young Drinkers*, Tavistock, London

O'Connor, J. (1978) *Cultural Influences and Drinking Behaviour – Drinking in England and Ireland*, Tavistock, London

Ogbourne, A.C. and Smart, R.G. (1980) 'Will restrictions on alcohol advertising reduce alcohol consumption?', *British Journal of Addiction, 75*, 293-6

O'Malley, B. (1979) 'Cigarettes and sofas: how the tobacco lobby keeps the home fires burning', *Mother Jones*, (July), 56-62

OPCS (1978) *General Household Survey*, HMSO, London

Orford, J. and Edwards G. (1977) *Alcoholism*, Oxford University Press, Oxford

Pan, L.(1975) *Alcohol in Colonial Africa*, Finnish Foundation for Alcohol Studies, Helsinki

Partanen, J. (1982) 'The Philosophy of alcohol education', *proceeding of 28th International Institute on the Prevention and Treatment of Alcoholism*, ICAA, Lausanne

Partnanen, J. and Bruun, K. (1966) 'Inheritance of drinking behaviour', Rutgers Centre of Alcohol Studies, New Brunswick

Peck, D.F. (1982) 'Problem Drinking: Some Determining Factors', in Plant, M.A. (ed.), *Drinking and Problem Drinking*, Junction Books, London

Pequignot, G., Tuyns, A.J. and Bevta, J.L. (1978) 'Ascetic cirrhosis in relation to alcohol consumption', *International Journal of Epidemiology*, 7, 113-20
Pittman, D.J. and Lambert, M.D. (1978) *Alcohol, Alcoholism and Advertising*, St. Louis, Missouri
Plant, M., Peck, D. and Stuart, R. (1981) 'Self-reported drinking habits among a cohort of Scottish teenagers', *British Journal of Addiction*, 77, 75-90
Plant, M.A. and Pirrie, F. (1979) 'Self-reported alcohol consumption and alcohol related problems', *Social Psychiatry*, 14, 65-73
Robertson, L.S. (1976) 'Whose behaviour in what marketplace?', presented at the Steinhart Conference on Consumer Behaviour in the Health Marketplace, University of Nebraska, Lincoln
Robinson, D. (1979) *Talking out of Alcoholism*, Croom Helm, London
Roe, A. (1942) 'Legal Regulations on Alcohol Education', *Quarterly Journal of Studies on Alcohol*, 3, 433-64
Roe, A. (1943) 'A survey of alcohol education in the United States', *Quarterly Journal of Studies on Alcohol*, 4, 574-663
Rootman, I. and Moser, J. (eds.), (1982) *Community Response to Alcohol-Related Problems*, Report on a WHO project by an international group of collaborators, WHO, Geneva
Saunders, J.B., Davis, M. and Williams, R. (1981) 'Do women develop alcoholic liver disease more readily than men?', *British Medical Journal*, 282, 1140-3
Schweitzer, S.O., Intriligator, M.D. and Salehi, H. (1983) 'Alcoholism: an econometric model of its causes, its effects and its control', in Grant, M., Plant, M.A. and Williams, A. (eds.), *Economics and Alcohol: Consumption and Control*, Croom Helm, London
Single, E., Morgan, P. and De Lint, J. (1982) *Alcohol, Society and the State. Volume 2: The Social History of Control in Seven Countries*, Addiction Research Foundation, Toronto
Skog, O.J. (1982) *Estimating Magnitudes and Trends of Alcohol-Related Problems: A Critical Review*, National Institute for Alcohol Research, Oslo
Smart, R.G. (1974) 'Comparison of purchasing: self-service and clerk service liquor stores', *Journal of Studies on Alcohol*, 35, 1397
Smart, R.G. and Cutler, R.E. (1976) 'The Alcohol Advertising Ban in British Columbia: Problems and Effects on Beverage Consumption', *British Journal of Addiction*, 7, 13-21
Smart, R.G., Gray, G. and Bennal, C. (1978) 'Predictors of drinking and signs of heavy drinking among high school students', *Internatinal Journal of Addictions*, 13, 1079-94
Strickland, D. (1982) 'Parents, Peers and Problem Drinking: an analysis of interpersonal influences on teenage alcohol abuse in the USA', *Proceedings of 28th International Institute on the Prevention & Treatment of Alcoholism*, ICAA Lausanne
Strickland, D. (1983) 'Advertising Exposure, Alcohol Consumption and Misuse of Alcohol', in Grant, M., Plant, M. and Williams, A. (eds.), *Economics and Alcohol: Consumption and Controls*, Croom Helm, London
Sturgess, B.T. (1982) 'Dispelling the Myth: the effects of total advertising expenditure on aggregate consumption', *Journal of Advertising 1*,, 201-12
Savoy, P. (1981) 'The deregulators: legalizing corporate murder', *The Nation, 20*, 761-764
Terris, M. (1981) 'Epidemiology as a guide to health policy', *World Health Forum*, 2, 551-62
Thorley, A. (1982) 'The Effects of Alcohol', in Plant, M. (ed.), *Drinking and Problem Drinking*, Junction Books, London
Tones, B.K. (1977) 'Effectiveness and efficiency in health education: a review of

theory and practice', SHEG, Edinburgh

Trotter, T. (1804) *An Essay on Drunkenness,* Longman, London

US Department of Health, Education and Welfare (1978) 'Protection of Human Subjects: Research involving those institutionalised and mentally infirm', *Report and Recommendations,* Part III

Van Iwaarden, M.J. (1983) 'Advertising, alcohol consumption and policy alternatives', in Grant, M., Plant, M. and Williams, A. (eds.), *Economics and Alcohol: Consumption and Control,* Croom Helm, London

Walsh, B.M. (1980) *Drinking in Ireland,* Economic and Social Research Institute Broadsheet, No. 20

Waterson, M.J. and Hagan, L.W. 1980) *The relationship between alcohol advertising and consumption,* report prepared for the Independent Television Companies Association

Watts, A.G. (1975) 'Teaching Decision-Making Skills', *General Education,* No. 25

Watts, A.G. and Elsom, D. (1974) *Deciding,* Hobson Press, Cambridge

WHO (1952) *Expert Committee on Mental Health Alcohol Sub-Committee,* Technical Report Series 48, WHO, Geneva

WHO (1980) *Problems Related to Alcohol Consumption,* Technical Report Series 650, WHO Genva

WHO (1982) *Alcohol consumption and alcohol-related problems: development of national policies and programmes,* report on Technical Discussions of 35th World Health Assembly, WHO, Geneva

WHO (1983) *Community responses to alcohol related problems* (in preparation)

Williams, A. (1981) Comment in discussion at Conference on Economic Aspects of the Use and Misuse of Alcohol, University of Essex

Wilson, P. (1980) *Drinking in England and Wales,* DHSS/OPCS, London

Woozley, A.D. (1981) 'Law and the Legislation of Morality', in Caplan A.L., and Callahan D. (eds.), *Ethics in Hard Times,* Plenum Press, New York

INDEX

For Product Safety Concerns and Information please contact our EU
representative GPSR@taylorandfrancis.com
Taylor & Francis Verlag GmbH, Kaufingerstraße 24, 80331 München, Germany

www.ingramcontent.com/pod-product-compliance
Lightning Source LLC
Chambersburg PA
CBHW050434280326
41932CB00013BA/2105

9 7 8 1 0 3 2 6 3 9 9 2 5